FACES OF RENEWAL

FACES OF RENEWAL

Studies in Honor of Stanley M. Horton
Presented on His 70th Birthday

Edited by

Paul Elbert
Middle Georgia College

PEABODY, MASSACHUSETTS 01961-3473

ISBN 0913573-49-3

Excerpts from Gene A. Getz, *Sharpening the Focus of the Church* (Wheaton, Ill.: Victor Books, 1974), pp. 115–16, appearing in ch. 15, pp. 254–55, were used with permission.

TABLE OF CONTENTS

PART I: BIBLICAL STUDIES

EDITOR'S PREFACE

I T IS A PRIVILEGE to have been editor of an anniversary volume commemorating both the seventieth birthday and the faithful and industrious service of our colleague in Christ, Dr. Stanley M. Horton. A true servant of the church universal, his life has been distinguished by the principle *soli Deo gloria* and it is to this end that we dedicate these pages in his honor.

We have attempted to capture some, but certainly not all, of the relevant motifs of spiritual renewal as they apply to Christian life. At our present moment in history I sense, for example, a renewed interest in humility and the patient endurance of suffering as fruits of the Spirit. There is a serious interest in being diligent, so as to utilize as fully as possible in the face of human weakness those spiritual fruits and gifts which are so generously bestowed upon unworthy sinners. Coincident with this interest is a growing consensus that some historical formulations re the nature of Scripture and its interpretation do not at all properly extend so as to forbid or exclude any categories of varied gifts mentioned in Scripture.* Rather, I sense a maturing comprehension throughout Christendom that these manifold activities of the Holy Spirit are being given according to God's sovereign will in order to help us better understand and share experiential grace with others. There is a renewed perception of the gift of the Spirit as assisting phenomenologically in a multiplicity of Christian functions among believers. One observes in concert with this perception a renewed awareness of the importance of the dynamical interiority of the Spirit. Amidst such undeserved grace one must note as well an attitude of renewed love and obedience towards God and of compassion towards others.

There is also most assuredly a renewed emphasis on evangelical mission, quite consistent with that evangelical purpose detected both in Luke–Acts and in the work of the Holy Spirit today, an emphasis that is vigorously afoot in all the major denominations of Christendom. An explosion of charisms, some bearing similarity to those recorded in the Acts of the Apostles and suggested as narratively programmatic in chapter two, verses thirty eight and nine, is once again in our century contributing to an authentic and often zealous interest in Luke's subject, the salvation of the lost. I rejoice in this fact and see in it a reflection of the powerful resurrection life of the real New Testament Jesus. We are indeed indebted to the gracious ministry of our Lord to us and to capable stewards of his grace like professor Horton, who, in his turn, has set an example of charity which would be difficult to imitate.

It is a pleasure to take this occasion to thank all of the contributors for their efficient collaboration in the preparation of this volume. Their devotion to their tasks has been diligent and helpful. The comments of William Menzies on some points of historical detail are warmly acknowledged. Certain kind friends of scholarship whose support helped in times of difficulty are much appreciated; similarly, the secretarial skills of Heather Skipper and Robin Newman enabled our work to proceed. I am also grateful to Robert Graves for his help in the preparation of the indices.

I would surely be remiss if I were not to register my sincere appreciation to the libraries of London Bible College and Tyndale House at Cambridge for their hospitality during a part of this work and to colleagues at Middle Georgia College for a pleasant teaching atmosphere in which our festschrift could be completed.

It is indeed then a privilege at this time to extend birthday greetings and hearty congratulations to you, Stanley, on your seventieth birthday. We admire the ministry of teaching and pastoral scholarship which our Lord has accomplished through you. Your pioneering efforts as a servant of renewal merit our respect. May His Spirit strengthen and refresh as you continue to fulfill your mission. On behalf of your fellow workers and friends, many of whom are expressing sentiments via their enrollment on the *Tabula Gratulatoria*, I am very pleased to inscribe our heartfelt dedication.

O serve praeclare Domini Nostri, tibi hunc libellum dedicamus.

Nos locupletavisti quippe qui per totam vitam Jesu Christo
summa cum constantia serviveris,

Muneribus studiose perfunctus proposuisti nobis ergregium
exemplum cuius nec nos nec multi brevi obliviscemur,

Officium doctoris tam fideliter explevisti ut nos instinguas
ad exemplum tuum imitandum.

Animum demissum modestiamque tuam magni aestimamus,
nam per eos testaris Jesum Christum ac Sanctum
Spiritum interfuisse tuo labori.

Precamur tibi vitam longam et beatam;
Dominus tibi benedicat, O adjutor doctorum ac eruditorum,
Deo devote!

P.E.
Cochran, Georgia
1985

---

* E.g., cf. Heinz Schürmann, "Les Charismes Spirituels," *L'Église de Vatican II* (ed. Yves Congar; US 51b; Paris: Cerf, 1967) 541,570; Max Turner, "Jesus and the Spirit in Lucan Perspective," *TynB* 32 (1981) 39; "Spiritual Gifts Then and Now," *VoxEv* 15 (1985) 7–64.

TABULA GRATULATORIA

Ben Aker
Patrick H. Alexander
Donald L. Anderson
David W. Argue
Don Argue
French L. Arrington
Irene Arrowood
Richard Arrowood
J. Robert Ashcroft
George Assad

Donald E. Baldwin
Leroy Bartel
James M. Beatty
Bill Behr
Loida Behr
Zenas J. Bicket
Leroy Birney
Sarah Blackstone
Daniel L. Blanton
Edith Blumhofer
Paul Borka
James Breckenridge
Raymond T. Brock
David Bundrick
David D. Bundy

John Caplin
G. Raymond Carlson
William Carmichael
Wanda Carter

Augustus Cerillo, Jr.
Esther Cimino
Ralph L. Cimino
Barbara Clark
David C. Clark
David G. Clark
Gary K. Clark
Alex Coker
Robert E. Cooley
Eldin R. Corsie
Roger D. Cotton
J. H. Crouch
Clayton E. Crymes

Murray W. Dempster
Peter Dippl
Richard W. Dortch
Roland Q. Dudley
James D. G. Dunn

William G. Eastlake
Twila Edwards
Paul Elbert
Winston Elliott
Howard Ervin

Robert Faricy, S.J.
D. William Faupel
Gordon D. Fee
Raleigh Ferrell
George M. Flattery

Gerard J. Flokstra, Jr.
Irving F. Ford
J. Massyngberde Ford

Kenneth H. Gamerdinger
R. Hollis Gause
Sharron Linzey Georgianna
Roswith Gerloff
Thoralf Gilbrant
Kenneth Gill
Louis Goldberg
Robert Graves
Hobart E. Grazier
Charles E. Greenaway

H. Glynn Hall
Ian R. Hall
Fred Halton
Kenneth L. Hardin
Dale E. Harmon
Ralph W. Harris
Everett F. Harrison
Thomas F. Harrison
Ronald C. Haus
Nancy S. Heidebrecht
Stephen J. Hendrickson
James L. Hennesy
James D. Hernando
Robert W. Herron, Jr.
Galen Hertweck
Roger Heuser
Dexter B. Higgins
Peter Hocken
Melvin L. Hodges
Charles L. Holman
Jerry W. Horner

Harold Hunter
Robert A. Hunter
Larry Hurtado
Herb Hull

David Kent Irvin
Akiei Ito

Burton K. Janes
Stanley Jebb
Hugh P. Jeter
Joyce Denton Johnson
Sam Johnson

Cecil Kerr
Douglas Kinder
James King
Mark Kinney
Elmer E. Kirsch
Simon J. Kistemaker
Koichi Kitano
Harold Kohl
Wayne Kraiss
Richard Krüger
Peter Kuzmič
Ronald Kydd

Norm Labrentz
René Laurentin
Martin Lewadny
Edgar R. Lee
Jaebum Lee
Rodney Lensch
Verdell F. Longstaff
Richard Lovelace
Lowell Lundstrom

Frank Macchia
J. Gordon McConville
Andrew McDearmid
William G. MacDonald
Damous E. McGee
Gary B. McGee
John W. McKay
Basil McKinney
Everett L. McKinney
Ken McKinney
Basil McNeely
Larry McNeill
Jan Maempa
Howard F. Magnus
Michael Mattocks
Don Meyer
Robert Meyer
Thomas Wm. Miller
Rick D. Moore
Linda Morris

Douglas J. Nelson
H. Terris Neuman
Paul Newberry
Stephen L. Norman, Sr.

David Olford
Loek Oudeman

Anthony Palma
John M. Palmer
Daniel B. Pecota
Cody L. Pelham
David Petts
John P. Phillip
Donald E. Phillips

Theola Johnson Phillips
Garnet E. Pike
Jean-Daniel Plüss
O. W. Polen
Margaret M. Poloma
John M. Pope
Timothy Powell
Raymond V. Pruitt

Paul Radke
P. S. Rajamoni
Henry Ramaya
John Rea
Opal Reddin
David A. Reed
W. C. Richardson
David Ridge
Richard Riss
Cecil M. Robeck, Jr.
Louis P. Rogge, O.Carm.
Mark D. Romano
Jon Ruthven

James N. Sanders, Sr.
Jerry Sandidge
Trandafir Sandru
J. Paul Savell
Siegfried S. Schatzmann
Samuel J. Schultz
Michael D. Sharp
James B. Shelton
Royce M. Shelton
Hurley R. Shortt
Lowell G. Simmons
Walter A. Simmons
Mark Sims

Heather Skipper
Malcolm C. Skipper
Donald Smeeton
Henry J. Smith
Robert G. Smith
Wesley Smith
Carlton Spencer
Russell P. Spittler
Harold V. Spruill
George Stotts
Roger Stronstad
John Swails
Vinson Synan

John Tang
Del Tarr
Edmund Tedeschi
Oddvar Tegnander
John Christopher Thomas
Carley Touchstone
Robert E. Tourville

Reinhold Ulonska
J. Dalton Utsey

C. W. Van Dolson
Lawrence M. Van Kleek

Laud O. Vaught
Carl Verge

Philip L. Walker
Horace S. Ward
Julian Ward
Wayne Warner
Richard Waters
Adrian West
George W. Westlake, Jr.
Francis Whiting
Elizabeth Williams
J. Rodman Williams
Larry Williams
Ward R. Williams
William C. Williams
John Wilson
R. Paul Wood
James E. Worsfold

Johnny Yeoh
Ronald Youngblood

Christof Ziemer
Thomas F. Zimmerman

BIOGRAPHICAL SKETCH

William Menzies and Paul Elbert

S TANLEY MONROE HORTON WAS BORN MAY 6, 1916, to parents who participated in the pentecostal revival at the beginning of this century. Both of his parents were empowered for further service by a baptism in the Holy Spirit during 1906; his father in Winnepeg, Canada, and his mother at the Azusa Street revival in Los Angeles. Converted to Christ at the tender age of six, Stanley has continued to serve our Lord faithfully throughout his life as Bible student, pastor, teacher, administrator, and scholar.

He earned a B.S. from the University of California at Berkeley and was working in that state's bureau of chemistry laboratory when he was called into the teaching ministry. Obedient to this call, he pursued a lifelong course of biblical studies, specializing in Old Testament. He holds the M.Div. from what is now Gordon-Conwell Theological Seminary, the S.T.M. from Harvard University, and the Th.D. from Central Baptist Theological Seminary.

During his truly evangelical career he has evidenced a rare combination of gifts and graces as a Christian leader whose humble piety, intellect, disciplined study, and keen sense of practical ministry have commanded our respect and admiration. While teaching at the Metropolitan Bible Institute in New Jersey he was ordained by the Assemblies of God in 1946. He served as professor and chair of the biblical education division in Central Bible College, Springfield, Missouri, from

1948–1978. In 1978 a new men's dormitory on that campus was named the Stanley M. Horton Hall in his honor. He continues vigorously to this day as Distinguished Professor of Old Testament at the Assemblies of God Theological Seminary in Springfield. His spiritual wisdom and understanding, poured into the lives of thousands of students during forty years of classroom teaching, have had and continue to have a godly and steadying influence.

It is a privilege to share here in turn our own personal impressions of this pentecostal and charismatic scholar-teacher. My (WM) first contact with Stanley came in my freshman year in Bible college, where he was one of the younger faculty members. I often sought him out for counselling. His quiet manner and practical wisdom helped me greatly in those formative years. His commitment to scholarship demonstrated to me that piety and intellect could—and should—go together. I have never forgotten the model this youthful instructor set before me.

Years later, I was asked to join the faculty of the school from which I had graduated. Stanley and I were now colleagues; in fact, we worked together for many years, first at Central Bible College and in more recent years at the Assemblies of God Theological Seminary (then known as the "Grad School"). During these years my dear friend time and again displayed not only patience in times of crisis, but restraint and tolerance. His spiritual and intellectual maturity continually served as a source of inspiration and as a corrective to my own temptation to impatience and judgment.

My (PE) first contact with Stanley came through his written ministry, some of which is documented in the following bibliography. I was immediately impressed by the sober pastoral concern and the emphasis on spiritual reality in his writings. His devotion to serving our Lord through a thoughtful application of his distinctive charisma of pastoral scholarship led me to a deep appreciation of this genuine and humble servant. His generous friendship as a colleague has always been warm and courteous and his interest in the scientific underpinnings of much theological discussion is always dynamic and progressive. I believe that his unfailing attention to duty, his life-long obedience to God's call, and his charismatic and sacrificial love of God's people enable us to recognize his true stature as one who historically follows in the train of giants of inner spirituality like Donald Gee and Padre Pio.

A quiet man, Dr. Horton nonetheless has displayed courage and conviction on a variety of occasions. In the pioneer days of the Society for Pentecostal Studies, when many were reluctant to identify with an unproven association, Dr. Horton lent his influence and strength to this new creative venture, for in it he saw a possible forum wherein serious biblical and theological study might begin to flourish in the various charismatic traditions. Believing that sincere Christian scholarship should never be insular or suspicious, and that good teaching must be firmly based on serious biblical study, he has always encouraged those who would continue to study, learn, and grow, both academically and pastorally. With his gentle personality, completely free of anti-intellectualism and authoritarianism, he has steadfastly encouraged a scholarly and spiritually sensitive exploration for truth.

Dr. Horton is a life member of the California Scholarship Federation and the Phi Alpha Chi honor society. He has been a member of the Evangelical Theological Society since 1951 and has served on the Theology Commission of the National Association of Evangelicals. He is listed among the Outstanding Educators of America. His professional associations also include the American Scientific Affiliation, the Society of Biblical Literature, the American Association of Professors of Hebrew, and the Near East Archaeological Society. Dr. Horton has served as a guest professor at the Near East School of Bible and Archaeology, Jerusalem (excavating ruins at Dothan); at Southern Asia Bible College, Bangalore, India; at the East Africa School of Theology, Nairobi, Kenya; at the Berea Bible School, West Berlin; at Continental Bible College, Brussels, Belgium; and at the Far East Advanced School of Theology, Manila, Philippines.

As a person, then, Dr. Horton has lived out before us those qualities of Christian grace worth emulating. In addition to these personal graces, faithfully and unpretentiously shared, the Lord's servant has placed before us some important theological and biblical insights. These may well serve to chart a helpful course for younger leaders and thinkers to consider and have always been submitted in the spirit of Bengel's dictum, *Te totum applica ad textum . . . rem totam applica ad te*, for Stanley is not only a man of the Spirit, but a devoted student of Scripture. Equipped with a command of the biblical languages and insight into the scholarly literature of biblical studies, he has synthesized his biblical understanding and his fellowship with Christ into a thoroughgoing evangelical world view. His pen has perhaps fashioned the most significant theological affirmations in the classical pentecostal tradition. For example, one highlight of his pastoral scholarship is the work, *What the Bible Says About the Holy Spirit* (1976), which has been translated into French, Spanish, Chinese, German, Korean, Portuguese, and Tamil. Similarly, *The Book of Acts* (1981) has also been translated into several languages.

As Stanley approaches the sunset of a fruitful career of service it is indeed fitting that many of his friends, former pupils, and professional colleagues should seek to honor him with a collection of essays. And so it is with warm feelings of appreciation and thanksgiving for his ministry that we offer him this volume on his seventieth birthday. We believe him to be eminently festschrift-worthy and wish him and his wife Evelyn, who is organist at their local church, many happy and peaceful years together.

A SELECT BIBLIOGRAPHY OF THE WRITINGS OF STANLEY M. HORTON, 1949-1983

1949
"We Need the Scripture Today!" *PE* (February 12) 2,6; reprinted (October 9, 1966), 2,3.

1955
Into All Truth (Springfield, Missouri: Gospel Publishing House).
"How Old is Man?" *PE* (December 11) 3,4.

1961
"A Suggestion Concerning the Chronology of Solomon's Reign," *BETS* 4/2 (October) 3,4.
Panorama of the Bible: A Teacher's Manual (Springfield: Gospel Publishing House).

1962
Great Psalms: A Teacher's Manual (Springfield: Gospel Publishing House).

1963
Bible Prophecy: A Teacher's Manual (Springfield: Gospel Publishing House).

1964
"How Deep are Child Conversions?" *PE* (June 7) 6-8.

1965
Gospel of John: A Teacher's Manual (Springfield: Gospel Publishing House).
"The Biblical Basis for Church Membership," *PE* (March 14) 2,3.
"They Were All Filled," *PE* (May 2) 8,9.

1966

"God-breathed Words," *Advance* (September) 4,5.
"Why I Believe the Bible is True," *PE* (September 4) 8,9; reprinted (December 13, 1981), 4,5.
"A Righteousness that Will Stand," *PE* (November 6) 5,6; reprinted (February 5, 1984) 3,4.

1967

The Promise of His Coming (Springfield: Gospel Publishing House); reprinted in paper as *Welcome Back Jesus.*
"Paraclete—What Does it Mean?" *Paraclete* 1/1 (Fall) 5–8.

1968

"The Holy Spirit and Christ's Coming," *Paraclete* 2/1 (Winter) 12–16.
"Not by Might nor by Power," *Paraclete* 2/4 (Fall) 15–19.

1969

"The Holy Spirit in the Book of Judges," *Paraclete* 3/2 (Spring) 9–14.

1970

"Computerized Fallacies," *PE* (January 28) 10,11.
"Is Mark 16:9-20 Inspired?" *Paraclete* 4/1 (Winter) 7–12.

1971

"When is a Gift of Utterance in Order?" *Paraclete* 5/4 (Fall) 9–17.
"The Best Loved Book," *Advance* (December) 16,17.

1972

"Word Study: God's Mighty Hand," *PE* (May 28) 12.
"New Translations Keep Coming," *Advance* (August) 10,11.
Desire Spiritual Gifts (Springfield: Gospel Publishing House).

1973

"Why the Bible is Reliable," *PE* (January 14) 8–10.
"Lachish," *Encyclopedia Americana* 16 (ed. Bernard Cayne; New York: Americana) 615.
"Word Study: Delight," *PE* (November 18) 15.

"Sir Flinders Petrie," *Encyclopedia Americana* 21 (ed. Bernard Cayne; New York: Americana) 678.

1974
Ready Always: A Devotional Commentary on I and II Peter (Springfield: Gospel Publishing House).
"NIV—A New Testament Favored by Evangelicals," *PE* (September 8) 8,9.

1975
"Word Study: Tribulation Now," *PE* (January 19) 9.
"Pisgah," *Wycliffe Bible Encyclopedia* 2 (eds. Charles Pfeiffer, Howard Vos and John Rea; Chicago: Moody) 1347.
It's Getting Late: A Devotional Commentary on I and II Thessalonians (Springfield: Gospel Publishing House).
"Word Study: The Indelible Sin," *PE* (August 10) 19.
"Shittim," *Wycliffe Bible Encyclopedia* 2 (eds. Charles Pfeiffer, Howard Vos and John Rea; Chicago: Moody) 1582.

1976
What the Bible Says About the Holy Spirit (Springfield: Gospel Publishing House).
"The Bible and the Homosexual," *PE* (February 29) 4,5.
"Word Study: When God Repents," *PE* (March 14) 8,9.
"Word Study: A Rod of Iron," *PE* (April 11) 10,11.
"Word Study: Manifesting His Name," *PE* (December 19) 5.

1977
"Guilt for the Death of Christ," *PE* (March 20) 8–10.
"I Will Put My Spirit within You," *Paraclete* 11/2 (Spring) 8–11.
"Word Study: Rejected—Yet Beloved," *PE* (May 8) 13.

1978
"Word Study: Can Spiritual Gifts be Lost?" *PE* (March 12) 8.

1979
The Holy Spirit: A Study in Pneumatology (Brussels: International Correspondence Institute).
"Twenty Five Years after Pentecost," *Paraclete* 13/1 (Winter) 5–8.

"Many Gifts—The Same Spirit," *Paraclete* 13/2 (Spring) 27–31.
"Old Testament Foundations of the Pentecostal Faith," *JSPS* 1/1 (Spring) 21–30.
"Unity by the Spirit," *Paraclete* 13/3 (Summer) 28–31.
"Many Members—One Body," *Paraclete* 13/4 (Fall) 14–18.
"Prophecy in the Old Testament: Its Definition, Form, and Function," *Redemption Tidings* (October 18) 10–13.

1980

"Love is Indispensable," *Paraclete* 14/1 (Winter) 19–27.
"Word Study: Consecration, Commitment, Submission," *PE* (February 10) 20,21.
"One Purpose—Edification," *Paraclete* 14/2 (Spring) 23–29.
"Worshipping with Heart and Mind," *Paraclete* 14/3 (Summer) 26–31.
"In Good Order," *Paraclete* 14/4 (Fall) 5–8.

1981

The Book of Acts (Springfield: Gospel Publishing House).
"Decently and in Order," *Paraclete* 15/1 (Winter) 9–13.
"Prayer—Communion with the Triune God," *PE* (August 23) 6.
"Word Study: Confess It!" *PE* (September 6) 10,11.
"Another New Bible Version: The New KJV," *PE* (December 7) 12,13.

1982

"The Pentecostal Explosion at the Azusa Street Mission," *Assemblies of God Heritage* 2/3 (Fall) 2,3,6.

1983

"Great Joy," *Advance* (December) 4,5.

Dr. Horton authored the entire volumes of *The Adult Teacher*, a weekly Sunday school periodical published by his denomination for use in adult Bible classes, annually from 1952–1971. He contributed the biblical exposition to issues of the *Teacher* from 1971–1978 and has written about half of each volume since that time.

ABBREVIATIONS

AB   Anchor Bible
Acts Thom.   Acts of Thomas
AnBib   Analecta biblica
AUSS   Andrews University Seminary Studies
ATLAMS   American Theological Library Association Monograph Series
BAGD   W. Bauer, W. F. Arndt, F. W. Gingrich and F. Danker, *Greek-English Lexicon of the New Testament and Other Early Christian Literature*
Barn.   Barnabas
BBB   Bonner biblische Beiträge
BC   F. J. F. Jackson and K. Lake, eds., *The Beginnings of Christianity*
BDF   F. Blass, A. Debrunner and R. W. Funk, *A Greek Grammar of the New Testament and Other Early Christian Literature*
BETL   Bibliotheca ephemeridum theologicarum
Bib   Biblica
BJRL   Bulletin of the John Rylands University Library of Manchester
BNTC   Black's New Testament Commentaries
BTB   Biblical Theology Bulletin
BWANT   Beiträge zur Wissenschaft vom Alten und Neuen Testament
BZNW   Beihefte zur *Zeitschrift für die neutestamentliche Wissenschaft*
CalTheoJ   Calvin Theological Journal
CBC   Cambridge Bible Commentaries
CBQ   Catholic Biblical Quarterly
Corp. Herm.   Corpus Hermeticum
CT   Christianity Today
Did.   Didache: The Teaching of the Twelve Apostles
Ed.   Editor
EQ   Evangelical Quarterly
ET   English Translation
EvT   Evangelische Theologie
ExpTim   Expository Times

FThSt   Frankfurter Theologische Studien
HNT   Handbuch zum Neuen Testament
HNTC   Harper's New Testament Commentaries
HTKNT   Herders theologischer Kommentar zum Neuen
    Testament
ICC   International Critical Commentary
IDB   G. A. Buttrick, ed., *Interpreter's Dictionary of the Bible*
IDBSup   Supplementary volume to *IDB*
Int   Interpretation
JBL   Journal of Biblical Literature
JETS   Journal of the Evangelical Theological Society
Jos. *Ant*   Josephus, *Antiquitates*
Jos. *B.J.*   Josephus, *de Bello Judaico*
JSNT   Journal for the Study of the New Testament
JSNTS   Journal for the Study of the New Testament Supple-
    ment Series
JSPS   Journal of the Society for Pentecostal Studies
JSS   Journal of Semitic Studies
JSSR   Journal for the Scientific Study of Religion
JTS   Journal of Theological Studies
KJV   King James Version
LQ   Lutheran Quarterly
LSJ   H. G. Liddell, R. Scott and H. S. Jones, *A Greek-English
    Lexicon*
LXX   Septuagint (earliest Greek version of the OT)
MeyerK   H. A. W. Meyer, Kritisch-exegetischer Kommentar
    über das Neue Testament
MSS   Manuscripts
MT   Masoretic Text
NAS   New American Standard
NCB   New Century Bible
NEB   New English Bible
NICNT   New International Commentary on the New Tes-
    tament
NIDNTT   C. Brown, ed., *New International Dictionary of New
    Testament Theology*
NIGTC   New International Greek Testament Commentary
NIV   New International Version
NKJV   New King James Version
NovT   Novum Testamentum

NT   New Testament
NTS   New Testament Studies
OBO   Orbis Biblicus et Orientalis
OT   Old Testament
PE   Pentecostal Evangel
1 QH   *Hôdāyôt (Thanksgiving Hymns)* from Qumran Cave 1
1 QS   *Serek hayyaḥad (Rule of the Community, Manual of Discipline)*
    from Qumran Cave 1
RB   Revue biblique
RevExp   Review and Expositor
Rpt.   Reprint
RSV   Revised Standard Version
RTP   Revue de théologie et de philosophie
SBLSBS   Society of Biblical Literature Sources for Biblical
    Study
SBT   Studies in Biblical Theology
SJT   Scottish Journal of Theology
SNTSMS   Society for New Testament Studies Monograph
    Series
TDNT   G. Kittel and G. Friedrich, eds., *Theological Dictionary*
    of the New Testament
ThRen   Theological Renewal
T. Levi   Testament of Levi
TNTC   Tyndale New Testament Commentaries
TQ   Theologische Quartalschrift
Tr.   Translator
TWOT   R. L. Harris, G. L. Archer and B. K. Waltke, eds.,
    Theological Wordbook of the Old Testament
TynB   Tyndale Bulletin
US   Una Sancta
VoxEv   Vox Evangelica
WMANT   Wissenschaftliche Monographien zum Alten und
    Neuen Testament
WUNT   Wissenschaftliche Untersuchungen zum Neuen
    Testament
ZKT   Zeitschrift für katholische Theologie

PART I:
BIBLICAL STUDIES

1

THE EXPERIENCES OF DERELICTION AND OF GOD'S PRESENCE IN THE PSALMS: AN EXERCISE IN OLD TESTAMENT EXEGESIS IN THE LIGHT OF RENEWAL THEOLOGY[1]

John W. McKay

OUR CENTURY HAS WITNESSED a worldwide revival of charismatic Christianity without precedent in the history of the church. Laity, pastorate, and scholarship of every denominational and credal shade have been influenced by it in some degree, though sadly its impact on OT scholarship has been fairly minimal to date. It is therefore a wonderful privilege to be contributing to this anniversary volume in honour of one fellow OT scholar who has faithfully served the cause of Pentecostalism for many years.

In the Gospels of Mark and Matthew the only words of Jesus from the cross are the cry of dereliction that opens Psalm 22: "My God, my God, why hast thou forsaken me?" (Mark 15:34; Matt 27:46, RSV). While most commentators seek to assert the reality of Jesus' experience of dereliction—however that is to be understood—the sense of embarrassment at finding these words on the lips of the Son of God is never far from the surface, and the reader is generally reminded that Psalm 22 culminates in a note of triumphant faith.[2] And at that point we find ourselves thrown back on the interpretation of the psalm itself.

The psalm falls neatly into two parts, a cry for help (vv 1–21) and a hymn of praise (vv 22–31), where both parts seem to relate to the psalmist's present condition. The psalm is neither a hymn of praise for deliverance from past suffering, nor simply a promise of praise conditional upon future deliverance from present suffering, but a prayer for help in present distress together with an offering of praise to God for giving it. Some commentators have therefore argued that Psalm 22 is made out of two originally independent psalms, a lament and a hymn of thanksgiving. Others have maintained that it was composed for the use of the Jerusalemite king as he participated in the different stages of a festival drama which portrayed his initial humiliation before the onslaught of inimical powers of evil and chaos and his final restitution and victory as God's viceregent and the champion of cosmic order. A further possibility is to relate the psalm to the ritual of an individual who in his suffering presents his cause before priest and congregation and utters praise in anticipation of healing, prompted by an oracle or a blessing pronounced between his recitation of the two parts.[3] Each of these suggestions contains its own difficulties inasmuch as it depends on assumptions, literary or ritual, that cannot be proved from the OT text itself.[4]

Furthermore, the problem of the structure of Psalm 22 is one shared by almost every other lament of the individual worshipper—and these psalms of lament constitute by far the largest single category in the psalter (about 40 psalms altogether). Some of these are too short to be easily divisible into two psalms (e.g., Psalms 13 and 54) and it seems unreasonable to assume that most of them were written for the king's use at festival time without clearer evidence to that effect. Nor does the theory of interruption by a priestly oracle suffice in every instance, since the praise element sometimes precedes the lamentation (as in Psalms 27 and 40) and occasionally the two are intermingled throughout the psalm (as in Psalm 31). Of course there is bound to be variety in a book like the psalter and the theory that explains one lament need not necessarily be the correct one to explain another, but scholarship has until now been much preoccupied with precisely this problem, of discovering some kind of reasonable comprehensive setting (*Sitz im Leben*) to which the majority, if not all of the psalms can be attached. Since the determinative work of Gunkel, that setting has been seen in the religious life of the worshipping community rather than in the private experience of an individual, such as David, and discussion and research have therefore tended to focus on determining the nature of Israel's (festival) worship to which the psalms are presumed appropriate.[5]

This is, of course, a valuable pursuit in itself, but it has tended to remove attention from the strongly experiential language of the psalms. It is like reconstructing the festival atmosphere and the seasonal rituals of the Church of England from *The English Hymnal* without being overly concerned about the profound inner spirituality to which many of the hymns attest. My purpose here is to look for a moment beneath the skin of (reconstructed) rituals in an attempt to tap the heartbeat of religious experience in many psalms of lamentation that speak of dereliction and longing for the presence of God,[6] and ultimately to return through Psalm 22 to the experience of Jesus.

When we begin to probe the psalmist's experience in the laments, we are immediately confronted with the problem of identifying the nature of the sufferer's complaint. Sometimes he tells of illness (Psalm 6), or of false accusation (Psalm 17), or of assault by nightmarish (demonic?) creatures (22:12f), or of persecution by his fellow countrymen and former friends (Ps 55:12f).

These and other similar circumstances have sometimes been treated as determinative for distinguishing a psalm's specific purpose and setting, but the images must often be read as typical and poetic, presenting a whole panorama of suffering which permits the psalms to be used in a variety of circumstances. This impression finds ample confirmation in Psalm 22 itself, where in vv 6–8 and 12–18 the categories of mockery, nightmare, fever, hostility, and persecution are ranged side by side. It is hardly to be assumed that this particular psalm is only suitable for use by one whose plight is that he has been struck down with malaria in an African jungle while a crowd of wild beasts prowl and growl around him and a tribe of headhunters leer at him through the undergrowth. The imagery is clearly fluid and symbolic, but more than that, it is cumulative, building up a heightened impression of that tendency to death about which the sufferer complains so frequently in the laments (e.g., Pss 6:5; 22:15; 28:1; 69:1f). It is in this fear of death that these typical pictures find their coherence and meaning. Death represents the antithesis of all that God represents. It is the other shepherd from whose power God has to ransom the righteous (Ps 49:14f). Its domain is Sheol, a place of silence where God's praise is not sung (Ps 6:5) and where the dead lie forgotten by God (Ps 88:4f). It signifies horror, insecurity, abandonment. It is what the psalmist fears most of all because it spells dereliction. Hence his cry of agony, for he sees his present condition, whatever it be, as one that draws him nearer to that terrifying darkness. Yet his sense of dereliction is also a present reality and not just a fear of future abandonment in the grave. Already in this life he feels the power of death at work in his body and already he feels that God is no longer vitally present with him.

In order to probe more deeply into the experience of the psalmist, it is necessary at this point to introduce a distinction between the language of "intrinsic" experience and that of "theological" interpretation. The terminology is partly prompted by Dorr's study of the theological vocabulary of renewal in which he distinguishes between "intrinsic" and "imposed" categories in discussing the experience of baptism in the Spirit.[7] The distinction made here, however, is not exactly the same as Dorr's though there are similarities between them. The "intrinsic" is basically what a man himself feels about what happens to him and the "theological" is his view of what God's part is in the event. In discussing religious experience the two categories must inevitably overlap at certain points, but the broad distinction is a convenient one for our present purposes.

The intrinsic vocabulary falls into three broad subdivisions. First, there are the pictures of physical illness and debility (Pss 6:2; 22:14f; 38:3,5) and, of course, of the dominating tendency to death (Ps 22:15). Second, there is the more psychological language of spiritual distress (Ps 42:5), guilt feelings (Ps 38:4), uncertainty about the way of faith (Ps 25:4f), depression and hopelessness (Ps 102:3f), sorrow, sadness and tears (Pss 6:6; 30:5; 69:3), and nightmarish horror (Ps 22:12f, 16f,20f). Third, there are the social portraits of loneliness (Ps 25:16), rejection by friends (Pss 38:11; 69:8), betrayal (Ps 55:12f), mockery (Pss 42:3; 69:12), and most frequently of unspecified besetting enemies (Ps 13:2,4). The one word that seems best to embrace these various aspects is that used at the beginning of Psalm 130, namely "depths": "Out of the depths I cry to thee, O Lord!" The psalmist has hit rock bottom in this life; to sink any lower must be to sink into Sheol. He is helpless to raise himself and God seems to be doing very little to help him, to be very absent indeed.

But with that thought we come to the vocabulary of theological interpretation that describes God's part in the experience. The psalmist prays that God may not "forget" him (Ps 13:1), or "hide his face" from him (Ps 13:1), or "forsake" him (Ps 22:1), or "be far from" him (Ps 22:1), or "be deaf" to him (Ps 28:1), or "be silent" to him (Ps 28:1), or "be angry" with him (Ps 6:1), or "cast him off" (Ps 88:14). These phrases are drawn from the prayers of the psalmist, not from doctrinal statements, but they clearly do presuppose an accepted theological interpretation of God's role in human suffering. On the surface this may look like an interpretation that stands in contrast to the confident expressions of belief in God's perpetual presence even amid the direst distress such as are to be found in Psalm 23, or in the NT in Rom 8:39, but it must be admitted that it is one that coheres admirably well with the mood of inner agony presented in the intrinsic vocabulary of the psalms. In principle God may be eternally present, but experience does not always conform to the expectations of rational and dogmatic principle, as the perplexed "Why?" or the weary "How long?" so forcibly attest. The psalmist is preoccupied with his innermost feelings of desolation, and it is those feelings that his prayer vocabulary reflects rather than any refined theology he may care to uphold in his less troubled moments. Nonetheless, his cries of dereliction do indicate a yearning for the vindication of a faith that has its roots in a doctrine of God's eternal presence.

The experience of the presence of God is the direct counterpart to the experience of dereliction and it naturally plays a considerable part in the psalms we are examining here. The intrinsic expressions again fall into three broad categories. First, there is the physical manifestation of the psalmist's mood in rejoicing (Ps 13:5), singing (Ps 13:6), dancing (Ps 30:11), shouting (Ps 71:23), lifting the hands in worship (Ps 63:4), and praising God (Ps 30:12). Second, there is the more emotional language of peace (Ps 4:8), security (Ps 31:20), satisfaction (Ps 63:5), release from fear (Ps 27:1f) and guilt (Ps 32:1f), the reviving of the heart (Ps 69:32), and exuberant joy (Ps 4:7). Third, there is the social aspect of worship in the temple (Ps 27:6), praying for the same experience for others (Ps 28:9), witnessing to others about the experience (Pss 22:22; 69:32), rejoicing in the company of the faithful (Ps 22:22,25), even joining in the song that the whole of creation sings to God's glory (Ps 69:34). In sharpest contrast with the depths-language of dereliction, this is the song of the man whom God has "set on high" (Ps 69:29). It is the language of thrilled rejoicing and praise, of deep peace and security, of excited song and witness—everything that Christian renewal stands for (cf. especially Ps 4:7–8).

The vocabulary of theological interpretation relating God's part in the experience is very rich and varied, but attests to the same kind of enjoyment of warmth, assurance, and vitality. God hears (Ps 6:8), he answers (Ps 13:3), he turns or comes back (Ps 6:4), he draws near (Ps 69:18). God heals (Ps 6:2), saves (Ps 6:4), and delivers (Ps 6:4). He dispels the foe (Ps 6:10) and lightens human sorrows (Ps 13:3). He is gracious (Ps 6:2) and bountiful (Ps 13:6). He pardons (Ps 25:11) and reassures about the way of faith (Ps 25:4–10). He brings release from death (Ps 13:3), he brings life (Ps 30:3), he gives his Spirit (Ps 51:10f). His presence is mediated in his house (Ps 27:4f) or his sanctuary (Ps 28:2) where the sufferer is, as it were, brought into the security and warmth of God's own home (Pss 23:6; 43:3). God's presence is variously described as his shelter (Ps 31:20), the shelter of his wings (Ps 61:4), his strength (Ps 28:7f), images betokening security, or as his face (Ps 22:24), his beauty (Ps 27:4), his light (Ps 43:3), his power and glory (Ps 63:2)—all of which suggest the radiant warmth and splendour that evoke reverence and joyous praise; or again God's presence is conveyed as his truth (Ps 43:3), his goodness (Ps 27:13), his integrity and uprightness (Ps 25:21), and most frequently his love (ḥesed, Ps 31:16), qualities that inspire a sense of reassurance and trust; and finally as his Spirit (Pss 51:10f; 143:10) that restores vitality and joy and that leads in the paths of righteousness.

Despite the great variety in the terminology, the impression of an overall picture is easily formulated. God's presence means integrated wholeness, physical, spiritual, and social. It means release from physical torment, from spiritual anxiety, and from social scorn or oppression. More positively it means physical healing and rejoicing, spiritual peace and security, and social harmony in the worshipping community of the faithful. It effects passage from the realm of death into the vital and joyous realm of life. Intrinsically it is the turning of weeping into joy, or mourning into dancing (Ps 30:5,11); theologically it is the restoration of God's favour or his presence (Ps 30:5,7).

At this point we may return to the initial problem of the connection between the two contrasting elements in the laments and approach it afresh through the images of dereliction and God's presence that we have extracted from them. Although these psalms may have been recited in festival or private ritual contexts, and while they may be appropriate for use in time of bodily illness, or on the eve of trial in court, or in the face of demonic wizardry, or in the teeth of persecution, or in other similar circumstances,[8] they are not prayers simply for physical healing, or simply for spiritual deliverance, or simply for the repairing of relationships. Their intrinsic language, it must be reiterated, draws total, cumulative pictures. These psalms cry out for fullness of life in all its aspects, for renewed, total, integrated wholeness—that wholeness is epitomized in the psalmist's overarching theology of the presence of God. The main difference between the intrinsic and the theological expressions is that the former speaks of what is humanly or scientifically quantifiable, while the latter uses language that is only meaningful in the context of religious belief. That is, the vocabulary of the theological interpretation is the vocabulary of faith. And it is at this faith level, it would seem, that the link between lamentation and praise in the psalms must be established.

Occasionally the laments hint that the cause of dereliction may be sin (e.g., Pss 6:1; 38:1,4,18), but generally no explanation is offered. Dereliction is rather presented as an experience about which the sufferer does not care to rationalise. He complains, he begs, he agonizes, he pleads, he prays and cries

out, *why?* or *how long?* but he does not want reasoned explanations such as a Job's comforter might care to offer. The only
answer he is prepared to accept is complete restoration, which,
he knows and as Job also discovered, is to be found in the
vision of the face of God and there alone. *He seeks not explanations, not consolations, not even cures, but God himself.* He likens
himself to one dry and weary (Pss 42:1; 63:1; 143:6) crying for
water from the very ends of the earth (Ps 61:2), crying out for
God (Ps 42:2). Hence, coupled with the language of faith we
have also the language of longing, and it is these two dispo-
sitions, faith and longing, that forge the link between the
contrasting elements in the psalms of lamentation.

Thus, whereas the psalmist sometimes suggests confession
of sin as the channel of transfer from death to life (e.g., Psalms
25, 38, 51), more often he speaks of confession of faith (Ps
31:4) or trust (Pss 13:5; 22:4; 28:7), sometimes stimulated by
meditation on God's great acts in creation and past history or
on God himself (Pss 63:6; 77:3f). Coupled with his expression
of trust is the oft-repeated theme of waiting in hope for God
(Pss 27:14; 31:24; 38:15) or of longing for him (Pss 38:9; 42:1f;
63:1; 84:2). In other words, the psalms of dereliction and God's
presence are essentially psalms of longing and waiting, of faith
and trust. (Perhaps it would be more useful and less confusing
to refer to them by some such title as "psalms of trustful longing" rather than by the designation "laments," which, though
it may be appropriate for other psalms, is somewhat mislead-
ing when applied to many of these that use the language of
dereliction or of God's presence.) They speak of a religion that
is satisfied with nothing less than God himself and is prepared
to wait and wait for him (cf. also Job and Habakkuk). And
undergirding this religion of longing and waiting are the conviction and trust that God acts to revitalize the languishing
body and the broken heart, a conviction and trust that are
prepared to stake everything on the reliability of God himself
to such a degree that already in the midst of sorrow and
rejection the sufferer can look to God's tomorrow with a
yearning and confidence that enables him or her to view the
restoration as already a reality, if not yet historically realised.

Let us now return to Psalm 22 and then to the crucifixion. In
Psalm 22 the theme of trust is explicit in the psalmist's medi-

tation on the faith of his forefathers in vv 4–5 where the verb "trust" is used three times. It also underlies the mocking taunt of his enemies in v 8 and his expression of his belief that God has been his protector from birth in vv 9–10. The theme of longing is more implied than explicit, but it can be traced in the words of dereliction themselves as represented in vv 1,11,19, in the unresting prayer for hearing in v 2 and in the expression of faith in v 26 that those who seek God will be satisfied. There can be little doubt that, although the actual words "long," "wait," or "hope" are not found in the text, this is in fact a psalm of trustful longing like so many others in which the distressed sufferer reaches out for God's presence.[9]

In the Gospels of Mark and Matthew, Jesus is portrayed as one who, after his struggle in Gethsemane, accepts his destiny and, like Isaiah's servant, "gives his back to the smiters and his cheek to those who pull out the beard" (Isa 50:6). He is resigned, unresisting to his Father's will, and yet also resigned, unresisting to the abuse of his enemies. He is, in fact, permitting himself to live out the double experience of Psalm 22 and all the other similar psalms in the OT, but permitting himself to do so in the fullest confidence and trust such as no other man had ever been able to muster. He is indeed the perfect figure of trusting and waiting, quite unlike the warrior who faces the prospect of death with gritted teeth or with unthinking abandon, quite unlike the philosopher who drinks the hemlock with logical repose, quite unlike the martyr who hungers for his fiery crown. His cry of dereliction is no cry of victory. On the cross Jesus has plumbed the depth of human misery where only the grave remains; his sense of alienation must have been very real. But neither is his cry simply one of despair. Much rather it is a cry of deep and desolate longing, but yet of a longing that has shown itself to be undergirded by such faith and hope that it could not but be rewarded with its Easter.

Is not the pattern found in Psalm 22 and on the cross that of renewal? We Christians speak of receiving God's blessings by faith, but perhaps we need to learn more of the lessons of the Psalms and of Jesus about longing, hope, trust, and endurance as we seek this renewal. Again, we may long for the intrinsic experiences of joy and consolation, but they will only be real

and lasting to the person of faith if they are sought directly in
what the psalmist so often and so fondly refers to as "the face
of God." And as we wait with longing and trust, we must also
learn to confess that trust "in the midst of the congregation"
(Ps 22:22) with words of faith and praise, though not simply
with shallow lip service, but with the confidence that is prepared to go with Jesus into the very depth of real dereliction
knowing that God has the power to redeem and glorify.

> *One thing* have I asked of the Lord,
>   that will I seek after;
>   . . . to behold the beauty of the Lord.
> Thou hast said, "Seek ye my face."
>   My heart says to thee,
> "Thy face, Lord, do I seek."
> I believe that I shall see the goodness of the Lord
>   in the land of the living!
> Wait for the Lord;
>   be strong, and let your heart take courage;
>   yea, wait for the Lord!
>
>   (Ps 27:4,8,13f)

Notes

1. The editor would observe that Dr. McKay will perhaps be
familiar to most readers for his stimulating and timely study of
Elihu's contribution to the debate about suffering in the book of Job,
"Elihu: A Proto-Charismatic?" *ExpTim* 90 (1979) 167–71. Formerly
Senior Lecturer in Theology in The University of Hull, and subse-
quently, Rector of St. Ninian's Church (charismatic Scottish Epis-
copal), Prestwick, Ayrshire, Dr. McKay has now taken up the post of
Director of Studies at the newly formed Roffey Place Christian Train-
ing Centre, Faygate, Horsham, West Sussex, England RH12 4SA.
Roffey Place is associated with the international ministry of Colin
Urqhart and fills an important need in the British charismatic scene.

Dr. McKay's interest in preparing his contribution to this festschrift was at first prompted by a paper on death read to the department of Theology in the University of Hull by a former colleague,
Rev. I. P. Ellis. Further motivation came during the preparation of an
address on the presence of God in the Psalms for a diocesan clergy
conference in York, and through a reading of *Remove the Heart of Stone:
Charismatic Renewal and the Experience of Grace* (Dublin: Gill and Mac-
Millian, 1978) by the pastoral missionary theologian Donal Dorr.

The basic theology of dereliction, presence of God and trustful longing, as many OT students have realized, already underlies Dr. McKay's exegesis in J. W. Rogerson and J. W. McKay, *Psalms* (CBC, 3 vols.; Cambridge: University Press, 1977), where some of the points of detail raised in his present contribution may be explored further.

2. Cf. C. H. Dodd's contention that such quotations are intended to recall their whole context in the OT, *According to the Scriptures* (London: Nisbet, 1952) 97. An early stage of the embarrassment about the words of Jesus may be reflected in the variant manuscript traditions and in the Gospel of Peter, cf. K. Stendahl, *The School of St. Matthew and its use of the Old Testament* (Lund: Gleerup, ²1968) 83–87. For an account of some of the main theories about the use of Psalm 22 in the passion narrative, particularly as found in Mark, cf. J. H. Reumann, "Psalm 22 at the Cross: Lament and Thanksgiving for Jesus Christ," *Int* 28 (1974) 39–58. For an overall treatment, cf. D. J. Moo, *The Old Testament in the Gospel Passion Narratives* (Sheffield: Almond, 1983), who argues that the evangelists did not alter history in relation to Psalm 22 in the crucifixion narrative.

3. For a concise presentation of the most widely held view of the interpretation of the laments, cf. J. H. Hayes, *Understanding the Psalms* (Valley Forge, Pennsylvania: Judson, 1976) 57–84. The theory of their use by the king in the festivals has been restated by J. H. Eaton, *Kingship and the Psalms* (SBT 2/32; London: SCM, 1976); cf. D. E. Aune, *Prophecy in Early Christianity and the Ancient Mediterranean World* (Grand Rapids: Eerdmans, 1983) 84–85.

4. Cf. particularly the careful criticism of D. J. Clines, "Psalm Research since 1955: I. The Psalms and the Cult," *TynB* 18 (1967) 103–6.

5. For an outline of the history of modern Psalm-studies, cf. R. E. Clements, *A Century of Old Testament Study* (London/Philadelphia: Lutterworth/Fortress, 1976) 76–98.

6. The psalms under discussion here are listed in Rogerson and McKay, *Psalms* 1:13f, under the heading "Prayers of the individual in time of need." It is, of course, only possible to give a few select references in the text of this article, but a general reading of most of these psalms should be sufficient to show how the arguments presented here apply to them.

7. Dorr, *Remove the Heart of Stone*, 36–54.

8. Ibid., 36; Hayes, *Understanding the Psalms*, 57–84.

9. One of the best expositions of Psalm 22 along similar lines that I know is that of J. McLeod Campbell, *The Nature of the Atonement* (London: Macmillan, ⁶1886) 236f, though he stresses the trusting, rather than the longing aspect of the psalm.

2

RENEWAL AS RESTORATION IN JEREMIAH

J. G. McConville

IT IS WELL-KNOWN that the term "new" in the OT (*ḥādash*)
usually has the connotation "renewed."[1] This is true even
where the thing that is said to be new appears to be radically
so. The latter part of the book of Isaiah witnesses to this,
when, even as it exhorts not to remember "the former things"
(43:18), it yet conceives its promised "new thing" (43:19) in
terms which can only be understood in relation to what
has gone before. Thus newness is postulated, in one way or
another, of Jacob (41:15) and of the heavens and the earth
(65:17; 66:22), recalling Gen 1:1. Even in 43:18–21 the language
used implies that newness is in terms of familiar creation—and
election—theology. This suggests that whatever renewal might
have meant in OT Israel's experience of God, it can at most
have been a transposition into a higher key of experience
already in their past.

What is true of the book of Isaiah is true also of that passage
which is the almost obligatory "text" for any investigation of
renewal in the OT, namely the New Covenant prophecy of Jer
31:31–34. The *similarity* between this New Covenant and already existing covenantal formulae has led scholars to admit
that the exact nature of the newness here is elusive, to disagree over what it is, and in some cases to deny that there is
anything really new here at all.[2] The following study will, I
hope, make an indirect contribution to this debate.

Our present concern, however, is not with the New Covenant passage itself, but with its context in the book of Jere-

14

miah's theology of restoration, without which it can hardly be properly understood.[3] Our method will be to examine the usage of the verb *shub* in the book, a verb which can be rendered "return," "restore," or "repent," according to context, and which is used, in all senses of both Israel and Yahweh.[4] Our contention is that the usage of *shub* well illustrates the point that renewal in the OT is a returning, and also that the promise of a New Covenant—and any "renewed" relationship with Yahweh—presupposes such "returning."

Jeremiah's appeal to wayward Judah is most typically a call to "return" (Jer 3:7, 10; 4:1; 5:3 etc.). Jeremiah 2 pictures a nation which has defected from Yahweh in order to pursue other gods. Her present disloyalty, furthermore, is in contrast to an earlier period in which she enjoyed a harmonious relationship with her God, who had delivered her from Egypt (2:2f). The prophet's appeal, therefore, has this last period as its background, and summons Judah to enjoy it again, by a return to her former faithfulness.

The return required of Judah is not an entirely independent act, but rather part of a complex one involving Yahweh also. This emerges from a number of word-plays involving the verb *shub*. The most important kind of word-play is that in which a causative form of the verb, with Yahweh as subject, is closely linked with a simple form, applied to Judah. Thus in Jer 31:18 Ephraim (standing poetically for Israel) prays: "Bring me back (causative of *shub*) that I may be restored (*shub*)" (RSV). A restoring activity on the part of Yahweh is a prelude to, or at least a concomitant of, the repentance that reestablishes the relationship. Similarly in 15:19 the Lord says to Jeremiah: "If you *return*, I will *restore* you." (Again—and henceforth—the italicized words are forms of *shub*.) A comparison of the two passages shows that it is impossible to determine a chronological relationship between God's part and humanity's; in this case, unlike 31:18, the human part seems to come first. In fact one can say no more than that the act of restoration involves both God and humanity.

It is important, before proceeding, to identify to what Israel is required to return and be restored. Fundamentally, she must return to the worship of Yahweh from that of Baal. The point is conveniently made by 4:1-4, where we see something of the cash-value of true religion (truth, justice, uprightness, v 2), and the need for allegiance to be heartfelt, (v 4a). This much is clear. Ambiguity threatens to supervene when we ask what is meant by Yahweh "returning" Judah. This is because at one level the activity seems to be a straight, physical one. Beyond the judgment (which is exile) he will restore Judah to her land (e.g., 29:14). Our remarks in the preceding paragraph suggested, however, that there was a moral dimension to Yahweh's activity. And this remains true. Both elements—namely the bringing to repentance and the return to the land—constitute Yahweh's restoring activity. Jeremiah 15:19 illustrates the former; 29:14 exemplifies the latter. Passages such as 31:18 are nicely ambiguous.

This ambiguity is important, however, because it tells us more than anything the answer to the question posed above. The "returning" activity of Yahweh is both a bringing to repentance and a restoration to the land, understood as the fruits of obedience, or the currency of covenant. In renewed obedience, Judah will rediscover the blessing that is properly hers.

So far, we have observed that renewal in Jeremiah involves a return to a place formerly occupied. The idea of returning, however, can be used not only in a good sense but also in a bad one. That is, one who is faithful can return to former wicked ways (cf. 3:19; 8:4-6; 11:10). Indeed, so much is this a danger, that the moral condition of Judah can in effect be pictured as consisting in a tension between the demand to "turn" in one direction and the compulsion to "turn" in another that is diametrically opposed. Jeremiah 3:12 captures this so neatly that it can hardly be adequately reproduced in English. The RSV has: "Return, faithless Israel." The word "faithless," however, like "return," is a form of *shub* (KJV's "backsliding" does more justice to the word-play). The same verb, therefore, appears twice in quick succession, the one meaning "return to God," the other "return to wicked ways." The contradictory tendencies within Judah could hardly be captured in a more picturesque way. (3:14 and 22 are similar cases). It follows from passages like these that returning, for Judah, is no simple matter. It is not a case of proceeding from Point A to B, nor indeed from a neutral position to a committed one. There is no neutrality here. Rather, as in the theology of Paul, there is a battle. Restoration is a return to God on the part of those who have once known him and it occurs in the face of powerful, spiritual compulsion not to do so.

It is worth pausing over Jer 15:19, to notice how this verse combines a number of the points we have considered. Jeremiah is himself rebuked here because of his own doubts. We have observed above the relationship between the human and divine parts in the restoration envisaged, the human part here being Jeremiah's. (The passage thus warrants the view that our observations apply on an individual as well as a corporate level.)[5] The last part of the verse is also a play on *shub* of the second sort we noticed: let the people "return" to Jeremiah (implying a repentance toward God), but he must not "return" to them (meaning that he must not join them in their defection from God).

To complete the picture of the analogy between God's responses and those of humanity we notice finally that God too can "return" both to and from Judah. In 4:28 we read how he will not *turn back* from his purpose to destroy the sinful nation. In 32:40, beyond the promise of restoration in the New Covenant prophecy, he declares that he will no longer *turn away* from doing good to Judah. This undertaking is closely linked with a statement (in the same verse) of his intention that *they* should no longer *turn* from him. There is, therefore, a correspondence between the "turning" of people and God not only in the act of restoration but both before and after the act as well. The relationship between people and God is thus portrayed as always dynamic. Restoration itself partakes of this dynamic quality.

Conclusions

What can our study of Jeremiah say to our contemporary spirituality? At the outset it must be said that any properly biblical assessment of renewal must take into account many strands of teaching, and that the book of Jeremiah is only one such strand. To characterize renewal as restoration or return is not to preclude other related ideas such as growth. However, the word that came to God's people of the OT through

Jeremiah comes to his people still, and we can, I believe, draw three conclusions.

The first is simply that all renewal has some basis in what has already been known. New knowledge of Christ is knowledge of the *same* Christ. There is in all healthy spirituality a returning—a remembering of what it was that first produced a response to God—and a discipline in doing so.

Secondly, the act of returning to God is inseparable from his act of bringing, and indeed his *promise* to bring. We began by putting the New Covenant promise in the context of Jeremiah's wider theology of repentance. We now reverse the emphasis. Our duty to return to God is undergirded by his enabling promise. Jeremiah 24:7, whose terms are so close to those of 31:31–34, but which makes clearer the relationship between promise and repentance, illustrates the point. In the struggle of life with God, in which there is that in us which impels us away from him, it is an indispensable encouragement to hear the words: "I will put the fear of me in their hearts, that they may not turn from me" (32:40).

The third point concerns that battle for the human soul. Our study showed that there was for Judah no neutral point of equilibrium. The only options were to hurry in either one direction or the other, and there were powerful factors pulling both ways. Any return to God is in the context of such a battle, and therefore only by his power and human vigilance. The point illustrates the appropriateness of the Reformation principle according to which the church is *"semper reformanda"*— always to be reformed. It applies also to individuals, of course, and here (as in other respects) Jeremiah stands close to Paul, with his realistic understanding of the perpetual struggle between the old, carnal man and the new, spiritual one (1 Cor 3:1–4 and—in my view[6]—Romans 7). Renewal for Jeremiah is standing, by God's power, in the place of obedience.

Notes

1. Cf., e.g., F. F. Bruce, "New," *IDB* 3:542–43; G. A. F. Knight, *Law and Grace* (London: SCM, 1962) 55–60.
2. Cf. H. W. Wolff, *Confrontations with Prophets* (Philadelphia: Fortress, 1983) 49–62. Some scholars wax lyrical about Jeremiah's New

Covenant as a high point in OT theology, cf. J. Bright, *Jeremiah* (Garden City, New York: Doubleday, 1965) 287; G. von Rad, *The Message of the Prophets* (London: SCM, 1968) 181f. For the contrary view, cf. R. P. Carroll, *From Chaos to Covenant* (London: SCM, 1981), 215–33. For the present writer the newness consists in a greater immediacy in human knowledge of God, superseding even the need for teachers (Jer 31:34).

3. We cannot engage here the complex question of the authorship of Jeremiah. We shall draw for our argument upon strands of the book which are widely considered diverse in origin. The case for unity of authorship has been made by important scholars such as J. Bright, "The date of the Prose Sermons of Jeremiah," *JBL* 70 (1951) 15–35; H. W. Weippert, *Die Prosareden des Jeremiabuches* (Berlin, de Gruyter, 1973).

4. For a comprehensive treatment of the usage of the verb *shub*, cf. W. L. Holladay, *The Root shubh in the Old Testament with Particular Reference to its Usage in Covenantal Contexts* (Leiden: Brill, 1958).

5. For a profound treatment of the relationship between Jeremiah's experience and that of the whole people, cf. T. Polk, *The Prophetic Persona* (Sheffield: JSOT, 1984).

6. Cf. James D. G. Dunn, "Romans 7:14–25 in the Theology of Paul," *Essays on Apostolic Themes* (ed. Paul Elbert; Peabody, Massachusetts: Hendrickson, 1985) 49–70.

3

ROMANS 12:1-2: THE GOSPEL AND RENEWAL

David L. Olford

> *Superficiality is the curse of our age. The doctrine of instant satisfaction is a primary spiritual problem. The desperate need today is not for a greater number of intelligent people, or gifted people, but for deep people.*[1]

W ITH THESE WORDS, R. Foster, begins his presentation of the spiritual disciplines that he views as the "door to liberation,"[2] or "the path to spiritual growth."[3] Many would agree at least with the thrust of Dr. Foster's statement, and many do desire a deeper spiritual commitment and experience for themselves, for their churches, or for the church as a whole. Later in the book, when discussing corporate disciplines,[4] Dr. Foster describes a community characterized by what we might call a "deep" corporate spiritual life or experience.

> Such a community would live under the immediate and total rulership of the Holy Spirit. They would be a people blinded to all other loyalties by the splendour of God, a compassionate community embodying the law of love as seen in Jesus Christ. They would be an obedient army of the Lamb of God living under the Spiritual Disciplines, a community in the process of total transformation from the inside out, a people determine to live out the demands of the gospel in a secular world. They would be tenderly aggressive, meekly powerful, suffering and overcoming. Such a community, cast in a rare and apostolic mold, would constitute a new gathering of the people of God.[5]

Our concern in this article is not to discuss spiritual disciplines as such, but to consider afresh a biblical text that calls the individual and the community to a "deep" response and commitment to God. The Apostle Paul cannot be accused of calling forth "superficiality" from his readership in Rom 12:1-2. Paul challenges his readers and hearers to a life of complete dedication and transformation. Viewing Paul's challenge (again) may help us to consider the individual and corporate response to the gospel that is necessary for a community to be cast in a specifically "apostolic mold." Romans 12:1-2 takes us from "the splendour of God," as demonstrated in the *apostolic* gospel (note Rom 11:33-36), and leads us into *apostolic* directives for a community, including the "law of love as seen in Jesus Christ" (Rom 12:1-2 is a text that can be viewed as summarizing the "demands of the gospel" for God's people living "in a secular world." Within this present festshrift, which considers various aspects of renewal, Paul's exhortation may be of special relevance, for Rom 12:1-2 is a text that speaks of a transformation and renewal that is, because of God's mercy and grace, "from the inside out."

We will consider first of all the significant role of Rom 12:1-2 as an introduction to the directives that follow it. We then will discuss Rom 12:1-2 itself, considering the important words and phrases of the sentence.[6] Lastly, our conclusion will attempt to view the text as whole, and we will consider various implications for Paul's readers today. For if we desire apostolic guidance for renewal in our lives or within the church, a careful consideration of the implications of Rom 12:1-2 may prove to be helpful.

I. Romans 12:1-2 and Paraenesis[7] in Romans

If W. Wuellner is correct in viewing Rom 1:18-15:13 as a unity, giving it the label "*Confirmatio*," then we need to attribute to 12:1-15:13 its due significance within the letter.[8] Wuellner does use the label "digression" for this section of the letter, but this in no way denies its importance.[9] This does not minimize the fact that "Rom 12:1-15:13, spells out the practical commitment of those who took part in the argumentation."[10] At the same time it is an "*exemplum* or paradigm of Paul's basic thesis."[11] The relevance of Rom 12:1-2 to the thesis of Paul's letter has been stated strongly by V. P. Furnish:

The exhortation of Rom. 12:1-2 and the specific appeals which are thus
introduced summarize and focus the whole preceding argument. The first
verses of chap. 12 offer a fresh statement, now in the imperative mood, of
what it means to receive by faith the revealing of God's righteousness
(1:16-17).[12]

It does seem correct to view the paraenesis, and Rom 12:1-2,
as relevant to Paul's purpose and presentation in the letter.
This can be shown without proving that each ethical directive
is somehow developed with a particular theological statement
in mind. Rather, it is the relevance of the paraenesis in general
that is our concern, and therefore the relevance of Rom 12:1-2
as the transition and introduction to the paraenesis.

Paraenesis is common in the Pauline corpus (Rom 12:1-
15:13; Gal 5:13-6:10; 1 Thess 4:1-12; 5:1-22; Col 3:1-4:6; and
Eph 4:1-6:18),[13] and it may include general ethical instructions
as well as directives particularly relevant to the community
addressed.[14] What needs to be remembered as far as Romans is
concerned is that: (1) Paul had never been to Rome (1:10); (2)
Paul recognizes the faith, tradition, and maturity of the believers in Rome (1:8,12; 6:17; 15:14; 16:19); and (3) Paul planned
to visit Rome and to be sent from Rome to minister in Spain
(15:24). Thus, it is probable that Paul's paraenesis, as well as
his gospel, affirms his apostolic standing and ministers to the
community in the light of his future visit.

Wuellner's work on rhetoric in Romans lends support to the
idea that the paraenesis in Romans functions as Paul's "appeal
to commitment" to his gospel, and therefore his ministry.[15]
Pauls' authority is implicit in the giving of such paraenesis and
in the expectation of response. His reference to his *charis*,
"grace," at the beginning of his paraenesis (Rom 12:3), which
is unique in the Pauline corpus, may suggest this. One needs
also to keep in mind the apologetic for writing that follows the
ethical section in 15:14-21. Here again Paul refers to the *charis*
given to him by God (15:15). When added to Paul's affirmation
of his grace and apostleship at the beginning of the letter (1:5),
these texts communicate Paul's authority. Also, in Romans
Paul makes it clear that his teaching stands in the tradition
of the teaching that he is "supplementing" (1:8; 6:17; 15:14;
16:17-19). Appealing to the tradition already received must
have caused the readership in Rome to recognize further the
validity of Paul's gospel and apostleship.

J. L. White refers to the use of paraenesis as "a fourth medium of Paul's authority,"[16] which is one aspect of how Paul refers "to one or another aspect of his apostolic presence."[17] White suggests that

> Paul appears to bring the full weight of the Christian apostolic tradition to bear upon the more specific claims of the letter by his use of paraenesis. This aspect of Paul's apostolic presence indicates that his authority was not primarily individualistic or esoteric in intent.[18]

White believes that by nature paraenesis "is general in intent and shows the relevance of Paul's situational types of advice in connection with the preparation of Gentile congregations for the day of Christ."[19] This may be true as one views the paraenesis as a whole, even if Paul's directives are written with the situation in Rome in mind.

As we consider Rom 12:1-2 carefully below, it is important to keep in mind this Pauline paraenesis. Such paraenesis provides an "apostolic mold" for community living that is commensurate with the gospel already presented. These ethical instructions, beginning with a proper self- and community understanding (12:3-8) and ending with a call to practical unity in Christ (15:1-7; note 8-12 also), presuppose and affirm the authority of the apostle. They are clearly presented as "apostolic." Also, these instructions present a "mold" to form community living. They are what gospel-living is to look like in the community(ies) in Rome. Romans 12:1-2 introduces this "apostolic mold" by calling for the dedication and transformation that is the appropriate response to the gospel of which Paul is not ashamed (1:16).

II. Exegesis of 12:1-2

Romans 12:1-2 links the previous material to the paraenesis that we have considered above. This connection has been described as response or obedience to grace or the gospel,[20] the relation of ethics to theology,[21] the application of previous discussion,[22] exhortation based on previous material (especially chs. 5-8),[23] and as exhortation taking the place of dogmatic teaching,[24] among others. There are affinities between 12:1-2 and a number of the previous section of the letter.[25] Thus, the preceding argument is relevant to what is now being said. The use of *oun*, "therefore," in 12:1 indicates an inferential exhortation based on this preceding material, while signaling a new section.[26]

Verse 1a: Parakalō oun hymas, adelphoi, dia tōn oiktirmōn tou theou.
Therefore I exhort you, brothers, by the mercy(ies) of God.

Parakalō oun hymas, adelphoi indicates the change of mode in communication to direct appeal, or exhortation.[27] Frequent uses of *parakalō* by Paul indicate its importance in what he is seeking to communicate in his letters by way of exhortation.[28] Although the word need not have an authoritarian tone to it,[29] I believe that Cranfield is right when he suggests that here there is a "note of authority."[30] He states, "it denotes the authoritative summons to obedience issued in the name of the gospel."[31] It is appropriate as an introduction to a section of paraenesis.

Dia tōn oiktirmōn tou theou is part of the rhetorical appeal. Schlier views "das Erbarmen Gottes" as the primary subject and the apostle as secondary in the appeal to the community.[32] Schlier's emphasis on the mercy of God appealing though Paul, in parallel with Christ working through Paul, does lay stress on words that may be put aside too quickly.[33] But, more important is the rarity of such a phrase in the Pauline corpus. The theocentric nature of the *dia*-phrase most likely reflects the theocentric argument of the whole letter, and especially the concern just concluded. The plural abstract noun *oiktirmōn*,[34] within the *dia*-phrase, point back to Paul's argument, although it is as rhetorically significant as it is theologically significant.

Verse 1b: parastēsai ta sōmata hymōn thysian zōsan hagian euareston tō theō, tēn logikēn latreian hymōn
to present your bodies a living holy acceptable to God sacrifice, your reasonable worship (service)

Paul's exhortation is given in two parts with the second part consisting of both contrasting and complementary directives. We consider here the first part of the exhortation, an exhortation that involves the forceful and unique use of sacrificial language.

Paristēmi with *thysia* is one way of saying "present a sacrifice." This is true in extrabiblical Greek, whereas the closest the LXX readings get to this meaning is priestly or levitical service or presentation (e.g., Deut 17:12; 18:5, 7; Judg 4:14; 11:13).[35] Paul's uses of the words *paristēmi* and *paristanō* reflect diversity (Rom 6:13[twice],16,19; 12:1; 14:10; 16:2; 1 Cor 8:8; 2 Cor 4:14; 11:2; Eph 5:27; Col 1:22,28; also 2 Tim 2:15; 4:17). An important set of occurrences are presented in 6:13–19, although sacrificial language is not explicit. In 12:1, though, the presentation is sacrificial with *ta sōmata hymōn* entering the consecrated realm of that which is given completely to God. *Paristēmi* is the action Paul calls for, an action that may have both priestly and sacrificial connotations, since the sacrifice involves self-presentation.

Sōma refers to the whole selves, the persons, the individuals' concrete lives. These are the victims, so to speak, in this presentation of a sacrifice. Cranfield states, "The Christian is to offer himself to God entirely—himself in the whole of his concrete life."[36] R. J. Daly comments concerning the concreteness of Paul's image using *sōma*, noting that it is "more material in emphasis than Greek religious thought."[37] R. Jewett suggests in a summary fashion that "presenting the bodies as a sacrifice . . . means to place them entirely in God's service and under his rule."[38] Jewett, furthermore, sees Hebrew sacrificial thought as lying behind the image, with the sacrifice being placed completely at "God's disposal."[39] (Jewett considers the emphasis on the living body to be a counter to "enthusiastic-gnostic theology prevalent in Corinth," and "pneumatic libertinism in Rome.")[40] Paul's image does seem to bring together ethical and cultic thought in a particularly concrete way, having a Hebrew flavor, but not dependent upon a specific OT image. Thus, whatever the specific source of Paul's imagery, the use of *sōma* seems to place it firmly outside of a strictly philosophical or mystical approach to sacrifice which Paul could have drawn on. The image is too concrete for dependence on such sources.

Käsemann has suggested great significance to the use of *sōma* here. *Sōma* represents "our being in relation to the world,"[41] which leads Käsemann to see a close relationship between 12:1 and 12:2. Käsemann views the cultic "transposed into eschatology" here as a baptismal exhortation "in which levitical demands are simultaneously adopted and adapted."[42] He sees Paul's application as emphasizing the rule of God over the lives of the bodies involved. Each one of the *adelphoi* is exhorted, therefore, to present himself in his concrete bodily existence.

Paul's use of the word *thysia* is limited (Rom 12:1; 1 Cor 10:18; Phil 2:17; 4:18; Eph 5:2). The use of *thysia* in Rom 12:1 is the only time it is used within a direct exhortation, although the sacrificial description of the love of Christ in Eph 5:2 implies that Christian love should please God in the same way.[43] Philippians 2:17 may provide a parallel reading, depending on how one deals with the hendiadys and the difficult genitive *tēs pisteōs hymōn*.

A significant and clear parallel outside of Paul's own use of *thysia* is 1 Pet 2:5.[44] Here, the elect (1:1) are living stones (2:4), identified with the living stone that was rejected by men but elect and precious with God. The spiritual sacrifices mentioned (2:5) are not specified, but are an extension of the image of a holy priesthood, which in fulfilling its responsibilities offers such sacrifices. The sacrificial image flows from the priestly description, and it would seem to speak of lives and/or actions consistent with divine election in Christ.[45] Its presence in a section on purity and maturity (1:13–2:10), and the subsequent exhortations beginning with *agapētoi, parakalō* (2:11), also make this text worthy of mention here.

It is interesting to note the undeveloped nature of Paul's cultic language in Rom 12:1 in comparison to 1 Pet 2:5. There is no explicit description of the presenters as priests, and the idea of a dwelling place or temple is lacking.[46] There is no mention of the mediating role of Christ, and the emphasis is on the appeal itself based on the mercy of God. Thus the image is not overtly tied into a christological frame in any way, but is framed by the appeal and the complementary directives to follow (12:2).

The use of *thysia* in this context takes on an ethical significance, as the three descriptive phrases, the surrounding appeal, and the paraenesis to follow indicate. In Heb 10:5–14 the body offered in accordance with the will of God is the sacrifice (10:10). In Rom 12:1 the bodies of the brethren, offered in response to the gospel, is the sacrifice Paul encourages.[47] This presentation of the body is preliminary and complementary to the commands in 12:2, which result in the proving and discerning (in a complete sense) of God's will.[48]

Zōsan hagian euareston tō theō should be translated together modifying *thysian*.[49] Having said this, *zōsa* will prove to reveal a particular emphasis that is worthy of special attention. *Zaō* and *zoē* are used significantly in Romans, beginning with 1:17.[50] Cranfield suggests that the sacrifice "is to be 'living' in a deep theological sense," since in fact when sacrifices were offered they were living, and the contrast of dead and living sacrifices is hardly "worth mentioning."[51] If this is the case, then we are dealing with what may be a carefully created liturgical introduction that has used significant words in the letter. At the least, the use of *zōsa* with *thysia*, clarifies the fact that this sacrifice involves bodily living, or existence. It is living to the Lord (14:8), indeed serving Christ according to the directives of the kingdom that pleases God (14:18). This would seem to be the ethical emphasis of the word *zōsa*, but we must consider the broader context in the light of the significance of "life" in Romans.

The death-life construct is crucial in Paul's understanding of justification and salvation, and it acts as the paradigm (at times with the help of the image of Christian baptism) for Christian experience and obedience. Righteousness, so crucial to the message of Romans, is reckoned "to those who believe upon the one who raised Jesus our Lord from the dead, who was delivered on account of our trespasses and raised for our justification" (Rom 4:24b-25). Life is possible because of the death and resurrection life of Christ. The Christian is to walk in "newness of life" (Rom 6:4), he is to consider or reckon "himself dead to sin and alive to God in Christ Jesus" (6:11).[52] The Christian is to present himself "to God as alive from the dead" (Rom 6:13). Death in Christ has delivered the Christian from the law and enables the believer to "bear fruit to God" (Rom 7:4) and "to serve in the newness of the Spirit" (7:6). As the Christian awaits the redemption of the body (Rom 8:23), he or she must "put to death the deeds of the body by the Spirit" and in so doing live (8:13). These ideas above must be remembered when viewing Rom 12:1. They are not overtly stressed in Rom 12:1-2, although they may be presupposed.

The use of *zōsa* in 1 Pet 2:5 needs attention. The living
nature of the stones of God's real dwelling and the spiritual
nature of acceptable sacrifices are emphasized. These qualities
are dependent on the life of the rejected stone, Christ himself,
and his mediation that allows the spiritual sacrifices to be
rendered acceptably to God (1 Pet 2:4–5).[53] The use of *zōsa* and
pneumatikos in 1 Pet 2:4–5 does not directly criticize ritual practice, but such a criticism may be implied. The same may be said
for the use of *zōsa* in Heb 10:20, and even in 7:25, 9:14, and 17.
The permanent, final, and sufficiently efficacious is declared in
contrast to the limited, temporary, and therefore insufficient.
When one remembers the use *logikē latreia* in Rom 12:1, the
same type of implicit comparison to some type of false, in-
adequate, or surpassed worship may be being made. This is
more probable when Paul's reference to the corrupt worship
of humanity is kept in mind (1:25). Regardless of the possibility
of some type of implicit comparison, *zōsa* has a strong positive meaning indicating the nature and quality of the sacrifice
offered on the basis of the gospel. Because of the sacrificial
context *zōsa* may have a nuance slightly different from previous uses in Romans. *Zōsa* together with the other qualifiers
of *thysia*, stresses the authentic or acceptable nature of this
sacrifice.

The use of *hagios*[54] and the phrase *euareston tō theō* further indicates Paul's emphasis on the nature of this sacrifice presented.
For Paul the state of being *hagios*, or the actions associated with
it, involve the call of God (1:7), the presence and work of the
Holy Spirit (15:16), and the active personal response of the
Christian expressed in bodily slavery to righteousness (6:12,
13,19,22). This last emphasis has the strongest precedent in
the letter and seems most appropriate here, although the idea
of a holy or pure sacrifice is straightforward enough. We do
not want to read too much into this word, but *hagios* may have
an ethical thrust in view of the actual sacrifice referred to by
Paul. Furthermore, *euareston tō theō*, appropriate within a cultic
setting,[55] is used more generally in Rom 14:18, and is used in
language affirming a particular action in Phil 4:18. It is a phrase
that has usage in ethical contexts.[56]

A cultic motif in the introduction to a section of ethics is not
surprising in general. Cultic language was appropriate within

an ethical context in Greco-Roman texts of the period, not to mention the OT and the literature of intertestamental and early rabbinic Judaism.[57] At the same time, it needs to be stated that Paul's particular image of presenting bodies as a living sacrifice is unprecedented. The image is distinctive in the Pauline corpus as well. He does use cultic language somewhat similarly in places (1 Cor 3:16f; 5:7-9; 6:19; 2 Cor 6:16; Phil 4:18?; Eph 5:2),[58] but the distinctive aspect of 12:1 is the sacrificial presentation of bodies. The distinctiveness of Paul's words here is emphasized further by the unique combination of *logikē* and *latreia*.

The phrase *tēn logikēn latreian hymōn* is a summary statement that captures the significance and implication of the sacrifice described. This phrase is more than liturgical summary. It is appositional "to the idea of the sentence,"[59] affirming the exhortation given. The phrase reminds one of the language used in contexts where the nonliteral and metaphorical uses of sacrificial language are found (e.g., *T. Levi* 3:5,6; *Corp. Herm.* 1:31, 13:18,19). This phrase could designate noble, spiritual, or real worship emphasizing the mind and the supra-physical, implicitly questioning the value of traditional worship or sacrifice that lacks philosophical illumination.[60] This is not Paul's particular emphasis, though, and describing the presentation of bodily existence as in some sense constituting reasonable worship or service by means of the metaphorical use of sacrificial language is unique in the relevant literature.[61]

Paul does not use *logikos* elsewhere. A word with some overlap in meaning, *pneumatikos*, does occur often in the Pauline corpus,[62] including three uses in Romans (1:11; 7:14; 15:27). *Pneumatikos* appears twice in Romans in a contrast between flesh and spirit (7:14, 15:27). But Paul is not using flesh/spirit language in this context. He is using an unusual combination of cultic words that leads into a stylized text (12:2) that has a number of rare words.[63] Paul continues in 12:2 to call for the transformation of the readers through the renewing of the mind. With this type of emphasis, complementary to the thought in 12:1, it is understandable that *logikos* would be used. The *nous* is the focal point of the renewing process.

A text that may be of help in discerning the meaning of *logikos* is 1 Pet 2:2. In a context filled with cultic language, *spiritual* in the phrase *"spiritual* unadulterated milk" transfers the image of babies drinking milk directly to the Christian sphere that it seeks to describe. Thus, we are speaking of a spiritual feeding, and a spiritual milk which is the pure teaching of the word (1:25). Implicit here is not only "spiritual" in the sense of nonliteral, but authentic and real for the realm of salvation. It is interesting that *logikos* is used in relation to teaching and growth (1:25–2:2), whereas *pneumatikos* is used to "spiritualize" house and sacrifices in 2:5. It may be that the reference to *logos* (1:23) and the exhortation that implies learning may have directed in the use of *logikos* here, because it implies the growth of the Christian mind and character through teaching.

The above use of *logikos* may give us insight into the use of *logikos* in Rom 12:1.[64] *Logikos* conveys the reasonable, the rational, the spiritual, effectively the authentic, that in this case is the call of the apostle. The emphasis is on the genuine character, the reasonable and rational (in the sense of appropriate) response to the gospel. The authentic willful and conscious presentation of the body in a life pleasing to God is the reasonable worship of a person whose mind is renewed. A further support of his emphasis may be Rom 6:11–13. In Rom 6:11 Paul calls his readers to "reckon" (*logizesthe*) themselves "dead to sin but alive to God in Jesus." One's living is to be guided by thinking that is patterned by the death and resurrection of Christ. The self-presentation in Rom 6:13 is the logical or appropriate outworking of one's faith and baptismal union with Christ.

Logikos in Rom 12:1 is descriptive of *latreia*.[65] The noun *latreia* only appears one other time in the Pauline corpus, in Rom 9:4. Any contrast drawn between 9:4 and 12:1 must note the positive nature of Paul's reference to Israel's worship in 9:4. Although Paul employs language in Rom 12:1 that resembles language used elsewhere to criticize the limitation of the cult (note especially Hebrews 7:10), Paul's language in Rom 12:1 offers no explicit comparison. Paul focuses on the appropriate response to God that the gospel demands. Also, *latreia* is one in a list of privileges mentioned there. It is unlikely, therefore, that Paul has this specific text in mind in Rom 12:1. More significant may be Paul's use of the verb *latreuō* (Rom 1:9,25;

Phil 3:3; 2 Tim 1:3).[66] Paul speaks of his ministry in the gospel using *latrueō* and qualifying it with *en tō pneumati mou*.[67] This is a unique description of ministry. It has an apologetical sense to it, although it is not as polemical as the identifying phrase *hoi pneumati theou latreuontas* in Phil 3:3. In both texts the meanings of "service" and "worship" overlap, since the word is appropriate to the cultic setting or to general service. The authenticating note, and indeed the apologetical sense is present in Rom 12:1, although the reference to *pneuma* is lacking.

Directly relevant for comparison is Rom 1:25. Mankind has exchanged the truth for a lie, and has reverenced and worshipped the creature rather than the creator. Romans 12:1 declares by the mercy of God, the alternative to such worship. This worship is not caught in a lie, but is the authentic and appropriate response of mankind in the body. It is the response to the truth of the gospel. It is the rational response—in the sense of reasonable in view of the gospel presented in 1:16–11:36—to God. The relationship between 1:18–32 and 12:1–2 is further suggested as one notes the movement of ideas in both sections. In 1:18–32 one can outline a movement from wrath (1:18), to bodily corruption (1:24), to false worship (1:25), and to a worthless mind (1:28). Although more concise and interrelated, 12:1–2 can be outlined in a similar fashion (mercy of God–bodily presentation–rational worship–transformation by the renewing of the mind). Thus there is a reversal of the situation under the wrath of God that is based upon the argument of Paul. Cranfield seems to be right when he states that for Paul "true worship is rational . . . in the sense of being consistent with a proper understanding of the truth of God revealed in Jesus Christ."[68]

Verse 2: kai mē syschēmatizesthe tō aiōni toutō, alla metamorphousthe tē anakainōsei tou noos eis dokimazein hymas ti to thelēma tou theou, to agathon kai euareston kai teleion.
    and do not be conformed to this world, but be transformed by the renewal of the mind so that you approve (discern) what the ([good and acceptable and perfect]?) will of God is, the good, and acceptable and perfect.

The *kai* in 12:2 suggests the continuation of Paul's exhortation. It is the exhortatory frame that holds 12:1 and 12:2

together. The transition from a cultic image does not disrupt the exhortation. *Tēn logikēn latreian hymōn*, although appositional to the first part of Paul's exhortation, is not inappropriate before the second part of Paul's challenge. The movement from the presentation of the body to the renewal of the mind is straightforward enough. Romans 12:1–2 presents a comprehensive challenge, addressing the *adelphoi* in terms of their bodies and their minds. The trilogy of descriptive words following *to thelēma tou theou* parallels the trilogy of descriptive words following *thysia* in Rom 12:1. This parallel construction helps to bind the exhortation together structurally.[69] The hortatory context holds the cultic and the eschatological-ethical and transformational language together.[70]

The movement from body to mind reminds us of Rom 1:24–28, which we have already noted in relation to *logikē latreia*. The *adelphoi* are not those who are given over by God *eis adokimon noun* (1:28). They are not those that live a lifestyle deserving of death and are totally morally perverse (1:18–32). Those addressed in Rom 12:2 are evidently (as in Eph 2:2) not to walk or live according to the age, order, or way of this world. They are evidently not to think according to this world (note 1 Cor 1:18–2:16). Rather, they are to be those who are being transformed by the renewing of the mind (note Eph 4:17–24), which results in the ability to discern and approve[71] God's will—the good, acceptable, and perfect (12:2). Paul's readers already have heard from him that God's purpose for them is conformity to the image of Christ (Rom 8:28–30), which to us would seem to be the opposite of conformity to the world. Paul's language in Rom 12:2 does not explicitly point back to Rom 8:29, but Rom 8:29 should not be forgotten when considering the transformation that Paul desires.

Paul has spoken already concerning the body and the mind in Romans 6–8. The view of the *nous* in 7:22–25 is in interesting contrast to the use of *sōma* in 7:24. At the same time, an interesting precedent in the letter is the yielding or presenting of the body (Rom 6:11–13), which is dependent upon a reckoning shaped by the gospel. Since this reckoning is not done by the mortal body, the members, or the flesh, it is probably done by the mind, although Paul does not state this.

This discussion in chap. 6 is not completely unrelated to 7:23-25, nor is it unrelated to 8:5ff. The mind seems to be open, according to Paul's argument in chap. 7, to serving the law of God (7:25), although the flesh or one's members seem to serve the law of sin. But God's salvation through his Son frees one from the law of sin and death (Rom 8:2-4) and offers "the law of the Spirit of life in Christ Jesus" (8:2). The present situation seems to be, regardless of how one relates chaps. 7 and 8, that those who are in Christ Jesus (8:1) are called upon to think a particular way. They are to set their minds on the things of the Spirit, not on the flesh (8:5). In principle, the body is to be considered dead (8:10), and life is to be lived according to the Spirit (8:4,9,13-14). The Spirit is involved even in the putting to death of the deeds of the body (8:13).

It is not surprising, therefore, that Paul's thought in 12:1-2 develops from bodily presentation that speaks of yieldedness or obedience without allegiance to the flesh to transformation by the renewal of the mind. If one reads Paul's earlier discussion into the text at this point, a few things may be clarified or may be seen as preliminary to renewal. Bodies are to be presented to God, dedicated to God, although the redemption of the body (one could speak of renewal) is still in the future (8:23). At the present, the one baptized into Christ is to live with the *understanding* that he is set on the desires of the Spirit (8:5), the Spirit associated with future life (8:11). In essence this means that the gospel ethic is to be that of the future age, living as if alive from the dead, living as heirs with Christ in this time of suffering (8:17). Why is the Christian not to be conformed to this world?—because the Christian has died and lives a new life according to the Spirit. Such a perspective would seem to be included in or presuppositional to Paul's call for nonconformity to this age (world) and the further call for transformation by the renewal of the mind.[72]

One needs to remember Col 3:1-4 and Eph 4:17-24 when considering Rom 12:2 further. Both passages are introductory to ethical instructions and speak of the mind. In Col 3:2 the mind is to be "set on things above, not on things on the earth" (NKJV). This is because of the Christian's death and the resurrection with Christ (Col 3:1,3). In Eph 4:17-24, living that is the result of the futility of the Gentile mind is to be shunned (Eph 4:17–19), and the spirit of the mind is to be renewed (Eph 4:24). Thus, the Christian is to put off one pattern of living (old man) and put on a new pattern (new man) (Eph 4:22,25). Crucial to this process is the teaching concerning Christ that has been received (Eph 4:20–21), and surely this presents the basis for a renewal that results in the life of the new man. Thus, this mental renewal is dependent upon teaching concerning Christ and results in a lifestyle and ethical response, as we would suggest it is in Romans as well.

Although Paul's exhortation does not emphasize "process," but presentation, this call to nonconformity and transformation surely can be seen as a continuous call. The present tenses of the verbs would allow for this. Interestingly, Paul's only other use of *metamorphoō* occurs in a context that suggests a continuing or progressive transformation (2 Cor 3:18). The only other instance of *anakainōsis* refers to the renewing work of the Holy Spirit (Tit 3:5), a work of renewal that may be expressed or spelled out practically in Rom 8:1–17 as something that is continuous. Furthermore, 2 Cor 4:16–18 speaks of a day-by-day renewal that involves a recognition of the unseen and the eternal, while choosing not to focus on the visible and the temporary. Thus, despite the definiteness of Paul's exhortation in Rom 12:2, Paul is probably speaking of a continuous commitment to a process or pattern. The fact that the verbs are not active may suggest this also.

In Rom 12:2 avoiding conformity or being transformed can both be connected to the renewal of the mind, although the grammatical link is with *metamorphousthe* directly. In the final analysis the means or process of this renewal of the mind is not stated.[73] Paul obviously does not express himself fully at this point, but instead he states an introductory exhortation that summarizes his desired response to the gospel. At the same time, what Paul says depends upon the gospel that he has presented from 1:16 to the present point. Thus, the means of nonconformity and transformation may be suggested or derived from Paul's argument. One must consider first the Holy Spirit who enables the process of death of the deeds of the body (Rom 8:13) and who is involved in the life of the one in Christ (Rom 8:1–17). In 2 Cor 3:18, which contains the only other NT use of *metamorphoō* by Paul, he speaks of the Holy Spirit as involved in a process of transformation. Nevertheless, Paul is expressing himself formally as well as unusually in Rom 12:2, and thus he may be thinking more generally. He also does not mention the Spirit directly. The transformation he speaks of is at least the appropriate result of and response to the gospel. After all, Paul has taken his readers from the situation described in 1:18–3:20 to Rom 12:1–2. And as we have noted, Rom 12:1–2 can be compared and contrasted with 1:18–32. It is the gospel, the power of God resulting in salvation to everyone who believes, that makes the contrast between 1:18–32 and 12:1–2 possible.

Also suggesting this broad perspective is the fact that the renewal itself is not described directly, except in terms of its purpose and/or result (*eis to dokimazein*): the discerning, the proving, and possibly the implied conformity to the will of God. Paul does not only speak of the will of God, though, he speaks of the will of God that is *agathos* "good," *euarestos* "acceptable," and *teleios* "perfect" (12:2).[74] These words describe the will of God, but they may also connote the content of that will as well. In other words, if one removed the words *to thelēma tou theou*, one would read that the renewal of the mind is purposed for and results in the discerning of what is good, acceptable, and perfect. This again indicates the general and ethical flavor of Paul's exhortation. This discernment is based upon the renewal of the mind.

Just as one can look back at the gospel as the basis of transformation, it is safe to say that the renewal of the mind is likewise based upon the gospel. Paul is introducing instructions that are founded upon the gospel in the broadest sense (note Rom 12:3ff). These instructions begin by calling for proper thinking concerning one's self in relation to others (12:3), and for the recognition of the body-nature of the community (12:4–5). Thus, there is a unity and diversity that implies equality and respect for varying gifts (12:5–8). The transformation in or by the renewal and renewing[75] that Paul is speaking of in 12:2 leads into the Christian thinking and living expressed in this paraenesis to follow.

Surely the pattern of thinking or reckoning foundational and preparatory to the paraenesis equals thinking based upon the gospel. It is thinking that understands the wrath, justice, and goodness of God, and the sin, accountability, and judgment of humanity (Rom 1:18–3:20). It is thinking determined by the righteousness and grace of God revealed in the gospel and through the death and resurrection of Christ (Rom 3:21–5:21). It is thinking based upon the death and resurrection of Christ which have dealt with sin and death (Rom 6:1–8:4), and it is thinking directed to and by the Holy Spirit (Rom 8:1–30). It is thinking that recognizes the faithfulness of God towards Israel and his mercy towards all (Rom 9:1–11:36). This thinking is obviously not spelled out by Paul in an introductory text like Rom 12:1–2, but such thinking is literally preliminary to his exhortation. Thus, to hear Paul's call to dedication and transformation that leads into Paul's directives for an appropriate community lifestyle, the reader or listener must follow Paul's "deep" understanding and presentation of the gospel.

III. Conclusion

In this conclusion we want to make a few comments about Rom 12:1–2 as a whole, and then we will consider some implications for us today.

Romans 12:1–2

(1) Rom 12:1–2 is a structurally significant text; it is introductory to the paraenesis and inferentially related to the gospel presented earlier in the letter. The general nature, the rare words, and the liturgical structure of Rom 12:1–2 suggest that Paul is composing and possibly borrowing idioms that are appropriate to a liturgical situation. The image or occasion of baptism may provide some of the language of this exhortation, since a call for bodily presentation and nonconformity and transformation would be appropriate at a baptismal setting. Whether this is the case or not, the exhortation is formal in tone, introductory in function, and comprehensive in its broad implications.

(2) Paul's call is radical in the sense of being fundamental and it is general in the sense of being for all who hear his

words. Paul's appeal is not an appeal to enter into esoteric religion. The exhortation is based upon the gospel presented and leads into the community instructions to follow. Paul's call is a call to dedication and transformation for all who have followed Paul so far in his letter. Paul takes his readers from wrath (bodily dishonor), false worship, and a corrupt mind to this exhortation, which is by the mercies of God for bodily presentation—reasonable worship and mental renewal. This transition and transformation are based upon the gospel of the righteousness of God revealed in and through the death and resurrection of Christ.

(3) Romans 12:1-2 may illustrate Paul's own role as proclaimer of the gospel in an interesting way. The sacrifice and renewal to which Paul calls his readers is the appropriate response to the gospel he preaches. Speaking of his own ministry, after explaining his manner of writing, Paul refers to doing the "sacrificial service of the gospel of God in order that the offering of the Gentiles might be acceptable, sanctified in the Holy Spirit" (15:16). The sacrificial language of 12:1, although not precisely parallel to 15:16, may suggest that Paul is doing in Romans what he in fact does in his ministry. He is calling forth an offering (12:1, 15:16), and seeking to make sure that it is acceptable. In this respect, Romans is an example of Paul's ministry, with Rom 12:1-2 indicating the desired result of that ministry.[76] Paul calls people to living and thinking on the basis of the gospel. He calls for reasonable and authentic worship. When we take into consideration the situation of mankind (1:18-3:20) and the false worship that he speaks of in Rom 1:25, we can discern that Paul's challenge is indeed through or by means of the mercies of God.

Implications for Paul's Readers Today

If we consider Rom 12:1-2 to be a significant text, as its position in Romans suggests (above), then it may provide some "structuring" principles for the subject of renewal within the Christian community.

(1) The preaching of the gospel is the necessary basis for sacrifice and renewal in the church. Whatever sacrifice is to be offered and whatever transformation is to take place, it is

dependent upon and should be commensurate with the gospel. Indeed, the gospel, "the power of God resulting in salvation" (Rom 1:16), should be presented in order to bring about authentic worship and that which is according to the will of God. The content of the gospel proclaimed is significant, therefore, since it affects directly the nature of the response. It is the type of gospel that Paul proclaims, the apostolic gospel, that calls forth the radical and complete response described in Rom 12:1-2. If we are looking for renewal in the church along apostolic lines, we need to start with the proclamation of the apostolic gospel.

R. Lovelace, in his book *Renewal as a Way of Life: A Guidebook for Spiritual Growth*, speaks of the need for the "cultivation of the mind," and "the formation of Christian hearts and minds."[77] Lovelace addresses the need for "theological integration" on the part of Christians in our day.[78] Our concern here is not so much with Lovelace's specific concern for "theological integration" as it is with the matter of "the formation of Christian hearts and minds." As far as we can tell from Paul's letter to the Romans, his gospel goes a long way in establishing the fundamentals for forming a Christian mind (and heart for that matter). This gospel is not simplistic, nor is its challenge. Any preaching of the gospel that aspires to evoke renewal in our day must challenge its listeners to obedience and thinking that are radical and consistently Christian.[79]

(2) The direct challenge of the gospel is for total yieldedness to God and a commitment to mental transformation so as to discern the will of God. These are complementary responses that need to be interpreted individually and corporately in the light of the gospel. Before one should seek for particular changes within the community of believers, whether they be structural, ministerial, ethical, or whatever, the need is for a radical commitment to God through Christ on the part of the individuals of the community. Godward dedication and transformation are to result in practical gospel thinking and living in the community, but dedication and transformation are foundational, not secondary. Paul presents this foundational challenge before he speaks about a proper individual and community mindset, the importance of gifts and the essentials of lifestyle.

S. Horton, discussing "The Use of Spiritual Gifts," has stated, "It is not enough to have gifts, then. The motive, the love, the zeal, the state of the heart and mind of the person who exercises the gift is Paul's chief concern."[80] In Rom 12:1-2 Paul indicates his concern for lives given completely to God and completely changed by God before he discusses matters of community living. The very "state" of Paul's readers is challenged by the gospel and is to be a fundamental concern of those interested in renewal. Community Christianity needs to be committed Christianity.

(3) Paul's challenge is for all who believe. The obedience of the body and the renewal of the mind are the appropriate response of all who hear Paul's message. This is a call to all, not to the religious elite. But this is not just a call to everyone who believes, it is a call to anyone who believes. Any less of a response from anyone is less than what Paul sought for. Those interested in renewal should address all who believe, and should challenge anyone and everyone to the commitment Paul describes. In this way our challenge will move beyond the superficial to the fundamental, and we may see, by God's grace, a community "cast in a rare and apostolic mold" because its renewal is based upon an appropriate and authentic response to the gospel.[81]

Notes

1. Richard J. Foster, *Celebration of Discipline: The Path to Spiritual Growth* (New York: Harper & Row, 1978) 1; italics not in original.
2. Ibid.
3. This is the subtitle of the book.
4. Foster, *Celebration of Discipline*, 123-71. The following quote comes from a chapter called "The Discipline of Guidance," 150-62.
5. Ibid., 162.
6. Of most significance in dealing with the sacrificial language in the text are the following: Hans Wenschkewitz, "Die Spiritualisierung der Kultusbegriffe: Tempel, Priester und Opfer im Neuen Testament," *Angelos* 4 (1932) 125-27, 130-31; Philipp Seidensticker, *Lebendiges Opfer (Röm 12, 1): Ein Beitrag zur Theologie des Apostels Paulus.* (Neutestamentliche Abhandlungen 20; Münster, Westf.: Aschendorffsche, 1954); Heinrich Schlier, "Vom Wesen der Apostolischen Ermahnung

nach Römerbrief 12:1-2," *Die Zeit der Kirche: Exegetische Aufsätze und Vorträge* (Freiburg/Basel/Wien: Herder, [5]1972) 74-89; Ernst Käsemann, "Worship and Everyday Life," in *New Testament Questions of Today* (London: SCM, 1969) 188-95; Raymond Corriveau, *The Liturgy of Life: A Study of the Ethical Thought of St. Paul in His Letters to the Early Christian Communities* (Studia Travaux de Recherche 25; Bruxelles/Paris: Desclee de Brouwer, 1970) 155-85; Robert J. Daly's *Christian Sacrifice; The Judaeo-Christian Background Before Origen* (Catholic University of America Studies in Christian Antiquity 18; Washington, D.C.: Catholic University of America n.d.) 243-46. Other articles of significance not primarily concerned with sacrifice are by Horace E. Stoessel, "Notes on Romans 12:1-2 The Renewal of the Mind and Internalizing the Truth," *Int* 17 (1963): 161-75; Christopher Evans, "Rom 12. 1-2, The True Worship," *Dimensions De La Vie Chrétienne (Rm 12-13)* (ed. L. De Lorenzi: Monographique de Benedictina, Section Biblico-Oecumenique 4; Rome: Abbaye de S. Paul, 1979) 7-49; John Koenig, "Vision, Self-offering, and Transformation for Ministry (Rom 12:1-8)," *Sin, Salvation, and the Spirit: Commemorating the Fiftieth Year of the Liturgical Press* (ed. D. Durken; Collegeville, Minnesota: Order of St. Benedict, 1979) 307-23; and although not consulted in any detail the following work should be mentioned: Josef Blank, *Paulus. Von Jesus zum Christentum: Aspekte der paulinischen Lehre und Praxis* (München: Kosel, 1982) 169-91. Most of the material presented in this study was researched for and written in my unpublished thesis, "Paul's Use of Cultic Language in Romans: An Exegetical Study of Major Texts in Romans Which Employ Cultic Language in a Non-literal Way" (submitted to Sheffield University: Sheffield, England, 1985), 301-55. There is a greater emphasis on renewal in this paper.

7. "Exhortation. Passages with a strong exhortatory content in both OT and NT are termed paraenetic" (*NIDNTT* 1, Glossary, 65). Furthermore, "the promise of the gospel is the foundation and presupposition of the claims of the paraenesis (cf. Rom. 1-11 with 12-15)" (65). It is interesting that Romans is the example given in this definition.

8. Wilhelm Wuellner, "Paul's Rhetoric of Argumentation in Romans: An Alternative to the Donfried-Karris Debate Over Romans," reprinted in *The Romans Debate* (ed. K. P. Donfried: Minneapolis: Augsburg, 1977) 152-77 (168).

9. Ibid., 171. The term "digression" is used in a formal rhetorical sense, and should not be thought of as indicating a section that is not significant to Paul's overall purposes in the letter.

10. Ibid., 170.

11. Ibid., 171.

12. Victor Paul Furnish, *Theology and Ethics in Paul*, (Nashville/New York: Abingdon, 1968) 106. Daly states "there is every reason to consider these to be the most important verses of the letter," *Christian Sacrifice*, 243. Whether or not Paul intended these verses to be "the most important," they are certainly worthy of careful attention.

13. D. G. Bradley, "The *Topos* as a Form in the Pauline Paraenesis," *JBL* 72 (1953) 238–46, esp. 239–40. More recent and with some
correction is the work of T. Y. Mullins, "*Topos* as a New Testament
Form," *JBL* 99 (1980) 541–47.
     Concerning other matters: the relationship between *kerygma* and
didachē is not a simple matter, and it touches upon the broader question of the relationship between theology and ethics in Paul. It would
seem that James I. H. McDonald's recent study has shown the danger
of drawing too clear distinctions between the two in *Kerygma and
Didache: The Articulation and Structure of the Earliest Christian
Message* (SNTSMS 37, Cambridge: Cambridge University, 198). C. H. Dodd
made clearer distinctions than McDonald in *Gospel and Law: The Relationship of Faith and Ethics in Early Christianity* (Cambridge: Cambridge University, 1951). Also see Dodd's *More New Testament Studies* (Manchester:
Manchester University, 1968), "The 'Primitive Catechism' and the
Sayings of Jesus," 11–29; and "*Ennomos Christou*," 134–48.
     14. For the outlines of paraenesis, cf. William Doty, *Letters in
Primitive Christianity* (Philadelphia: Fortress, 1973) 43,59–60. A more
recent study that considers the nature of such paraenesis McDonald's
Kerygma and Didache, 69–100 and notes.
     15. Wuellner, "Paul's Rhetoric of Argumentation in Romans,"
170–71.
     16. John L. White, "Saint Paul and the Apostolic Letter Tradi-
tion," *CBQ* 45 (1983) 433–44 (441).
     17. Ibid., 439.
     18. Ibid., 441.
     19. Ibid., 441. This is an interesting observation in relation to
R. J. Karris' argument concerning the nature of Paul's paraenesis in
14:1–15:13 ("Romans 14:1–15:13 and the Occasion of Romans," reprinted in *The Romans Debate*, 75–99). Karris is arguing that such
paraenesis does not indicate that a specific situation is in mind when
Paul writes Romans. If White is right concerning the nature of paraenesis, then Karris' argument loses some of its strength, since the
nature of such paraenesis is to be general in form regardless of the
situation addressed. For a position completely opposite that of R. J.
Karris, see Paul S. Minear's *The Obedience of Faith: The Purposes of Paul in
the Epistle to the Romans* (London: SCM, 1971).
     20. C. K. Barrett, *A Commentary on the Epistle to the Romans* (BNTC;
London: A. & C. Black, 1957) 230; similarly C. E. B. Cranfield, *The
Epistle to the Romans* (2 vols; ICC: Edinburgh: T. & T. Clark, 1975–79)
2:595, and F. F. Bruce, *The Epistle of Paul to the Romans: An Introduction and
Commentary* (TNTC; London: Tyndale, 1963) 226.
     21. C. H. Dodd, *The Epistle of Paul to the Romans* (London, Hodder
and Stoughton, 1932) 188.
     22. W. Sanday and A. C. Headlam, *The Epistle to the Romans* (ICC,
Edinburgh: T. & T. Clark, 1897) 351.
     23. Heinrich Schlier, *Der Römerbrief* (HTKNT 6, Freiburg: Herder,
1977), 351.

24. F. J. Leenhardt, *The Epistle to the Romans: A Commentary* (ET; London: Lutterworth, 1961) 300.

25. Paul's appeal on the basis of the mercy of God reminds one of the significance of mercy in the preceding section (9:15,16,18,23; 11:30,31,32). The language of presentation has already been used in 6:13,16,19. Chapters 5–8, and especially 6–8 have other affinities with the extensive use of *zōē* and *zaō* (5:10,17,18,21; 6:2,4,10,11,13,22,23; 7:1,2,3,9,10; 8:2,6,10,12). *Sōma* is also significant in this section (6:6,12; 7:4, 24; 8:10,11,13,23); and *nous* in 7:23,25. Thus these chapters have a number of connections that will receive further mention below. Then the conceptual and linguistic connections with 1:18–2:16 must not be forgotten, especially with the emphasis on morality in this section. Romans 12:1–2 seems to be a fitting bridge between the two major sections of the body of the letter (1:18–11:36 and 12:3–15:13).

26. For use of *oun*, cf. BAGD, 597.

27. See 15:30 and 16:17 for other uses of *parakalō* in Romans.

28. 1 Cor 1:10; 4:16; 16:15; 2 Cor 2:8; 6:1 (in view of 5:20); 9:5; 10:1; 1 Thess 2:12 (note this use in relation to description of ministry when present); 4:1,10; 5:15; 2 Thess 3:12; Phil 4:2; Col 2:2 (another description of apostolic concern and ministry); Phlm 9,10; Eph 4:1; also 1 Tim 2:1; other NT uses of interest include Jude 3; 1 Pet 2:11; Heb 3:13; 10:25; 13:19,22. The verb occurs over 50 times in the Pauline corpus.

29. Carl J. Bjerkelund's study suggests this possibility, *Parakalō, Form, Funktion und Sinn der parakalō—Sätze in den paulinischen Briefen* (Oslo: Universitetsforlaget, 1967) 172,173,189. This is a work that is particularly significant to Ernst Käsemann's comments on 12:1–2, *Commentary on Romans* (ed. and tr., G. W. Bromiley; Grand Rapids: Eerdmans, 1980) 326–27.

30. Cranfield, *Romans*, 2:597.

31. Ibid., 597.

32. Schlier, "Vom Wesen der Apostolischen Ermahnung," 78.

33. Ibid., 79–80.

34. Nigel Turner, *A Grammar of New Testament Greek: Syntax* (Edinburgh: T. & T. Clark, 1963) 28; also cf. Cranfield, *Romans*, 2:596.

35. Cranfield, *Romans*, 2:598, for extensive references, the most important of which are Jos. *Ant.* 4.6.4 (113) and Jos. *B.J.* 2.6.2 (89). More references are given by Georg Bertram and Bo Reicke, "*paristēmi, paristanō*," *TDNT*, 5:837–841; also, BAGD, 633; and LSJ, 1340–41.

36. Cranfield, *Romans*, 2:599. Robert Tannehill states that in this context *sōma* need only be viewed as the self that "exists for or to something or someone" in *Dying and Rising with Christ; A Study in Pauline Theology* (Zeitschrift für die neutestamentliche Wissenschaft und die Kunde der Älteren Kirche 32; Berlin: Töpelmann, 1967) 72. Also, see Rudolf Bultmann, *Theology of the New Testament* 2 vols. (ET; London: SCM, 1965) 1:192–203; Robert Jewett, *Paul's Anthropological Terms: A Study of their use in Conflict Settings* (Leiden: Brill, 1971) 201–304; Robert

Gundry, *Sōma in Biblical Theology, with emphasis on Pauline Anthropology* (SNTSMS 29, Cambridge: Cambridge University, 1976) 34-36.
    37. R. J. Daly, "The New Testament Concept of Christian Sacrificial Activity," *BTB* 8 (1978) 99-107 (102).
    38. Jewett, *Paul's Anthropological Terms*, 301.
    39. Ibid., 301.
    40. Ibid., 302.
    41. Käsemann, *Romans*, 327.
    42. Ibid., 327.
    43. The reference to the sacrifice of Christ in Eph 5:2 follows a command to "walk in love," but it is separated from the command by *kathōs kai*, which clarifies the exemplary role that Christ's love and giving of himself has in these verses. Thus the use of *thysia* does not occur in the exhortation itself.
    44. Another interesting text is Heb 13:15-16. This text describes the praise and deeds of Christians sacrificially. This can be viewed with 4:14-16 and 10:19-25 in mind. In these texts the connection with the mediating role of Christ is clear, whereas in 13:15-16 the sacrificial picture is left undeveloped.
    45. D. Hill notes that the writer of 1 Peter draws "upon liturgical fragments and ideas in order to reinforce his affirmation of Christian faith and his exhortation to fortitude and fidelity," in "To Offer Spiritual Sacrifices . . . (I Peter 2:5): Liturgical Formulations and Christian Paraenesis in I Peter," *JSNT* 16 (1982) 45-62 (61). The language is used in a passage like 1 Pet 2:5, as in Rom 12:1, to exhort the listeners/readers to live Christian lives befitting a holy priesthood, as stated elsewhere (Eph 4:1).
    46. Temple language is not used explicitly in Romans. R. J. McKelvey is correct in not treating any passages in Romans under his theme, *The New Temple: The Church in the New Testament* (London: Oxford University, 1969). Receiving careful attention are 2 Cor 6:16-7:1; 1 Cor 3:16-17; 1 Cor 6:19-20; Eph 2:20-22, pp. 92-124 (and 1 Tim 3:15; Gal 2:9; 2 Thess 2:3-4, 1 Cor 10:4, pp. 133-38). Daly's suggestion of a temple theme in Rom 15:20 may be correct if such thought is implicit, but it is not explicit (*Christian Sacrifice*, 249).
    47. Barrett, *Romans*, 231.
    48. Paul's possible knowledge or use of Ps 39:6-9 as in the LXX readings, is an interesting possibility, but dependence on this text does not seem necessary for an understanding of Paul's image.
    49. Thus we agree with Cranfield that in translating the phrase to "living, holy, and pleasing to God," each part equally describes the sacrifice (*Romans*, 2:600). Paul only uses *thysia* in the strictest literal sense once (1 Cor 10:18). Paul never uses *holokautōma*, although he uses *prosphora* twice (Rom 15:16; Eph 5:2). Paul uses *thyō* twice, also (1 Cor 5:7; 10:20).
    50. *zaō*: 1:17; 6:2,10,11,13; 7:1,2,3,9; 8:12,13; 9:26; 10:5; 12:1; 14:7,8,9,11; *zōē*: 2:7; 5:10,17,18,21; 6:4,22,23; 7:10; 8:2,6,10,38; 11:15.

51. Cranfield, *Romans*, 2:600. He refers primarily to 6:4, but also 1:17; 6:11,13; 8:13b.

52. Faith is presuppositional or implicit in this discussion. It is the basis of union with Christ (6:8). Baptism is obviously closely associated with repentance and faith, as 6:1–14 indicates. Paul is not developing a new aspect of soteriology here in view of 1:16–5:21. It is just as appropriate to speak of faith-union with Christ as baptismal-union. For, although baptism is used to indicate realistic participation in and experience of the accomplishment of Christ through death and resurrection, the Christian must reckon himself now to have this new life in Christ so as to live to God and not to sin. In other words, the ethical truths implicit in the death and resurrection of Christ are not automatically experienced in the baptized one. There is reckoning that must take place, which involves the recognition of what real faith-union with Christ means, a new life to be lived to God. This is probably part of the obedience of faith that Paul calls for (1:5; 15:18; 16:26?), and expresses in 12:1–2.

53. The parallel between these passages is made clearer by virtue of the paraenesis that follows both cultic texts. We are not suggesting much agreement between the paraenetic material, but the structural similarity between them.

54. On *hagios*: Otto Procksch and Karl Georg Kuhn, "*hagios, ktl*," *TDNT*, 1:88–115; Horst Seebass, "Holy, Consecrate, Sanctify, Saints, Devout," *NIDNTT*, 2:223–38; BAGD, 8–10; LSJ, 9.

55. For development of this idea, see Daly's *Christian Sacrifice*, 70–86; Note especially in Paul the use of *osmē euōdias* with *thysia dektē*, and followed by *euarestos tō theō*. Here we see the combining of these three phrases that expand on each other, but all suggest the same thing, God's acceptance. The use of *euprosdektos* should be considered also, since the meaning is very similar to *euarestos*. Here we see the use of the word crossing from the cultic to the ethical in texts using cultic language (Rom 15:16; 1 Pet 2:5), and being used in the general sense of acceptable or pleasing (Rom 15:31; 2 Cor 6:2; 8:12).

56. Significant uses of *euarestos* indicating its basic ethical meaning (Rom 12:2; 14:18; 2 Cor 5:9; Eph 5:10; Col 3:20; Tit 2:9). Also note outside of Paul: Heb 13:21 (where God's working in the life is being referred to), and Wis 4:10; 9:10.

57. A number of significant studies give much of the evidence from primary sources: Otto Schmitz, *Die Opferanschauung des späteren Judentums und die Opferaussagen des Neuen Testamentes: eine Untersuchung ihres geschichtlichen Verhaltnisses* (Tübingen: Mohr, 1910) outside the NT, 9–195, which includes the OT material; Wenschkewitz, "Die Spiritualisie-rung," background to NT, 6–87; brief discussion in the light of the hermetic material, C. H. Dodd, *The Bible and the Greeks*, (London: Hodder and Stoughton, 1935) 194–98; R. K. Yerkes, *Sacrifice in Greek and Roman Religions and Early Judaism*, (London: Adam and Charles Black, 1953); Seidensticker, *Lebendiges Opfer*, background to NT, 1–120; Johannes Behm, "*thyō, ktl*," *TDNT*, 3:180–90, esp. for background to NT,

186-89; McKelvey, *The New Temple*, 42-57; Corriveau, *Liturgy of Life*, background in the light of Rom 12:1, 159-64; C. Brown, H.-G. Link, and F. Thiele, "Sacrifice," *NIDNTT* 3:415-38 including NT material; Daly, *Christian Sacrifice*, for OT—NT, 9-307, also note within the rest of the material a lot of material on Philo and Barnabas, 389-440; For various references see J. P. Brown, "The Sacrificial Cult and its Critique in Greek and Hebrew I," *JSS* 24 (1979) 159-73 and "The Sacrificial Cult and its Critique in Greek and Hebrew II," *JSS* 25 (1980) 1-21, for linguistic comparisons; J. W. Thompson, "Hebrews 9 and Hellenistic Concepts of Sacrifice," *JBL* 4 (1979) 567-78; Frances M. Young, *The Use of Sacrificial Ideas in Greek Christian Writers From the New Testament to John Chrysostom* (Patristic Monograph Series 5, Cambridge, Massachusetts: Philadelphia Patristics Foundation, 1979) 11-73; and Everett Ferguson's "Spiritual Sacrifice in Early Christianity and Its Environment," in *Aufstieg und Niedergang der Römischen Welt: Geschichte und Kultur Roms im Spiegel der Neueren Forschung (Vorkonstantinisches Christentum: Verhältnis zu Römischem Staat und Heidnischer Religion)*, 23/2 (ed. W. Haase; Berlin/New York: De Gruyter, 1980) 1151-89, for OT and NT background, 1152-62. Also, cf. G. W. E. Nickelsburg and M. E. Stone, *Faith and Piety in Early Judaism: Texts and Documents* (Philadelphia: Fortress Press, 1983) 51-88.

58. 1 Cor 5:7 and Eph 5:2 have soteriological implications as well, but they are not stressed within their contexts. We have not included Paul's references to himself or ministry with the use of cultic language.

59. Sanday and Headlam, *Romans*, 353.

60. See n. 57 for numerous studies that discuss the relevant material. Special emphasis on the philosophical material is presented at the beginning of Seidensticker's *Lebendiges Opfer*, 17-43. Helpful is the work of C. H. Dodd, especially concerning the *Corpus Hermeticum*, in *The Bible and the Greeks*, 194-98; also, *The Interpretation of the Fourth Gospel* (Cambridge: Cambridge University, 1953) 420-23; and a more general discussion, but in relation to the Fourth Gospel, "The Prologue to the Fourth Gospel and Christian Worship," *Studies in the Fourth Gospel* (ed., F. L. Cross; London: Mowbray, 1957) 9-22; Richard Reitzenstein, *Hellenistic Mystery-Religions: Their Basic Ideas and Significance* (3rd ed., ET; Pittsburgh: Pickwick, 1978) 415-21.

61. Seidensticker affirms the uniqueness of Paul's use of sacrificial language against the background of relevant literature. He attributes this to a "christologizing" process that is different from contemporary spiritualization, *Lebendiges Opfer*, 327-29. It must be stated, though, that Rom 12:1-2 reveals little evidence of a definite christological thrust. This thrust may be suggested by the use of *sōma*, or the use of sacrificial language itself. But Paul's use elsewhere does not demand such an interpretation, unless one is using the term "christologize" in the broadest sense.

62. 1 Cor 2:13,15; 3:1; 9:11; 10:3,4; 12:1; 14:1,37; 15:44,46; Gal 6:1; Eph 1:3; 5:19; 6:12; Col 1:9; 3:16.

63. *Syschēmatizō* appears only here in the Pauline corpus; *metaphor-phoō* occurs only in 2 Cor 3:18; *anakainōsis* appears only in Tit 3:5.

64. As Ernest Best (*1 Peter* [London: Oliphants, 1971] 98) and E. G. Selwyn (*The First Epistle of St. Peter* [London: Macmillan, 1946] 154–55) have suggested, specifically seeing Rom 12:1 as a similar and previous usage to that in 1 Peter.

65. Otto Michel speaks of *logikē latreia* as "Es gehort freilich in den Sprachgebrauch der hellenistischen Synagoge." Furthermore, Michel states that *"logikē latreia* und *logikē thysia* gehoren offenbar in die liturgische Sprache des hellenistischen Judentums, die auch philosophische Motive verarbeitet hat" (*Der Brief an die Römer* [MeyerK 4/14; Göttingen: Vandenhoeck & Ruprecht, ⁵1978] 370). This he states after references to Hellenistic materials, Qumran, and the common references to *T. Levi* 3:6 and *Corp. Herm.* I, 31; XIII, 18. His thought is also influenced by D. Hans Lietzmann, and R. Reitzenstein's interaction with 1 Pet 2:5 (Reitzenstein's perspective on Rom 12:1 and 1 Pet 2:5 is heavily dependent on discussion of "Hermetic thought" [416], *Hellenistic Mystery-Religions*, 415–21.) Our concern is rather to emphasize the meaning of this phrase in the Romans context.

66. We are dependent upon H. Strathmann's *"latreuō, latreia,"* TDNT, 4:58–65; also Klaus Hess, "Serve," NIDNTT, 3:549–51.

67. R. Jewett refers to "popular Hellenistic Christian usage" as determining the *pneumati mou* reading (such as 1 Cor 5:4; 14:14; 16:18), but he sees the Spirit refering to the "divine spirit which was apportioned to the apostle," *Paul's Anthropological Terms*, 198; note Eduard Schweizer on *pneumatikos* in *"pneuma, ktl,"* TDNT, 6:434–37.

68. Cranfield, *Romans*, 2:604–5. Cranfield's denial that Paul's concept of rationality involves "the natural rationality of man" (604) is surely right if it is separated from the idea of divine createdness and intention. But if this distinction is not made, then the denial of this by Cranfield may not be as necessary.

69. The "addition" of *hymōn* in Sinaiticus, D, Codex Athous Laurae, and others may indicate a further desire to parallel 12:2 with 12:1; i.e., the use of *hymōn* with *ta sōmata* and *logikēn latreian*.

70. Thus, Käsemann was right in noting the eschatological meaning to the cultic language, *Romans*, 327. We would still argue that the ethical is still intrinsic to the eschatological, and indeed baptism ritualizes this connection. If baptism is the background or origin of this type of exhortation, then this connection is affirmed even more.

71. BAGD, 201, "accept as approved, approve." The word suggests a recognition and positive assessment.

72. On *nous*, cf. Jewett, *Paul's Anthropological Terms*, 384–89, 450–51. "The *nous* in this context appears to be a constellation of thoughts and assumptions. These are made new by the gospel, and out of the new situation and understanding flows the new existence, which is, so to speak, reshaped or formed from the inside" (385).

73. For the purposes of this paper we are attempting to read some possibilities into Paul's exhortation language.

74. Each of these descriptive words could receive a lot of attention. Together they indicate the ethical implications of Paul's call for transformation. The discernment of the mind pertains to that which is "good," "acceptable," and "perfect."

75. The renewal that Paul is speaking of is obviously a Christian renewal. In this respect it is interesting that *anakainōsis* is found only in Christian writings in the relevant literature of antiquity (BAGD, 55).

76. I comment on "The Desired Result of Paul the Preacher" in a short article in *The Preacher* 4/1 (1985) 1-2.

77. Richard F. Lovelace, *Renewal as a Way of Life: A Guidebook for Spiritual Growth* (Downers Grove, Illinois: Inter-Varsity, 1985) 192.

78. Lovelace, *Renewal,* 184-93.

79. Lovelace's concern for "theological integration" is broader than what we are speaking of, but his book is a good example of how basic elements of the gospel can be viewed as fundamentals of and for renewal.

80. Stanley M. Horton, *What the Bible Says About the Holy Spirit* (Springfield, Missouri: Gospel Publishing House, 1976) 193-94; the section on "The Use of Spiritual Gifts" begins on p. 191. Romans 12:3-8 is mentioned.

81. Foster, *Celebration of Discipline,* 162.

4

A LESSON FROM MATTHEW'S GOSPEL
FOR CHARISMATIC RENEWAL

Charles L. Holman

T HE GOSPEL ACCORDING TO MATTHEW is hardly a part of the NT
to which we normally would turn for instruction which
bears upon charismatic renewal. And yet present-day Gospel
research has paved the way for recognizing more readily an
important truth in Matthew's Gospel that pertains to such
renewal.

Contemporary research has affirmed two explanations among
others for the origin of our four Gospels, both of which have a
direct bearing upon the subject at hand. First, the Gospels
came to be composed partly in order to provide a sound understanding of the deeds and teachings of Jesus in a day when
false belief and sub-Christian behavior needed to be counter-
acted (cf. Luke 1:1–4). Secondly, the distinctive characteristics
of each of the Gospels often provide substantial clues for our
discerning something of the needs of the respective addressees.
While there are very significant similarities in the contents and
literary structure of the Gospels, especially the first three, there
are likewise very significant differences. The way each evangelist utilizes the record of Jesus' deeds and teachings (the "Jesus-
tradition") in the composition of his Gospel reveals something
of his particular concerns for those whom he addresses.[1] In
arriving at a lesson for charismatic renewal from Matthew's
Gospel, it is useful to keep in mind both of these factors which
help to explain Gospel origins.

I. Indications that Matthew addresses a "Charismatic" Community

There are indications from Matthean distinctives that Matthew addresses a charismatically sensitive community.[2] Since our first Gospel is a Gospel of our Lord Jesus Christ and not a letter addressed to one of the early church congregations or its leaders, we may arrive only indirectly at some knowledge of those whom Matthew addresses. But as we "read between the lines" in observing *the way* Matthew presents his Gospel, some interesting evidence emerges concerning those who were most likely the recipients.

The most important passage for our consideration is 7:15–23, which exposes false *charisma*. We will look carefully at the structure of these verses and then consider them in their immediate and broader contexts in Matthew. We will ask ourselves why it is that Matthew emphasizes the themes of our passage in the way he does. Based upon the results of our investigation at this point, we will explore the possibility of *genuine* charismatic activity in the community addressed by Matthew.

That part of the "Sermon on the Mount" which elicits our attention may rightly be divided into two paragraphs, as it is found in the Nestle-Aland *Novum Testamentum* and the RSV, NEB, and NIV (7:15–20; 7:21–23); but there are, nevertheless, reasons for considering the two paragraphs as a unit.[3] Both paragraphs are concerned with "false prophets" (vv 15,22–23). This is the dominating concern of the first paragraph wherein the false prophets (*tōn pseudoprophētōn*) are characterized in v 15 as masquerading for true disciples, but are recognized or known for what they are by their "fruits" (vv 16a,20). In between the repeated statement which gives this criterion for recognizing false prophets (vv 16a,20), Matthew gives three illustrative contrasts (grapes versus thorns, figs versus thistles, and a good tree versus a decayed tree) to underscore his point that such "prophets" are really false and have nothing in common with true disciples of Jesus. This emphasis is necessary because the false prophets appear to be "Christian" (wolves in sheep's clothing, v 15). The deception corresponds with those in the second paragraph who call Jesus "Lord" and who prophesy in his name, but who are unknown by the Lord (vv 22–23). Another point in common between the two paragraphs is that each moves toward the goal of "knowing" or not "knowing." The deceivers are *known* by their fruits (v 20, cf. v 16a), *epignōsesthe autous*), and ultimately they will be declared to be *unknown* by the Lord (v 23, *oudepote egnōn hymos*). The more exact overall relationship between these two paragraphs seems to be that the circle of counterfeit disciples is widened in the second paragraph to include exorcists and miracle workers, in addition to prophets, who come under the condemnation of the Lord (cf. v 15 with vv 22–23). Furthermore, the statement of warning in v 15 progresses to a statement of final judgment in v 23. "In that day" there will be *many* who will seek to justify their entrance into the kingdom on the basis of their "charismatic" ministries of prophesying, exorcising demons, and working miracles (vv 21–22). That such persons identify with the believing community is stressed by Matthew in his use of the emphatic possessive adjective *sos* ("your") in conjunction with each of the charismatic ministries suggested in v 22. These individuals will claim to have ministered in none other than *Jesus'* name. But in the end they are exposed as unsaved "charismatics"! Their "fruits" betray them (vv 16a,20); *they have not done the will of God* (v 21). We will need to return to this judgment of such persons later.

There are at least four reasons for believing that Matthew has a special interest in developing the matter of false charismatic activity. Consideration of these will give force to the question of why Matthew has chosen to air this theme under the inspiration of God's Spirit.

(1) The explicit concern over charismatic pretenders in the present (rather than the future) is unique to Matthew's Gospel, as far as the sayings of Jesus go. Luke's parallel to this portion of Matthew does contrast the good tree with the bad, figs with thorns, and grapes with thorn bush (6:43–44), but the context there concerns the hypocrite who judges his brother and the evil man as opposed to the good man (6:41–42,45). There is no mention of false prophets. Likewise, the verse immediately following in Luke concerns calling Jesus "Lord, Lord" and doing his will (6:46), with the two "foundations"

(rock and ground) concluding the section of Jesus' sayings in Luke 6. But there is no word against those claiming charismatic powers as there is in the parallel passage in Matthew 7. Matthew's sayings passage at this point concludes similarly to Luke's with the presentation of two foundations (rock and sand), which illustrates the importance of heeding Jesus' teachings (7:24-27). Actually, Matt 7:15-27 essentially parallels Luke 6:43-49, but *also* includes allusions to false charismatic activity that are not found in Luke.

(2) The setting of Matt 7:15-23 within the Sermon on the Mount highlights the importance of the false charismatic for Matthew.[4] The warning and condemnation (vv 15,23) occur immediately after Jesus' words concerning the "narrow" and "wide" gate for entering one's eternal destination (7:13-14). The issue is narrowed down to doing God's will (v 21), but with the focus on false charismatics who will lose out eternally. Special force is given to these solemn words with the closing statements of the two foundations, although the closing verses perhaps serve as a conclusion for the Sermon as a whole. Elsewhere in the Sermon explicit reference to the importance of doing God's will is found (5:17-20; 6:10,33). Such emphasis finds a final expression (prior to the conclusion) in reference to *false charismatics*! Thus with respect to the structure of the Sermon, the Matthean comment on false charismatics is fairly prominent.

(3) The situation of *many* carrying on a pseudo-charismatic ministry *in the name of Jesus* (Matt 7:22) is much easier to imagine as occurring in the later decades of the first-century Christian church than in the three years or so that Jesus was on earth with his disciples. On the other hand, there is nothing in the text that demands that we think Jesus spoke of such a development emerging as early as the time of his earthly ministry, at least on this scale. We do have evidence, on the other hand, that in the early church there was concern over false prophets and that a need existed to test ministries carried on in the name of Christ (cf. 1 Cor 12:10; 2 Cor 11:4,13-15; 1 John 4:1-3; *Did.* 11:3-12).

(4) The false prophet emphasis in Matthew 7 reappears in Matt 24:11,24. The first reference in v 11 is unique to Matthew's version of the eschatological discourse in the Synoptics.

(As a matter of fact, *pseudoprophētēs* is more prominent in Matthew than in any other document of the NT except Revelation, each having three occurrences of the term.) In four ways the false prophet motif of Matthew 24 resembles that of chap. 7, which further helps us to appreciate Matthew's concern. First, both passages speak of an *abundance* of false prophets. "Many" (*polloi*) is used in 7:22 and in 24:11. In the latter passage the arrival of such persons is future (*egerthēsontai*) from the standpoint of Jesus' prediction. (This would seem to confirm our opinion that the fulfillment of Matt 7:22 is future from the standpoint of the early Jesus.) Matthew's use of the motif appears to say that the false prophet problem that will become rampant in the last days has already appeared.[5] Second, the *danger* of deception is underscored in both passages. In 7:15 we have "beware" (*prosechete*), and in 24:11 we read "they shall deceive many" (*planēsousin pollous*). Third, "lawlessness" (*anomia*) is associated with the false prophets in 7:23 (cf. v 22), and it is indirectly associated with such persons in 24:12 (cf. v 11). Fourth, the apparent miraculous "ministry" of false charismatics in 7:23 is paralleled by the great signs and wonders (*sēmeia megala kai terata*) performed by false Christs and false prophets in 24:24. It is the miraculous deeds which are so deceptive in 24:24 (= Mark 13:22, where a warning follows in the next verse). Thus the pertinence and the seriousness of Matthew's message in chap. 7 is further demonstrated in chap. 24.

Now we are prepared to raise the question of why Matthew's Gospel is so concerned with the problem of false prophecy and false charismatic activity. Is it possible that a situation (or situations) in the community has led Matthew to single out false charismatics? When we recall that the Gospels are not disinterested "objective" presentations of Jesus' life and teachings, but are *proclamations* of good news, designed to stimulate faith in and obedience to the one who is presented as the one who fulfills God's redemptive plan, then we must attempt to relate the distinctive emphases of Matthew's Gospel to the needs of his recipients. The question then becomes, what situation did the Spirit of God most likely use to prompt Matthew to warn of the danger of false *charismata*.

First of all, such persons were obviously present or near enough to be dangerous to the Christians addressed. The most natural conclusion is that such persons had contact with the community. Second, in what kind of situation would false prophets be successful in their deceptive "ministries"? We think of three possible answers: (1) where *charismata* had been previously unknown, so that an uninitiated audience is now "swept off its feet"; (2) where *charismata* were known, but not experienced very much, outside the practice of the deceived/ deceiving charismatics who say "Lord, Lord"; (3) where a community was sensitive to and had firsthand familiarity with charismatic experience such as is found in Matt 7:22. The first possibility is hardly conceivable, given what we know of religious experience in the Mediterranean world of the first century A.D.[6] The second option is more plausible than the first, but the best answer is the last. Let us see why.

(a) The presence of prophets in the community addressed by Matthew is suggested in a saying of Jesus in Matt 10:41 concerning "receiving" a prophet. *Matthew's Gospel is the only place in the Gospels that the saying is found.* Even as others would receive the apostles and would thereby be welcoming Jesus (v 40), those who would receive a *prophet* for what he was (i.e., a prophet) would receive a prophet's reward (v 41a). Likewise, reception of a righteous man brings a righteous man's reward (v 41b; we will return to this idea below). In commenting on these verses, Schweizer writes:

> Behind these sayings, but above all behind the middle one, we can glimpse the church in which Matthew lives: wandering missionaries, prophets, and righteous men, who presumably have authority to teach the commandments of God and their interpretation by Jesus, move from one congregation to another, often despised and persecuted, always dependent on hospitality, and bringing with them the living Word of God that sets its stamp on their lives.[7]

The expectation of prophets being persecuted finds a precedent in Matt 5:12 (= Luke 6:23) and its expressly stated in Matt 23:34 (= Luke 11:49). In light of the foregoing data, it is probable that the community addressed had firsthand acquaintance with the prophetic ministry. Montague holds that "the community was one in which prophecy was not only widely exercised but had become an identifiable office, both for service within the community and for missionary work too (10:41; 23:34)."[8]

(b) It is very understandable that a community predisposed to charismatic activity would be especially susceptible to others who would produce the signs of charismatic powers and thus would be in danger of deception on the basis of the *prima facie* evidence of such deeds being performed in the name of Jesus (Matt 7:22). In Schweizer's opinion "the very warning against false prophets must imply that there are true prophets within the community."[9] We can at least agree that false charismatics would operate most effectively in a community situation where others were exercising "similar" gifts, thus avoiding the special attention and scrutiny that novelty would bring.

(c) There are strong indications that the "charismatics" who are workers of "lawlessness" (*anomia*) in Matt 7:22–23 reflect a problem that has quite seriously affected the community (as we discuss below). This in turn suggests that these "charismatics" are "insiders" in the community and are part of the problem which we shall see is fairly widely reflected in Matthew's Gospel. If we are correct at this point, then we have a community that is very sensitive to and that welcomes charismatic activity. Otherwise, these individuals would not have been able to make the dangerous inroads that are suggested by the prominence of 7:15–23, as we discussed above.

Thus, we may safely conclude that in all likelihood Matthew has a message for a community that is sufficiently sensitive to charismatic ministries that we may reasonably describe it as a "charismatic" community.

II. Community Laxness and the Jesus Ethic

We have already witnessed Matthew's warning against inroads of adherence to a sub-Christian lifestyle within the Christian community. He indicates this indirectly in the way that he accents Jesus' exposure of false disciples, that is, those who have acted in Jesus' name but lack the fruits of their profession. We shall now see further how this concern is developed by Matthew through his choice of vocabulary and in

various themes he presents. It will be apparent that the warning is very pertinent for Matthew's community. We will relate
this warning to the character of the community as (most likely)
"charismatic."

Attention to religious and moral failure within the profess-
ing Christian community is heightened by Matthew in the
prominence of the terms *skandalon* and *skandalidzō*, which speak
of "offense" and "causing to stumble." Together these 2 words
are found 19 times in Matthew, with at least 15 of these instances suggesting religious or moral failure: 5:29,30; 13:21,41;
16:23; 18:6,7(thrice),8,9; 24:10; 26:31,33 (twice). By contrast,
the 2 words are found a total of 8 times in Mark and 3 times in
Luke. With only 15 occurrences of the 2 words in the rest of
the NT, the words seem especially important to Matthew. He
records several of Jesus' sayings in which stumbling (sinning),
or causing the same within the godly community, is exposed.

There is some reason to think that the possibility of deception is underscored by Matthew in his use of the verb *planaō*
("lead astray"), which is found eight times in his Gospel. It is
interesting to notice that Matthew uses *planaō* in the parable of
the "straying" sheep (18:12–14), whereas Luke records the
same parable in terms of the "lost" (*apolesas/apolōlos*) sheep
(15:4–7). Matthew's verb choice suits the motif of his Gospel,
which shows concern for wayward community members, a
theme which should become even clearer as we proceed. (The
fact that the last verse of Matthew's parable, which makes the
application, speaks of not *losing* "one of these little ones" could
indicate that Matthew is reverting at that point to a more
original version of the parable which is reflected in Luke.)
Except for 22:29, all of the other instances of *planaō* in Matthew
are in chap. 24 and constitute warnings against false Christs or
false prophets (vv 4,5,11,24). The repeated pairing of *planaō*
with the false prophet theme of chap. 24 is most significant in
v 11, since this verse is unparalleled in the other Gospels. The
danger of false charismatics in the Christian community is
suggested here and apparently helps to explain the moral laxity
in the community.

Matthew's use of the term *anomia* ("lawlessness") seems
especially revealing. Matthew is the only evangelist to use this
word (7:23; 13:41; 23:28; 24:12), and it only occurs in the NT

twelve more times. The first two instances in Matthew are of particular interest because parallel passages are wholly lacking in Mark and Luke, and because here in Matthew *anomia* is associated with other terms which we have seen to be significant to Matthew. In other words in 7:23 and 13:41 Matthean concerns are very visible. In 7:23 "workers of lawlessness" describes the false prophets; in 13:41 "those committing lawlessness" are associated with "the things that offend" (*ta skandala*). We have already observed Matthew's interest in the problems of false prophets and "offense" in the sense of religious or moral failure within the godly community. By relating both of these problems to *anomia*, we hear Jesus through Matthew singling out those persons who choose to live by their own code of conduct rather than by the will (or law) of God. But the point here is that in the community the problem of not conforming to the standard of godly conduct is serious enough that Matthew speaks to it indirectly in the distinctive ways in which he presents us with the Jesus-tradition. In the two passages found only in Matthew's Gospel (7:23, with vv 21–22, and 13:41, with vv 42–43) the prospect is eschatological judgment. In his rendering of the eschatological discourse, Matthew refers to Jesus as saying that with the abounding of *anomia*, the devotion of many will grow cold (24:12). This passage is only found in Matthew and it amounts to another warning of how a godly community can be affected with the spirit of lawlessness. In Matt 7:21–23 the workers of "lawlessness" are the false charismatics!

Another major part of our argument that Matthew addresses a (charismatic) community which tends towards moral and ethical laxity is the attention that he devotes to adherence to the Mosaic Law as interpreted by Jesus (5:17–48). Far from dispensing with the Law, in Matthew's Gospel Jesus warns against relaxing one of the least of the commandments (5:19). The term *dikaiosunē* ("righteousness") is practically a Matthean word in respect to the Jesus-tradition, since in the Gospels it only occurs elsewhere in Luke 1:75 and John 16:8,10. In Matthew we find the term in 3:15; 5:6,10,20; 6:1(?),33; 21:32. It is the righteousness of keeping the commandments that Matthew has in mind (note the explanatory "for" which links v 20 to v 19 in chap. 5).[10] It is God's kingdom *and his righteousness* that are to be sought (6:33; contrast with the parallel in Luke 12:31, where "and his righteousness" is not found). The term "righteousness" is unnecessary in a sense, for the idea is contained in "seeking God's kingdom." But the emphasis is important for Matthew. This is the "righteousness" which must exceed that of the scribes and Pharisees if one is to qualify for entrance into the kingdom (5:20). The meaning of this righteousness is detailed in 5:21-48. The moral injunctions of the Mosaic Law are seen as "fulfilled" (5:17) through the reinterpretation of the Law given by Jesus. Considerate and loving interpersonal relationships are very prominent in vv 21-48. Why does Matthew emphasize the "righteousness" theme in Jesus' teachings in the way that he does? When we recall the various Matthean distinctives that we have already presented, the particular needs of the Matthean community seem to come even more clearly into focus with Matthew's unique stress upon righteousness.

Finally, each of the Synoptic Gospels concludes the eschatological discourse with an admonition to be watchful for the *parousia*; but Matthew's Gospel goes far beyond Mark and Luke in its unique presentation of this concluding exhortation (Matt 24:37-25:46 with Mark 13:33-37 and Luke 21:34-36). While Matthew ordinarily presents Jesus' teaching in block form (in contrast to Luke who intermingles it with the overall narrative, e.g., Matt 24:37-41 = Luke 17:26-27; Matt 24:42-44 = Luke 12:39-40), in his final major presentation of Jesus' teaching, Matthew *progressively explains* the necessity of being alert and ready for the coming of the Son of man. First, the ideas of watchfulness and preparedness are latent in the saying of Jesus in Matt 24:36 ("and concerning that day and hour no one knows"). Then two pericopes develop the idea of watchfulness: one based on a "days of Noah" model (24:37-41) and another based on the analogy of the nocturnal thief (24:43). A parable concerning both the faithful (*active*) and unfaithful servant who must reckon with the return of the absent master on an unexpected "day" and unknown "hour" illustrates further the meaning of being prepared for the *parousia* (24:45-51). Yet another parable (of the maidens and the bridegroom) demonstrates the meaning of preparedness for the *parousia*, with the "day" and "hour" unknown (25:1-13). This passage is unique to Matthew's Gospel. A final parable follows concerning servants entrusted with the master's talents (25:14–30) and strongly suggests that to be ready for that great day means to be active. Matthew concludes his version of the discourse with a dramatic presentation of the *kind* of activity that receives the divine approval in the last day, again a statement unique to his Gospel. In apocalyptic language Jesus tells of the judgment of the nations as "sheep" and "goats" (25:31–46). The ones that enter into life will be those who have acted considerately and lovingly toward Jesus' brothers, in other words toward the people who belong to Jesus (v 40). Jesus' brothers are those who do the will of God (cf. Matt 12:46–50 = Mark 3:31–35 = Luke 8:9–21). Once again the Jesus ethic is defined in terms of interpersonal relationships, in this case concerning those who are in need. To be ready for Jesus' return means to be active in serving him by serving his people. Although this admonition in Matthew is in reference to the nations of the world, its climactic prominence in Matthew's Gospel, against the background of the kingdom ethics of chap. 5, clearly forms a word of exhortation for Matthew's community as well.

Based upon the foregoing evidence, we may conclude that Matthew is addressing a situation where the strictures of Jesus' ethical teaching were weak, probably due to the influence of certain "charismatically" powerful figures in the community who either minimized the importance of the moral and ethical teaching of the earthly Jesus or practically abandoned it altogether (cf. 7:21–23). In a day when the church often had to rely more on the *oral* tradition of Jesus' words and deeds, such error and deception is all the more easily understood. It is crystal clear in Matthew's Gospel that those who enter the kingdom of heaven are those who do the will of God as reflected in Jesus' kingdom teaching.

There are two separate passages that help to confirm the above conclusion, both of which are distinctive to Matthew. In Matt 18:15–35 we find guidelines for church discipline, when one brother "sins" (*harmartēsē*) against another (vv 15–20), and for forgiveness by the offended person in such circumstances (vv 21–35, with v 21 linking the two paragraphs together around the thought of the "sinning brother"). Matthew expands greatly what covers only two verses in Luke's Gospel (17:3-4) and is not found at all elsewhere in the NT. We must ask ourselves what circumstances would call forth such an emphasis in Matthew's Gospel. In light of our foregoing discussion, the answer is apparent. Amidst charismatic demonstration there is a tendency (perhaps to put it mildly) to neglect Jesus' teaching concerning kingdom ethics. In addition, the Great Commission in Matthew is unique in its dominical exhortation to the disciples to go and teach the nations to "keep all things as much as I have commanded you" (28:19-20). This can refer to nothing other than the *teachings* of Jesus as found in Matthew's Gospel, which are now declared to be for all disciples throughout the world.

There is no real indication in Matthew that he is against *charismata*. To the contrary, Matthew magnifies the "mighty works" of Jesus' ministry. This is evident in the summary statement of Jesus' healings and exorcisms in 4:23-25, in which more attention is given to Jesus' miraculous works than to teaching and preaching in his itinerant ministry. Following the Sermon of chaps. 5-7, the varied miracle ministry of Jesus dominates chaps. 8-9. It was such deeds, along with the preaching of the gospel to the poor, that were intended to convince John the Baptist that Jesus was indeed the Christ (11:2-6). The miracles (*hai dynameis*) performed by Jesus in Chorazin, Bethsaida, and Capernaum should have brought these cities to repentance (11:20-24; cf. 7:22). The exorcisms of Jesus by the Spirit were signs of the presence of the kingdom of God (Matt 12:28 = Luke 11:19). Especially significant is the fact that in Matt 10:5-15, Jesus' commission to his twelve disciples stresses a ministry of miracles (vv 5-8) more than in the parallel portions in Mark (6:7-13) or in Luke (9:1-6; cf. 10:1-12). This commission has great relevance for Matthew's community, since in vv 16-23 he blends in the yet future ministry of the disciples (future in respect to Jesus' earthly ministry), wherein the disciples are to stand before governors, kings, and the Gentiles, v 18. In fact, the substance of vv 16-23 appears as part of the *eschatological* discourse in Mark 13:9-13 and Luke 21:12-19. It is further along in this same block of teaching that

Matthew speaks positively of receiving the prophetic ministry, v 41. Thus Matthew has a very positive presentation of a charismatic ministry by Jesus' disciples.[11]

What Matthew *is* concerned about are those who justify their standing in the godly community on the basis of their "charismatic" credentials *at the expense of* adhering to the ethics of Jesus and the kingdom of God. Matthew parallels the reference to receiving a "prophet" (10:41a) with receiving "a righteous man" (*dikaion*, 10:41b). For Matthew the two must go together. The enthusiasm of a life of faith inspired by the risen and exalted Lord must in no way overshadow the supreme importance of following the teaching of the earthly Jesus, who expresses God's final authoritative word for the Christian community. It is by *revelation* that the authority of the *earthly* Jesus is recognized (Matt 16:15–17)! This same Jesus promises that his spiritual presence is with even two or three gathered in his name (18:20); as the risen Christ he promises that his presence will continue with his disciples to the end of the age (28:20). Each of these three statements of spiritual experience is unique to the First Gospel. Matthew would have his readers recognize continuity between the earthly Jesus (whose teaching fulfills the Law and the Prophets, 5:17–20 with 5:21–48) and the risen Christ who inspires prophecy and other charismatic manifestations. The "charismatic" Christ also has commissioned his disciples to teach all nations to observe his commands.

III. Conclusion

It is very difficult to know exactly how to understand the religious experience of those in Matt 7:22–23 who are charismatically active in Jesus' name and who yet never had any real part in Jesus. In this study we have sought to understand what the problem of false *charismata* meant to Matthew and those whom he addressed.[12] It may be that Matthew intends us to understand that psychic or demonic powers could counterfeit the true work of the Spirit and deceive others by operating in the name of Jesus. (The text nowhere suggests that the miraculous works were unreal and tricks of some sort. The more natural sense is that they truly occurred.)[13] Matthew at the same time would encourage his community in *genuine* charismatic experience. But what is important is that in the charismatic experience of the community the moral and ethical teachings of the earthly Jesus be not compromised by some "higher" revelation of "prophets" speaking in Jesus' name or by the example of impressive supernatural ministries of some who neglect the tradition that goes back to Jesus of Nazareth. As a matter of fact, the criterion by which the authenticity of ministries purporting to be Christian is to be decided is nothing other than the Jesus-tradition.

One of the great surprises from God of our times is the widespread charismatic renewal of the church. But our response to this movement of the Spirit of God seems inevitably to bring pitfalls to be avoided. One of these is the neglect of the teachings of Jesus with respect to morality and ethics in everyday life. It is true that the sayings of Jesus must be carefully interpreted and properly applied to contemporary life situations. But at the same time such sayings are to be taken seriously. At no time must we allow the "Spirit" in our lives to become a functional arbiter in deciding on kingdom righteousness, irrespective of the teachings of the earthly Jesus. Because I have "peace" about a moral decision does not *necessarily* mean it is right. "Success" in a Christian ministry does not justify compromising the Jesus ethic with respect to the marital vows and/or sexual purity, or any of the other areas of life in which we may feel the pull of contemporary society toward the ethics of secular humanism. In a day when the church is arriving at a new appreciation for charismatic renewal, may we also pray for a renewal of kingdom righteousness and holiness. May it be said of us as it was long ago of Barnabas: "He was a good man, full of the Holy Spirit and of faith" (Acts 11:22).

Notes

1. The recognition of this phenomenon in Gospel composition need not lead us to suppose a radical reconstruction of the Jesus-tradition by the evangelists, as is found in the conclusions of radical redaction critics. For a helpful discussion see S. S. Smalley, "Redaction Criticism," in *New Testament Interpretation* (ed. I. H. Marshall; Grand

Rapids: Eerdmans, 1977) 181–95; for a broader introduction to issues
in Synoptic criticism, cf. G. E. Ladd, *The New Testament and Criticism*
(Grand Rapids: Eerdmans, 1967) chaps. 5–6, along with the background issues treated by C. F. D. Moule, *The Birth of the New Testament*
(3rd ed.; London: Black, 1981), especially chap. 5; "The Intention of
the Evangelists," *The Phenomenon of the New Testament*, (2nd ed.; London:
SCM, 1981) 100–14.

2. I use the name of "Matthew" in this essay without seeing the
need to discuss the issue of identity of the author of the Gospel,
which is actually anonymous, although traditionally it has been considered the work of Matthew the apostle.

3. Various scholars have observed a significant unity between
vv 15–20 and vv 21–23. Cf. D. E. Aune, *Prophecy in Early Christianity and
the Ancient Mediterranean World* (Grand Rapids: Eerdmans, 1983) 222–23;
D. Hill, *The Gospel of Matthew* (NCB; London: Marshall, Morgan and
Scott, 1972) 151; E. Schweizer, "Observance of the Law and Charismatic Activity in Matthew," *NTS* 16 (1970) 224; G. Barth, "Matthew's
Understanding of the Law," in *Tradition and Interpretation in Matthew*
(eds. G. Bornkamm and G. Barth; Philadelphia: Westminster, 1963)
162. D. Hill, "False Prophets and Charismatics: Structure and Interpretation in Matthew 7, 15–23," *Bib* 57 (1976) 339–40, apparently
takes back what he said earlier in his commentary, now denying that
the false prophets of v 15 are to be identified with those condemned
in vv 22–23. While it is possible that the condemned "charismatics" in
vv 22–23 are not to be restricted to the "false prophets" of v 15, I
think that links between the two passages are sufficiently strong to
indicate some identity between the two groups. At least both may be
characterized as *false* charismatics.

4. The following facts lead me to believe that Matthew himself
has edited or summarized what Jesus taught on the occasion represented in chaps. 5–7. The Sermon begins with the disciples being
addressed (5:1); the Sermon concludes with *the crowds* being astonished
at Jesus' sayings; the Sermon as found in Matthew would take approximately fifteen minutes if given verbatim. Thus what Matthew
has editorially *selected* to present his readers may be regarded as significant for them.

5. Similarly, the end-time preaching of the gospel among all
nations (24:14) is underway by the time Matthew writes (cf. "until
today" in Matt 28:15 with 28:18–20). I have explored further where
Matthew sees himself in the eschatological timetable in *Eschatological
Delay in Jewish and Early Christian Apocalyptic* (Ph.D. thesis, University of
Nottingham, 1983) 276–84.

6. In the case of prophecy, Aune, *Prophecy in Early Christianity*, esp.
139–338, has made an important contribution.

7. E. Schweizer, *The Good News According to Matthew* (London:
SPCK: 1975) 253.

8. G. T. Montague, *The Holy Spirit: Growth of a Biblical Tradition*
(New York: Paulist, 1976) 309.

9. Schweizer, *Matthew*, 179.

10. J. D. G. Dunn, *Unity and Diversity in the New Testament* (London: SCM, 1977) 247.

11. Cf. Hill, "False Prophets and Charismatics," 337. Other facets of this argument are helpfully found in E. Schweizer, "Matthew's Church," *The Interpretation of Matthew* (ed. G. Stanton; Philadelphia: Fortress, 1983) 130–33.

12. Many scholars prefer Syria as the location of the community which Matthew addressed, cf. W. G. Kümmel, *Introduction to the New Testament* (London: SCM, 1975) 119; Hill, *Matthew*, 50–52, but cf. B. T. Viviano, "Where was the Gospel according to Matthew Written?" *CBQ* 41 (1979) 533–46.

The fact that Matthew singles out "Syria" as the place throughout which Jesus' fame spread is particularly interesting (4:24). Several scholars have associated Syria with the origin of the Didache, and in *Did.* 11:3–12 the test of a prophet who "speaks in a spirit" (*lalounta en pneumati*) is his behavior, cf. R. A. Kraft, "Apostolic Fathers," IDBSup, 36–37.

The final redaction of the Didache is usually dated in the late first or the second century. A majority of critics have dated Matthew after A.D. 70, although others would argue for an earlier date, e.g., J. A. T. Robinson, *Redating the New Testament* (London: SCM, 1976) 13–30, 86–117; and R. H. Gundry, *Matthew: A Commentary on His Literary and Theological Art* (Grand Rapids: Eerdmans, 1981) 599–609, who argues for a date earlier than A.D. 63.

We may observe that, regardless of the exact date and provenance of these two documents, the evidence points to both the Matthean and Didachean communities as having faced similar problems re false charismatics.

13. Hill, "False Prophets and Charismatics," 340–41, maintains that the condemned persons of 7:22–23 are Christians who seek admission to the kingdom on the basis of their involvement with charismatic gifts. At the risk of minimizing Matthew's thrust at this point, I suggest that Matthew does not intend us to place *genuine* Christians in this category.

5

DISCIPLESHIP IN MARK'S GOSPEL

John Christopher Thomas

A PROPER UNDERSTANDING of biblical discipleship is essential if spiritual renewal is to be productive and continual. But, what does it mean to be a disciple? What is the basis of discipleship? Is there any one way of making disciples, or are there a number of options available? This study will examine the issue of discipleship in order to discover a biblical paradigm for discipleship which might be used by those interested in renewal. This will necessitate an entrance into the debate concerning Jesus' role as teacher, which will lead to a consideration of the relationship Jesus had with the disciples. The results of this investigation will then be tested by examining a few significant passages in the Gospel according to Mark that are particularly pertinent for understanding discipleship. Finally, a section will be devoted to applying those conclusions to the contemporary situation.

It is an honor to be able to offer a contribution on Marcan discipleship for this important occasion. Dr. Horton has contributed much to me over the few years I have been privileged to know him. Through scholarly productions, enlightening dialogues, and refreshing times of fellowship, he has been a source of great inspiration. Thank you, Stanley, for the many fine things you have brought to us all.

Jesus As Charismatic Leader

Without a doubt, the Gospels testify to the fact that Jesus was looked upon as a teacher by his contemporaries. *Didaskein* (to teach) appears over 90 times in the NT with about two-thirds of those occurrences being in the Gospels and the early parts of Acts.[1] Jesus is frequently referred to as *rabbi* and *didaskalos* (teacher). Traditionally, scholars have understood this to imply that Jesus was a rabbi. Bultmann's comments are representative of this view.

> The title (rabbi), which in the Greek gospels is usually rendered by the ordinary Greek form of address (Lord, Sir), marks Jesus as belonging to the class of scribes. And that implies, if it is to be taken seriously, that Jesus, being a scribe had received the necessary scribal training and had passed the requisite scribal tests. . . . But if the gospel record is worthy of credence, it is at least clear that *Jesus actually lived as a Jewish rabbi.* As such he takes his place as a teacher in the synagogue. As such he gathers around him a circle of pupils. As such he disputes over questions of the Law with pupils and opponents or with people seeking knowledge who turn to him as the celebrated rabbi. . . . As it is important that he is addressed as rabbi, so also it is significant that his adherents (not the twelve) are called pupils (disciples). That too is a technical term, and designates the pupils of a rabbi, not the members of a religious fellowship. . . . We cannot doubt that the characteristics of a rabbi appeared plainly in Jesus' ministry and way of teaching, unless the tradition has radically distorted the picture.[2]

As Bultmann observed, there are a number of similarities between Jesus and the rabbis. He is called rabbi (cf. Mark 9:5; 11:21; 14:45; John 1:39,49; 3:2; 4:31; 6:25; 9:2; 11:8) He teaches in the synagogues (Mark 6:1; Luke 4:16–30). He sits when he teaches (Matt 5:1). He has a group of followers (*mathētai*), and he is asked to render decisions on points of Torah. Despite these similarities, a number of real differences between Jesus and the rabbis have also been emphasized. Even Birger Gerhardsson, an advocate of using rabbinic methods of oral transmission as the paradigm for explaining early Christian transmission of tradition, criticizes Bultmann for not placing enough emphasis on the differences.[3]

The number of significant differences between Jesus and the rabbis are far reaching. (1) Jesus speaks on the basis of his own authority (*exousia*). He was not like the scribes who tended to cite other teachers as authorization for their message. (2) He does not recite the introductory quote from the Hebrew Scriptures, "Thus says the Lord," but replaces it with "truly I say to you." In doing this he speaks as God, at least implicitly. (3) Jesus seems less concerned with the letter of the Law than do the rabbis, for at many points he moves beyond it to the

Torah's original intent (cf. Mark 10:1-12). (4) Ordinarily, he
resorts to rabbinic exegesis only when drawn into debates.
This should not be taken to imply that he normally approached
Scripture in this manner.[4] (5) Jesus holds a position above the
Torah for his disciples. This certainly distinguishes him from
the rabbis. (6) One of the most characteristic differences between Jesus and the rabbis concerns the method of discipleship. Ordinarily, prospective students would join themselves to
a rabbi of their own choosing. However, Jesus' disciples re-
sponded to *his* call. The disciples' commitment to him far transcends that expected of a rabbinic pupil. Rabbinic students are
trained to replace their masters, yet Jesus is indispensable to
his disciples, even after his death. The rabbis seem reluctant to
teach in the open, but Jesus teaches wherever an appropriate
situation arises. Finally, Jesus teaches certain individuals who
would in no respect qualify as rabbinic students: sinners,
taxcollectors, women, prostitutes, and even children.[5] Consequently, while he may have borne an outward similarity to the
rabbis, Jesus was different from them in many respects.

The question remains, was Jesus a rabbi? After all, Jesus is
addressed as rabbi. However, several scholars are concluding
that the term rabbi would have had different nuances in A.D. 30
than during the latter part of the first century. Hengel observes
that "as an established title—despite the rabbinical tendency to
date back the forms of their own period into the past—'Rabbi'
only appears from the time of Johanan ben Zakkai and his
disciples, i.e., very probably only after 70 A.D."[6] Neusner
would be in basic agreement with this assessment.[7] It seems
better to view *rabbi, didaskalos,* and *kyrios* as synonymous during
the life of Jesus.[8] If this is true, then Jesus would not have to
be trained as a rabbi to be called teacher. Even if an ordained
rabbinate existed at his time, there were other individuals in
close temporal proximity who also served as teacher, but were
not rabbinic figures. First-century Palestinian Judaism was far
more sectarian than the surviving sources suggest, and no
group of consequence existed very long without a teacher.[9]
Additionally, Jesus' prophetic role need not be emphasized to
the exclusion of his teaching role. (These roles seem to have
been combined at Qumran.) Even at the end of the first century a prophetic figure like John the Baptist can be referred to

as rabbi.[10] This also demonstrates that a prophet could, at the same time, be a teacher. The Samaritan Taheb seems to have combined these two roles. Consequently, to speak of Jesus as teacher is a necessity. Yet, despite the similarities, it may do more harm than good to identify him as rabbi, especially with its Mishnaic meaning.[11]

A much more probable explanation of Jesus' role would be the identification as prophet. Most scholars agree that there are "indubitably authentic materials" present in the canonical Gospels which identify Jesus as prophet.[12] Not only is Jesus regarded as prophet by the people at large (cf. Mark 6:15; 8:27,28), but he implicitly accepts the title at Nazareth (Mark 6:4). Not only is he "a prophet like one of the prophets" (Mark 6:15), but eventually "the prophet" (Matt 21:11). Cullmann concludes, "The application of the concept of *the* Prophet to Jesus explains perfectly, then, both his preaching activity and the unique authority of his eschatological vocation and appearance in the end time."[13] But, even this designation does not go far enough in understanding Jesus,[14] for he transcends the jurisdiction of the prophets. *He* forgives sins. *He* casts out demons. *He* speaks on God's behalf, as God (in some real sense). *He* has authority over the Sabbath. *He* goes behind the Law to its original intention. These considerations lead Hengel to the conclusion that Jesus was an eschatological figure who acted on the basis of "a charismatic authority which wholly transcended that of contemporary apocalyptic prophets."[15] This is best explained as messianic authority.

The Disciples as Charismatic Followers

If rabbi is not the best descriptive title for Jesus, then the disciples are probably not best understood as rabbinic students.[16] How are the disciples of Jesus to be understood? Hengel suggests that the best parallels to Jesus' disciples are to be found in charismatic-prophetic-eschatological contexts. Beginning with the call of Elisha by Elijah, Hengel surveys the uses of "following" and "call" in various eschatological texts. Of particular interest is Mattathias' call in 1 Macc 2:27,28:

Mattathias cried out throughout the town in a loud voice, "All who are zealous for the sake of the Torah, who uphold the covenant, march out after me (*exeltheto opiso mou*)!" Thereupon he and his sons fled to the mountains, leaving behind all their possessions in the town (*enkatelipon hosa eichon en te polei*).[17]

Others considered are Ehud and Barak following Deborah (Judg 3:28) and Josephus' list of "prophets"—particularly Judas the Galilean. He concludes with an examination of the followers of John the Baptist.[18] The context of the majority of these cases includes the disintegrating of society. Out of this matrix comes a charismatic figure who calls for radical obedience, a forsaking of possessions, a breaking away from family, and so complete an identification with the leader or master that even the death of the follower on the master's behalf was not out of the ordinary. These examples come closer to explaining the relationship of Jesus and his disciples than the rabbinic model. Yet, due to Jesus' unique messianic authority, even these analogies are far transcended by Jesus' call of the disciples. Hengel concludes:

> Just as in the Old Testament God himself called individual prophets from work and family—"and Yahweh took me from the flock and said to me 'Go and prophesy against my people Israel'" (Amos 7:15)—so Jesus also calls individuals away from all human ties to follow him. . . . "Following" means in the first place unconditional *sharing of the master's identity*, which does not stop even at deprivation and suffering in the train of the master, and is possible only on the basis of complete trust on the part of the person who "follows"; he has placed his destiny and his future in his master's hands.[19]

Consequently, Jesus is best understood as a charismatic leader and his disciples as charismatic followers.[20]

An Examination of Pertinent Marcan Texts

At this point some NT texts will be consulted, in an effort to better determine if the proposed hypothesis concerning discipleship is well founded. Several passages from the second Gospel will be examined.

Two passages specifically describe a calling of disciples: Mark 1:16–20 and 2:13–14. *Deute opiso mou, aphentes*, and *ekolouthesan* are prominent terms found in these passages. In Mark 1:16–20

Simon and Andrew respond in a way reminiscent of those discussed previously (i.e., Mattathias). Mark describes their decision to follow as immediate (*kai euthus*) with far-reaching implications (*aphentes ta diktua*). The radical nature of the acceptance of this call is further heightened in the response of the sons of Zebedee. Simon and Andrew leave their livelihood, but James and John leave both their business and their father. The sudden decision of Levi (Mark 2:13,14) is no different. Just as the fishermen left their means of support, so does the tax-collector. Without hesitation, Levi responds and follows him.[21]

These two passages tend to indicate that the call of the disciples is a unique invitation rooted in the authority of Jesus himself. His charismatic authority evokes positive decisions to follow him. As Martin observes:

> The closeness of the bond between Jesus and his chosen followers is a matter of unusual significance. . . . He boldly innovates a new type relationship, of which the rabbinic "master-pupil" model is only dimly adequate as a precedent. . . . The disciples respond to this relationship by their acceptance of his sovereign call and their yielding to his claims.[22]

The Purpose of Discipleship

Mark 3:13–19 is devoted to the choosing of the Twelve. This passage, more than others in Mark, discusses the purpose of Jesus in choosing disciples. Consequently, this pericope deserves somewhat closer attention than the two calling-passages discussed above.

The evangelist describes Jesus as going up into the mountain. It is virtually impossible to identify this site. Fortunately, it does not appear that the geographical identification was as important for Mark as was the theological significance. More than likely, the evangelist is emphasizing the traditional setting for divine revelatory acts.[23] The use in v 13 of *proskaleitai* (he called) indicates that this call was no mere invitation, but a command. In the LXX such a summons depicts a high-ranking person calling subordinate individuals or groups. These include: parents calling children (Gen 24:58), rulers calling subjects (Exod 1:18; Judg 12:1), and Moses calling the elders (Exod 12:21; 19:7).[24] The use of *ēthelen autos* (he desired) puts additional emphasis upon Jesus' initiative in the call.[25] Mark simply states that the disciples' response was affirmative.

Not only did he call them, but he appointed (*epoiēsen*; 3:14,16) the Twelve. As Taylor observes, *epoiēsen* probably means "appoint," reflecting the LXX rendering of *ʿāśā ʿasah* when it is used for appointing priests (1 Kings 12:21; 13:33; 2 Chr 2:18) and for appointing Moses and Aaron (1 Sam 12:6).[26] In light of the earlier actions of the Marcan Jesus, it is probable that divine appointment is in mind here.[27]

Central to the present inquiry is the reminder of 14 and the whole of 15. Here, the purpose of discipleship is made clear. Mark employs two *hina* clauses. Both clauses denote purpose, with the second clause growing out of the first. The first reason given for the disciples' call is "in order that they might be with him." If Jesus' call is understood as a charismatic one, then the disciples' being with Jesus would demonstrate their solidarity with his identity. In the Marcan narrative world, the disciples spend time with him and observe his teaching and miraculous works before they are sent out (Mark 6:6b-13). Not only do they identify with him, but during this time are equipped to share in his work. In other words, the disciples' later service is a direct result of their being with Jesus. The tense of *ōsin* (present) indicates that a continuous communion is described.[28] However, the disciples' call was not for them to become an introverted group glorying in their religious experiences. The next *hina* clause spells out that they were to share in the mission of their leader. There is a double emphasis in the next clause. "In order that he might send them to preach and to have authority to cast out demons." The disciples' task is to participate actively in the work of Jesus. They were to do the things that he was doing. Previously, Mark has described Jesus as preaching and driving out unclean spirits. In the next three chapters both of these characteristics are explicitly emphasized. The following part of the Marcan narrative includes several parables (with space devoted to an explanation of the purpose of parables), a pericope devoted to the question of the basis of Jesus' authority (3:20-30), and the healing of a Gerasene demoniac (5:1-20). The disciples were to be Jesus' fellow workers. No doubt they were to proclaim the same message that Jesus proclaimed: the kingdom of God. Having learned about the authority to cast out demons (3:20–30), they are given such authority by Jesus (6:7). Their authority was in actuality the authority of Jesus transferred to the disciples. His authority is the unique authority of the Messiah. More than likely, *exousia* technically denotes power granted by a higher norm, which confers "the right to do something or the right over something."[29] This higher power is Jesus, in whom *exousia* (authority) and *dynamis* (power) are combined. Consequently, the disciples are equipped by Jesus to perform the very things that he is doing, which includes having authority over Satan. According to 6:30 the disciples were able to accomplish their assigned tasks.[30]

It appears that this understanding of the purpose of discipleship coheres better with the charismatic leader-follower analogies than the rabbinic model. In the majority of places where a charismatic call has been discussed, the followers participated in the work of their leader (i.e., Elisha, Ehud and Barak, Maccabees, Essenes, and Zealots.)

The Conditions of Discipleship

It should surprise few that attention is now given to Mark 8. The emphasis of the present examination falls upon vv 34ff. The full implications of this passage become apparent only when this pericope is viewed in its proper location in the Marcan narrative. Until this point, a number of deeds and incidents from the life of Jesus have been raising the question, who is Jesus? The first half of this Gospel seems devoted to setting the reader in the proper frame of mind for this passage. Peter's confession is placed at the center of the Gospel. A number of themes are brought together. Both the confession and ensuing discussion set the stage for the remainder of the Gospel.

Not only are these passages located in a strategic position in the Gospel narrative, but they also have a significant immediate context. Both Best[31] and Achtemeier[32] have identified Mark 8:22–10:52, the central section in the Gospel, as being wholly devoted to discipleship. This is highlighted by the fact that the section begins (8:22–26) and ends (10:46–52) with the story of a blind man receiving his sight.

With Peter's confession drawing attention to Jesus' true identity, the Lord begins to discuss the major part suffering plays in his own mission. Peter is totally unprepared for this disclosure and promptly "began to rebuke him." With his disciples in view, Jesus places Peter's admonitions in the same category as Satan's. Peter is advocating a kingdom without a cross. (Matthew and Luke record that Satan made a similar offer in the wilderness temptations). It is not without significance that the discussion of the conditions of discipleship so closely follows Jesus' teaching about his own suffering.[33]

According to Mark 8:34, Jesus and the Twelve are joined by the crowd (*ton ochlon*). The presence of the crowd is theologically significant. Its appearance indicates that the conditions of discipleship are the same for everyone. This universal note suggests that the Twelve are no different than others. These conditions are for all.

Jesus prefaces three conditions for discipleship by the general call, "If anyone desires to come after me." This is reminiscent of Mattathias' call. Here, in the clearest possible language, is the charismatic leader calling potential followers. As Best concludes:

> "Come after me" is a general command which specifically links discipleship of Jesus. . . . The call is not to accept a certain system of teaching, live by it, continue faithfully to interpret it and pass it on, which was in essence the call of a rabbi to his disciples; nor is it a call to accept a philosophical position which will express itself in a certain type behavior, as in Stoicism; nor is it a call to devote life to the alleviation of suffering for others; nor is it the call to pass through certain rites as in the Mysteries so as to become an initiate of God, his companion—the carrying of the cross is no rite! It is a call to fall in behind Jesus and go with him.[34]

Jesus calls disciples to identify with his mission, which involves suffering and death. Busemann is right on target with his analysis of Mark as one who is trying to communicate a vision of the Christian message which states: discipleship is the way of the cross with Jesus.[35]

The meaning of what it costs to follow Jesus is spelled out in 8:34. First, it involves self-denial (*aparnēsasthō heauton*). The tense and mood of the verb (aorist imperative), together with the context, suggests[36] that this denial involves a definite decision or ongoing set of decisions. The disciple, who here is the object of the verbal idea, must say no to making self the goal of life. Such denial involves turning "away from the idolatry of self-centeredness."[37] It consists of making Jesus and his mission the object of life and learning so as to serve a new leader. Denial, then, is a forgetting of self in order to be at the full disposal of Jesus. Next, the disciple must take up the cross (*aratō ton stauron autou*). Jesus was quite possibly referring to the gruesome sight that had become common in first-century Palestine.[38] More exactly, what did bearing a literal cross entail in the ancient world?[39] Crucifixion was a political and military punishment inflicted primarily on the lower classes and was remarkably widespread in antiquity. Serving as a deterrent, it was carried out publicly and usually included flogging. This humiliating penalty involved a naked victim publicly displayed at a prominent place. Quite a few of the victims were never buried which further aggravated the humiliation. There is no suitable contemporary analogy for the cross. It appears to have been the most excruciating death possible. The horror of crucifixion for Jews was heightened by Deut 21:23, "Anyone who is hung on a tree is under God's curse." The imperative *aratō* conveys intense metaphorical feelings of urgency and mission in the midst of suffering. The final command is to follow (*kai akoloutheitō moi*). That the rabbi-student analogy does not adequately define "following" is explicit here. "Following" entails a radical identification of the Lord and follower. As Schweizer concludes:

> Following Jesus means togetherness with Jesus and service to him. It entails giving up all other ties, to boat and tax-office, to father and mother, in short, to one's own life, to oneself. As Jesus' own way, by divine necessity, leads to rejection, suffering and death, and only so to glory, so also the way of those who follow him.[40]

Best's thoughts are in basic agreement:

> The way of the cross can only be a lonely way; as the disciple sees Jesus tread to the cry of dereliction he cannot but be frightened, and Mark depicts him as frightened, not only by the possibility of physical suffering, which for Mark's readers was a real possibility, but by the equally real possibility of mental and spiritual suffering. In responding to his call he has left behind everything and everyone and at the end of the road there may stand only a lonely cross. . . . Christians go the same way as their

> Lord but are always in the position of those who follow, never of those who have arrived. But if they are those who follow they are also those who are accompanied—by their Lord and by their fellow disciples. As long as the journey lasts Christians are never alone; the Lord is there to deliver and feed; they are together in the house, the ship and the temple as brothers and sisters.[41]

However, the paradox of the suffering Messiah was not the only dilemma for the disciples. Verses 35-38 explain that life itself is attainable only through the sacrifice of life. True life comes through following Jesus, even if it entails shame, humiliation, and/or death. For if life is lost, nothing can be exchanged for it. The loss is irrevocable.

Conclusions

1. To view Jesus primarily as a rabbi serves as a stumbling block in attempting to understand the biblical understanding of discipleship. A better analogy for Jesus and the disciples is the charismatic leader and his followers. Yet even this is not a true analogy, for Jesus is more than a charismatic leader. He has messianic authority.

2. Discipleship is to be understood as issuing out of a call by Jesus. This call is no mere invitation but is more of a command, which is based in the authority of Jesus himself.

3. Radical identification of the disciple with the Lord is one purpose of discipleship. This communion, or "being with," is a time of fellowship with Jesus, but is also a time of intense learning.

4. The disciple's communion with Jesus will result in a sharing in the work of Jesus. Proclaiming the kingdom of God and having authority over the demons are ways in which the disciples become Jesus' fellows-workers.

5. The conditions of discipleship involve both a denial of self and sharing the fate of the master on the cross.

Contemporary Application

At the present a plethora of models for advancing the kingdom are advocated. At this time evidence of success is being interpreted as affluence, numerical strength, social influence, and possession of motivational abilities. The surrounding Western society reinforces a concentration on the protection and development of the self. Ecclesiastical bodies seek to control internal as well as external situations by resorting to the world's power structures. Consequently, compromise and accommodation appear to be necessary evils.

The Marcan admonitions on discipleship indeed sound strange to the present situation. However, despite its foreign ring, these statements can be of genuine use to those interested in renewal through discipleship.

(1) There must be a continued emphasis upon the charismatic nature of Jesus' call. Never should this aspect be downplayed. There is an authority in the person of Jesus which must be encountered for a true call to take place.

(2) The purpose of discipleship must be constantly remembered. Spirit-movements have long emphasized a personal communion with the Lord. This fellowship is essential to discipleship. In the period of time between the call of the disciples and their being sent on a mission, Jesus taught them through parables and demonstrated his authority through exorcisms. They not only observed him but experienced him. Those presently wishing to make disciples would do well to emphasize the importance of integrating information and experience. The gifts and graces of the Holy Spirit cannot be presumptuously and artificially decoupled from the informational realm of the gospel. Discipleship may be choked in static liturgical soil, but it thrives on a dynamic relationship with the risen Jesus through Scripture and prayer.[42]

(3) In addition to communion, the believer must be acquainted with another purpose of discipleship. Jesus' call was for others to join in his work. Whether announcing the kingdom of God or exercising authority over demons, the disciple is to be Jesus' fellow worker. Both the message of the kingdom and the exercising of authority come through "being with" Jesus. Those familiar with charismatic experience(s) should seek humility so as to develop the spiritual sensitivity required for these tasks. The call of discipleship is for service.

(4) The conditions for discipleship must be held in their proper place. To follow Jesus entails self-denial and cross-bearing. Only in suffering does the Marcan Jesus manifest his

true messianic status in the fullest sense and, for Mark, a thoughtful comprehension of this fact must lead to taking up the cross in authentic discipleship.[43] It is unlikely that Mark intended to correct a one-sided belief in Jesus as a miraculous healer,[44] however, Mark may discredit a possible *theologia gloria* by stressing the cross and Jesus' passion in order to present a historically accurate *theologia crucis*.[45] This might be the most difficult aspect of discipleship to translate into 20th-century secular society with its strong emphasis on instant wealth and health. Those familiar with charismatic experience(s) should seek to balance their interest in diverse Pauline *charismata*, e.g., with equal attention to a Marcan theology of suffering. A radical identification with the suffering and death of Jesus must stand at the heart of a commitment to discipleship. In all likelihood it will be God's will for a disciple to endure suffering in some way. God may allow a disciple to suffer physically and/or mentally from illness or persecution.[46] Today the cross is an ornament, worn around the neck, sometimes casually placed in churches, and printed on bumper stickers. The horrible reality of the cross must be translated to the point that its essence (or dynamic equivalence) speaks to modern believers. Bruce Metzger suggests that one might ought to say, "In the electric chair or gas chamber of Christ do I glory." Discipleship embraces a death to self. This aspect of the gospel must not be allowed to be interpreted away in an affluent culture, but must experientially be a constant reminder of the transitory nature of discipleship.

(5) Authentic Christian existence is only available through a life given fully to Jesus. The total trust and confidence placed in the leader allows the follower to follow anywhere at anytime.

(6) In all points of discipleship the inevitable tension between Jesus' continuing call of discipleship and the call of self will always be present. This tension must never be resolved in favor of settling down in an affluent world. There may be some flexibility by the way in which particulars are worked out, but the heart of discipleship, and indeed of the gospel itself, is the message of the cross.

Notes

1. Karl Rengstorf, "*Didaskō*," *TDNT*, 2:138. R. T. France, "Mark and the Teaching of Jesus," *Gospel Perspectives: Studies of History and Tradition in the Four Gospels* (eds. R. T. France and D. Wenham; 3 vols., Sheffield: JSOT, 1980) 1:118,120, shows that 50% of Mark's gospel is devoted to presenting Jesus' teaching and that 35% of this teaching material is devoted to the theory and practice of discipleship.

2. Rudolph Bultmann, *Jesus and the Word* (ET; New York: Scribner's, 1958) 57–61, italics mine.

3. Birger Gerhardsson, *Memory and Manuscript: Oral Tradition and Written Transmission in Rabbinic Judaism and Early Christianity* (ET; Copenhagen: Munsgaard, 1961) n.4.

4. Cf. E. Earle Ellis, *Prophecy and Hermeneutic in Early Christianity* (Grand Rapids: Eerdmans, 1978) 237–53.

5. I am indebted to Bruce Metzger for several of these observations on the difference between Jesus and the rabbis. I also acknowledge his helpful contemporary analogue on discipleship quoted near the end of this study.

6. Martin Hengel, *The Charismatic Leader and His Followers* (ed. J. Riches; ET; Edinburgh: T. & T. Clark, 1981) n.22. Specialists in the NT will be more familiar with this work as *Nachfolge und Charisma* (BZNW; Tübingen: Mohr, 1967).

7. Jacob Neusner, *From Politics to Piety: The Emergence of Pharisaic Judaism* (New York: KTAV, 1979) passim; *The Pharisees: Rabbinic Perspectives* (New York: KTAV, 1985) passim; cf. Martin Hengel, *Judaism and Hellenism*, (2 vols.; ET; London: SCM, 1974) 1:81–83.

8. This should not be taken to imply that *kyrios* is never used as a christological title. It certainly has this implication in Mark 2:28. Cf. C. F. D. Moule, *The Origins of Christology* (Cambridge: Cambridge University, 1977) 35–46; Hans Bietenhard, "Lord," *NIDNTT*, 2:514.

9. Most certainly the Essenes had a teacher(s) and it is probable that the Zealots did as well.

10. If, as Leonard Gopplet, *Theology of the New Testament* (ed. J. Roloff; 2 vols.; Grand Rapids: Eerdmans, 1975) 1:16–17, suggests, the fourth Gospel was written to a community familiar with the Synoptic tradition, then a reference to the prophetic Baptist as rabbi indicates that the term was still somewhat fluid. Even without a knowledge of the Synoptic material, the reader of the fourth Gospel would be impressed with John's prophetic role, cf. Felix Porsch, *Pneuma und Wort: Ein exegetischer Beitrag zur Pneumatologie des Johannesevangeliums* (FThSt 16; Frankfurt: Knecht, 1974) 19–42.

11. Gerhard Friedrich, "*Prophētēs*," *TDNT*, 6:841–48 and Eduard Lohse, "*Rabbi*," *TDNT*, 6:965.

12. Reginald Fuller, *The Foundations of New Testament Christology* (New York: Scribner's, 1965) 125–31; Geza Vermes, *Jesus the Jew* (London: Collins, 1976) 86–102. Backgrounds to this Jesus material are

well set out by Gerhard Dautzenberg, *Urchristliche Prophetie* (BWANT 104; Stuttgart: Kohlhammer, 1975) 43–97. Jesus' prophetic status is assessed and confirmed by David Aune, *Prophecy in Early Christianity and the Ancient Mediterranean World* (Grand Rapids: Eerdmans, 1983).

13. Oscar Cullmann, *The Christology of the New Testament* (ET; Philadelphia: Westminster, 1963) 44; Jesus was surely well aware of his unique prophetic status, cf. James D. G. Dunn, *Jesus and the Spirit* (Philadelphia: Fortress, 1975) 84.

14. This is demonstrated in the fact that *prophētēs* seems to have fallen quickly out of usage as a conceptually adequate title, cf. Cullmann, *Christology*, 44–50; Aune, *Prophecy*, 189.

15. Hengel, *Charismatic Leader*, 64; cf. Joachim Jeremias, *New Testament Theology* (ET; Philadelphia: Fortress, 1971) 77, who observes that "Jesus, then, was regarded as a *charismatic* rather than a professional theologian," italics his.

16. Hengel, *Charismatic Leader*, 50–51, notes that there are no stories of calling and following in rabbinic literature comparable to those found in Mark and Q. In addition, the events of joining and learning was described by "learning Torah," never by "following after." When the latter thought does occur it is used solely to express the natural subordination of pupil to teacher.

17. Tr., Jonathan A. Goldstein, *1 Maccabees* (AB 41; Garden City: Doubleday, 1976) 234. See also the RSV's rendering.

18. Cf. Hengel, *Charismatic Leader*, 16–37.

19. Ibid., 71–72, italics his.

20. Gerd Theissen, *Sociology of Early Palestinian Christianity* (ET; Philadelphia: Fortress, 1978), observes that not only was Jesus a charismatic wanderer, but that the role of charismatic wanderer had a prominent place in the early church for a number of years.

21. Eduard Schweizer, *Lordship and Discipleship* (ET; London: SCM, 1960) 11f, finds that "There can be no doubt about the fact that Jesus called disciples to follow him."

22. Ralph P. Martin, *Mark: Evangelist and Theologian* (Grand Rapids: Zondervan, 1973) 132,133.

23. William Lane, *The Gospel According to Mark* (NICNT; Grand Rapids: Eerdmans, 1974) 132 and Colin Brown, "Wilderness," *NIDNTT*, 3:1009–10.

24. Lothar Coenen, "Call," *NIDNTT*, 1:272.

25. Cf. C. E. B. Cranfield, *The Gospel According to St. Mark* (Cambridge: Cambridge University, 1979) 126.

26. Vincent Taylor, *The Gospel According to St. Mark* (rpt.; Grand Rapids: Baker, 1966) 230. It should be observed that ʿāśā ʿasah is used in emphasizing God's acts in the sphere of history. It is also used interchangeably with bārā, baraʾ cf. Thomas McComisky, "ʿĀśā," ʿAsah *TWOT*, 2:701. In light of this, Mark's use of *epoiēsen* might be more than coincidence.

27. Mark's description of the purpose of the Twelve—to be with Jesus and to be sent out to preach and exorcise—is consistent with the concept of divine appointment.

28. Sean Freyne, *The Twelve: Disciples and Apostles* (London: Sheed and Ward, 1968) 119–38, argues that the whole of the second Gospel describes the process of "being with him."

29. Werner Foerster, *"Exousia," TDNT*, 2:562.

30. Robert P. Meye, *Jesus and the Twelve* (Grand Rapids: Eerdmans, 1968) 107, notes how Mark develops his material in that "Mark 1:17 is in fact to be linked to the appointment of the Twelve in 3:13–19 and the sending of the Twelve on mission in 6:7–13,30." Cf. his entire discussion, 106–10.

31. Ernest Best, "Discipleship in Mark: Mark 8:22–10:52," *SJT* 23 (1970) 323–37.

32. Paul J. Achtemeier, "'And he followed him': Miracles and Discipleship in Mark 10:46–52," *Semeia* 11 (1978) 115–42.

33. The fact that 32% of the sayings in Marcan Jesus material is concerned with elucidating the mission and passion of Jesus relates directly to Mark's understanding of suffering as a condition for discipleship, cf. France, "Mark and the Teaching of Jesus," 121.

34. Best, "Discipleship," 329.

35. Rolf Busemann, *Die Jungergemeinde nach Markus 10: Eine redaktionsgeschichtliche Untersuchung des 10. Kapitels im Markus-evangelium* (BBB 57; Bonn: Hanstein, 1983) passim. Perhaps a focal point of Mark's understanding of discipleship is in 8:34–38 which encapsulates his "discipleship of the cross," cf. Martin Hengel, "Enstehungszeit und Situation des Markusevangeliums," *Markus-Philogie. Historische, literargeschichtliche und stilistische Untersuchungen zum zweiten Evangelium* (ed. H. Cancik; WUNT 33; Tübingen: Mohr, 1984) n.136.

36. Cf. F. Stagg, "The Abused Aorist," *JBL* 91 (1972) 231; M. L. McKay, "Syntax in Exegesis," *TynB* 23 (1972) 46.

37. Cranfield, *Mark*, 281.

38. Hans Ruddi-Weber, *The Cross: Tradition and Interpretation* (ET; Grand Rapids: Eerdmans, 1979) 9, suggests that hundreds, possibly thousands, had been crucified by the time of Jesus' birth. Another factor latent in this saying is that Jesus probably understood his unique prophetic status as one which would inevitably involve suffering and rejection, cf. Aune, *Prophecy*, 156–59,187. This suggests that disciples who might prophesy or preach in his name could be expected to carry a similar, but much lesser, burden.

39. The following comments are based upon Martin Hengel, *Crucifixion in the Ancient World and the Folly of the Cross* (ET; Philadelphia: Fortress, 1977) 86–88.

40. Schweizer, *Lordship and Discipleship*, 20. Achtemeier, "Miracles and Discipleship," 136, detects as well that one can reach no other conclusion except that "Mark clearly thinks of discipleship primarily in relation to the passion of Jesus."

41. Ernest Best, *Following Jesus: Discipleship in the Gospel of Mark* (JSNTS 4; Sheffield, JSOT, 1981) 162,248. For Best, discipleship and Christology are thematically linked. Jesus lays down his life—so do the disciples; Jesus is a servant—so are his followers. What Jesus is and does—that is what the disciples are to be and do. However, even

in teaching this, Jesus remains distinct; his person and work are unique.

42. Re these latter categories, cf. Paul Hinnebusch, "Using the Scriptures for Prayer," *Scripture and the Charismatic Renewal* (ed. G. Martin; Ann Arbor: Servant, 1979) 59–75.

43. Cf. Martin Hengel, "Probleme des Markusevangeliums," *Das Evangelium und die Evangelien* (ed. P. Stuhlmacher: WUNT 26; Tübingen: Mohr, 1983) 237; "The Expiatory Sacrifice of Christ," *BJRL* 62 (1980) 461; and nn.33,35,40 above and 45 below.

44. J. Nissen, "The Problem of Suffering and Ethics in the New Testament," *Studia Biblica 1978, III: Papers on Paul and Other New Testament Authors* (ed. E. A. Livingstone, JSNTS 3; Sheffield: JSOT, 1980) 279.

45. John R. Donahue, "A Neglected Factor in the Theology of Mark," *JBL* 101 (1982) 582,586. Germane to our discussion is the thought that "Mark is seen as presenting the following of Jesus on the way to the cross as the Only Christian option. Suffering becomes almost equated with believing in the gospel" (586).

46. Such suffering, when it comes and in whatever form it comes, should be viewed christocentrically, i.e., from the perspective of the cross and resurrection. It should be viewed and experienced calmly (cf. my point 5 below), entering into the mystery of suffering with Christ and letting the benefits come as they may.

6

"FILLED WITH THE HOLY SPIRIT" AND "FULL OF THE HOLY SPIRIT": LUCAN REDACTIONAL PHRASES

James B. Shelton

L UKE EMPLOYS PHRASES that appear both traditional and Lucan in character to indicate the presence of the Holy Spirit in instances of inspired speaking. "Baptism in the Holy Spirit," "receiving the Holy Spirit," "the gift of the Holy Spirit," and "the Holy Spirit coming upon" an individual or group are apparently traditional phrases that Luke employs to express his specialized pneumatological interest, while "filled with the Holy Spirit" and "full of the Holy Spirit" have an unmistakably Lucan stamp, although the expressions themselves may antedate Luke. The concept of fulness in relation to the Holy Spirit has a specialized meaning in Luke's work regardless of its ultimate origin.

Luke uses the expression to provide crucial theological transition throughout his two-volume work of Luke–Acts. The phrase "filled with" or "full of the Holy Spirit" indicates primarily that inspired witness about Jesus or against the devil is occurring. Any other significance of the expression is probably peripheral to Luke's intentions. Its use in the infancy narratives, in the post-Pentecost church, and in the life of Jesus himself serves to cement the so-called three epochs of Luke[1] into an indivisible pneumatological unit.

Luke's overall program is one of witness to the Spirit-anointed Christ and his impending kingdom from Judea to Rome. By using the same phraseology for the witnesses provided by the precursors to Jesus, Jesus himself, and his

followers, Luke is declaring that the same provision of the
Holy Spirit authenticates the message of salvation. In this Luke
demonstrates that the kingdom movement—of which Zechariah, Elizabeth, Mary, John, as well as Jesus and his followers
are a part—is in the mainstream of Jewish salvation history.
This is the main task to which Luke addresses his pneumatology. If this is not understood then the wrong questions
about the Holy Spirit will be addressed to Luke and inevitably
the answers will be confusing and divisive. Specifically, Luke's
pneumatology does not exist to answer the question, "What
happens when believers initially receive the Holy Spirit?" Such
a question is only a peripheral interest to Luke at best.

I. "Filled with/Full of the Holy Spirit" and Authoritative Speaking

A. Specialized Meanings for "Filled" and "Full"?

Luke's presentation of the Holy Spirit is indeed varied. The
concept of "filled with the Holy Spirit" (*pimplēmi* + genitive of
Holy Spirit) is used perhaps to describe the reception of the
Holy Spirit (Acts 2:4) and to indicate that a special dispensation
of the Spirit was responsible for the authoritative speaking
of believers (2:4; 4:8,31; 9:17; 13:9). Even when the phrase
occurs where initial reception of the Spirit is mentioned, inspired speaking is also present in the context. The phrase, "full
of the Holy Spirit" (*plērēs* + genitive of Holy Spirit), also has
more than one use in Acts. It can refer to the quality of a
personality (6:3,5; 11:24)[2] or to the presence of divine power in
a person enabling him to speak or act authoritatively (e.g.,
7:55; Luke 4:1). Even the references to "full of the Holy Spirit,"
which apparently indicate quality of personality, reflect the
same pattern as the references to "filled with the Holy Spirit,"
since both are used in close proximity to the speaking ministry
of Spirit-filled persons.

It may be generally true that Luke uses "full of the Holy
Spirit" to express the character of a disciple and "filled with
the Holy Spirit" to indicate the empowering of an individual
on a specific occasion to speak authoritatively.[3] (Luke uses

"full" to indicate inspired speaking in 7:55.) The contexts for both expressions reveal Luke's interest in inspired speaking. Usually this is Luke's primary interest in referring to fulness of the Holy Spirit. (This would explain the use of *plērēs* instead of *pimplēmi* in 7:55.) "Filled with the Holy Spirit," used to express initial reception of the Holy Spirit, implies duration. Thus the uses of *plērēs* and *pimplēmi* do not always fit into this simplified order. Both expressions, however, occur in contexts in which inspired speaking is the major theme. Marshall notes the use of both "filled" and "full" to designate that believers spoke "effectively as witnesses to Christ."[4]

B. *Analysis of Passages with the Phrase, "Full of the Holy Spirit"*

1. *Stephen: Acts 6:3,5,8,10; 7:55.* It is significant that Stephen, who along with the other deacons is described as "full of the Spirit and wisdom" (6:3),[5] is later singled out and described with references to the Holy Spirit (6:5 and perhaps v 8)[6] immediately prior to the narration of his disputing with the men of the Synagogue of the Freedmen (6:9–12) and before his defense speech at his trial (7:2–53). It is clear that all of the deacons are full of the Spirit of wisdom or full of the Holy Spirit and wisdom (6:3), but in the actual list of names (6:5) only Stephen is described as "full of the Spirit and faith"! It is true that the expressions of fulness denote quality and that this quality may effect various manifestations (6:8).[7] The instances of "full of the Spirit" may be traditional descriptions of Jesus and his followers,[8] but *plērēs* is a Lucan preference word (in Luke–Acts 10 times; rest of NT 6) and especially so in association with the Holy Spirit. It would appear that Luke has his usual meaning in mind when he includes the phrase here, i.e., enabling to speak authoritatively. The observation is inescapable when one notices that after references to Stephen's spiritual fulness in 6:3,5,8 the main task in which that influence is employed is in speaking: "But they could not withstand the wisdom and the Spirit with which he spoke" (6:10).[9]

The capstone to this specialized use of "fulness" in relation to speaking occurs in 7:55 when Stephen, again described as "full of the Holy Spirit," sees a vision of Jesus with God[10] and relates it to his audience. Both the perception of the vision and

Stephen's description of it are results of being "full of the Spirit" (*hyparchōn*); for both *eiden* and *eipen* are parallel in form and connected by the coordinate conjunction *kai*. The *kai* here could be parataxis as it is in 7:58b,60b; and therefore one could argue that the vision was a result of "fulness" and not the speaking. But this interpretation is weakened by two points beyond the parallel verb structure and the coordinate conjunction. Grammatically, it should be noted that while 7:54–60 has some parataxis, *kai* is also used to connect similar verbal structures such as participles and verbs of identical person, number, and tense (e.g., vv 54,55–56,57–58; the second *kai* in v 58 may connect only the verbs, "stoned" and "cast down"). Thus the structure in vv 55–56 resembles this pattern of simple coordination and not stylistic parataxis. Furthermore, contextually, the force of the reference to the Holy Spirit and speaking in 6:10 cannot be ignored in 7:55. So even if the two events, the vision and the announcement of it to the audience, are considered separately, the fulness of the Spirit must be seen as the catalyst if not the prime force behind Stephen's declaration.

2. *Barnabas: Acts 11:24.* The last use of *plērēs pneumatos hagiou* in Acts occurs in 11:24. This reference to Barnabas is a description of his character, but Luke includes this description because of the activity of Barnabas in v 23. Barnabas exhorted (*parekalei*) the new church in Antioch. The *hoti* in v 24 functions as a causal conjunction and should be translated as "for,"[11] which is characteristic of Luke's usage elsewhere (Luke 9:12; 13:31; 16:24). (Note that in 9:12 Luke inserts this use of *hoti* into the Marcan material.) The question arises, Why does Luke call Barnabas "full of the Holy Spirit and faith?" Luke provides the answer: because of his exhortation.[12]

3. *Jesus: Luke 4:1,14.* These uses of "full of the Holy Spirit" parallel the uses in Luke's Gospel. Jesus is described as "full of the Holy Spirit" (4:1) after his baptism and prior to his temptation. Nowhere is evidence of Luke's redactional contribution clearer; for only Luke among the Synoptic Gospels inserts "full of the Holy Spirit" here (Matt 4:1; Mark 1:12; Luke 4:1). This is not just a superlative compliment to Jesus' nature and character nor just a summary of the results of his baptism; rather it explains how Jesus successfully combatted Satan in

the temptation. Jesus accomplished this not by means of miraculous self-attestation or through public wonderworking, but by inspired speaking while being "full of the Holy Spirit." In 4:14 Jesus is described as "full of the power of the Spirit." This does not show how he made his way back to his home community, but it anticipates his ministry there, which exclusively took the form of proclamation (see 4:18,19). Doubtless, Luke feels comfortable in allowing the phrase to be associated with the working of wonders (wonderworking is alluded to in Luke 4:23), but this effect does not occur in the ministry at Nazareth. In fact, Jesus refuses to perform wonders there. The ministry at Nazareth is inspired speaking. Thus the primary function of "full (plērēs) of the Holy Spirit" is to demonstrate that the speaker is divinely inspired. The anointing of Jesus in 4:18 and the fulness noted in 4:1 and the power in 4:14 effect the same result.

C. "Filled with the Holy Spirit" and the Reception of the Holy Spirit

1. *Pentecost: Acts 2.* "Filled with the Holy Spirit" (pimplēmi + genitive of Holy Spirit) also occurs in Acts in places where inspired speaking is the dominant theme. The classical passage around which much commentary and controversy revolve is Acts 2, Luke's Pentecost account. Interpretation of this event is crucial for all opinions concerning the classical Pentecostal and charismatic movements. Only here and perhaps in Acts 9:17 and Luke 1:17 is receiving the Holy Spirit described in terms of the fulness of the Holy Spirit. (In all of these inspired witness dominates the context. Initial reception may not be the main thought in these passages.) Elsewhere the experience is described as baptism in the Holy Spirit (Luke 3:16; Acts 1:5; 11:16); the Holy Spirit coming upon someone (Luke 24:49; Acts 1:8; 2:17; 19:6); receiving the Spirit or the power of the Spirit (Acts 1:8; 2:38; 8:15,17,19; 10:47; 19:2); the gift of the Holy Spirit (Acts 2:38; 10:45; 11:17); the promise of the Spirit (Luke 24:49; Acts 1:4; 2:33,39); and the Holy Spirit falling upon a group (Acts 8:16; 10:44; 11:15). Considering the frequency of the use of plērēs and pimplēmi in connection with the Holy Spirit in Luke, it is indeed surprising that a term so suited to the

description of the reception of the Holy Spirit by believers would be used so little in such contexts. It is true that Luke feels free to interchange the various phrases expressing the coming of the Holy Spirit; for we have seen this in his use of the Holy Spirit filling or coming upon someone in relation to inspired speaking. (Luke shows interest in the relationship of the Holy Spirit and inspired utterance in such expressions as, "come upon," "upon," "fell," etc., but it is not in the purview of the paper to examine these in detail.) This substitution of one phrase for another, while to a degree stylistic in places, cannot be viewed as a merely random variation. In each possible case where "filled with the Spirit" might indicate initial reception of the Holy Spirit, it occurs in the context of inspired speaking, in proclaiming the gospel and/or witnessing to the messiahship of Jesus.

The context in Acts 2 makes it clear that the experience of being filled with the Holy Spirit is responsible for inspired speaking that attracts the attention of the pilgrims in Jerusalem. The result is not ecstatic speech in the sense that the speaking is unintelligible or a catalyst for unintelligible confusion,[13] but the speaking in tongues provides a multilingual testimony to the mighty works of God (2:6,7,11). Here the result of being filled with the Holy Spirit is a proper, well-ordered evangelization complete with accommodation for those who were from foreign lands. Only those who do not recognize the foreign languages and therefore consider them unintelligible to anyone else accuse the disciples of being drunk. In fact, unintelligible speech is the only evidence the text gives for such an accusation. To assume that the audience condemned them for emotionalism or an altered state of consciousness requires a considerable amount of presupposition being read into the text.[14] The reaction in the text is to the language and may reflect the Judean prejudice that we meet elsewhere, "Can any good thing come from Nazareth?"

Here the main result of being filled with the Holy Spirit is inspired speaking, as is evidenced by the Galilean Peter, who astonishes the onlooking gainsayers by speaking to them in their own language: "Men of Judea and all you who live in Jerusalem" (v 14).[15] By expressing the reception of the Holy

Spirit in terms of "filled with the Holy Spirit" Luke is commenting not only on the inspired nature of the message in tongues, but also on the inspiration behind Peter's Spirit-directed interpretation of Scripture, the Christian presentation of the *Heilsgeschichte*, the confrontation of sinners with a call for repentance, and the Spirit-inspired promise of himself.

As noted above, the reception of the Holy Spirit has been described by various phrases. Specifically in reference to the reception on the Day of Pentecost we find: receiving power (Acts 1:8), clothed with power (Luke 24:49), baptized with the Holy Spirit (Luke 3:16; Acts 1:5; 11:16), the Holy Spirit falling on believers (Acts 11:15), a gift (Acts 11:17), the Holy Spirit or the promise of the Father coming upon the recipients (Luke 24:49; Acts 1:8), or the promise of the Father (standing as a substantive without a transitive verb, Acts 1:4). It would appear that Luke has explained the actual events in terms of filling because of the dominant role of inspired speaking and witness which abounds both in the predictions of the event and in the recounting of the event itself. Luke has superimposed the phrase, "filled with the Holy Spirit," upon the event here. Like the Holy Spirit coming upon (*epi*) someone, "filled with the Holy Spirit" can indicate both inspired speaking and reception of the Holy Spirit. Perhaps Luke feels justified in doing this because he has an OT precedent: when the Holy Spirit comes upon Saul at his anointing, divine speaking accompanies the endowment of the Spirit (1 Sam 10:6,10).

2. *Paul: Acts 9:17-20.* By all appearances the use of the phrase, "filled with the Holy Spirit," in connection with Ananias' laying hands on Paul is a reference to the reception of the Spirit (9:17,18). Apparently this occurs after Paul's conversion on the road to Damascus (9:3-8) when Ananias lays hands on him not only for the filling with the Holy Spirit but also for restoration of his sight.[16] (This double duty for laying on of hands is a typical Lucan presentation of salvation which sees the experience as all-inclusive, including healing.)[17] The result of Ananias' obedience is curiously expressed, for only the restoration of Paul's sight is mentioned. No reference to the reception of the Holy Spirit accompanies the confirmation of the healing (9:18) unless the result is implicit in the fact that

he then was baptized (v 19). So perhaps the phrase "filled with the Holy Spirit" is mentioned mainly for a reason other than to indicate initial reception of the Spirit. The subjunctive phrase, *plēsthēs pneumatos hagiou*, is left dangling with no explicit fulfillment in the indicative. It is, of course, not mandatory for Luke to give us an explicit indicative fulfillment paralleling each promised subjunctive action. The baptism could be seen as affirmation that the filling with the Spirit, which possibly connotes receiving the Spirit, has been fulfilled and that therefore reception did indeed occur.

The verses which follow, however, offer a better explanation of how Ananias' prayer for "filling with the Holy Spirit" was fulfilled. After noting that Paul (Saul) did not immediately leave the disciples at Damascus, Luke relates that he immediately (*eutheōs*) "began to proclaim" (*ekērussen*) that Jesus was the Son of God (v 20). *Eutheōs* places Paul's preaching into temporal proximity to the reference to "filled with the Holy Spirit," and it could well be taken that the expression of fulness modifies his preaching.[18]

Incidentally, this parallels the order of events in Stephen's ministry except that Paul just misses completing the parallel with his own martyrdom. Paul's conversion and subsequent preaching parallels Luke's prefatory observations to Stephen's inspired speaking where he describes Stephen in terms of the fulness of the Holy Spirit. There he uses the selection of the deacons as an opportunity to note that even prior to his defense speech before the council Stephen spoke under the direction of the Holy Spirit (6:10). Perhaps the observation that Paul, then Saul, was present at Stephen's martyrdom (7:58) is Luke's effort to parallel the two ministries. As a result of Paul's preaching in Damascus the parallel just misses completion when the new convert just misses martyrdom in the short term while in the long term it seems that it is only delayed. If this is a conscious parallel, then one could see how "filled with the Holy Spirit" in the subjunctive is fulfilled and confirmed in Paul's preaching which is expressed in the indicative.

Even if "filled with the Holy Spirit" refers to Paul's reception of the Holy Spirit, *double entendre* must be considered because of the force of *eutheōs* in v 20 and because of the dominant use of the fulness of the Spirit in relation to speaking. Peter's Pentecost sermon provides a parallel to this situation. After having received the Holy Spirit in terms of being filled (2:4), Peter is empowered (Luke 24:47–49; Acts 1:8) to proclaim the significance of the Pentecostal event through inspired exegesis, to proclaim Jesus as Christ and Lord and to offer salvation.

3. *John the Baptist: Luke 1:15.*   In his Gospel Luke presents a similar situation with the infant John. His description of John as "filled with the Holy Spirit from his mother's womb" (Luke 1:15) may be taken as a reference to the reception of the Holy Spirit unless it is argued that the Spirit influenced the child since his conception. But is initial reception the point Luke is trying to make? Is this a digression from Luke's usual use of the phrase or is inspired witness still the dominant theme in the phrase? Of course the infant John did not "speak" as such, but he did witness to the lordship of Jesus while still in the womb when he leaped for joy (Luke 1:45). Such a perception could only be by divine revelation, and his mother Elizabeth knew this was the reason for the baby's movement because she too was filled with the Holy Spirit and subsequently spoke words to affirm the action of the child (1:41–45). Luke may well have been of the opinion that the prenatal John's perception of Jesus was the moment when he was filled with the Holy Spirit and further that this filling with the Holy Spirit occurred to enable him to witness to Jesus' lordship. There is further evidence that John's witness to Jesus while still in the womb was what Luke had in mind when he recorded the angel's prophecy concerning John and the fulness of the Spirit. The angel described the future ministry of John primarily as proclamation of repentance (1:16). Moreover, Zechariah his father, filled with the Holy Spirit, described John's ministry in terms of prophetic exhortation in anticipation of the coming Messiah (1:67, 76–79). This is fulfilled in John's preaching in Luke 3. John, who was previously identified as filled with the Holy Spirit, began his ministry when the word of the Lord came upon (*epi*) him (3:2), a circumstance with striking parallels in Luke 2:27, Acts 1:8, and 4:31.[19]

4. *Origins of the phrase?*   It therefore appears that even though fulness of the Spirit is peripherally associated with receiving

the Spirit, inspired speaking is Luke's overriding theme. In the case of Pentecost, the reference to fulness is in Luke's own explanation of the event. In the case of Paul's conversion (Acts 9) and the beginning of his subsequent preaching ministry, and in the Baptist's prenatal ministry, the phrase occurs in monologues spoken by Ananias and by the angel of the Lord respectively. Elsewhere "filled with/full of the Holy Spirit" occurs only in Luke's own commentary and not on the lips of other persons. The incidents of the phrase occurring in speeches, which give evidence of being carefully composed, may indicate that the expression predates Luke and was descriptive of various people being "full of the Holy Spirit." Nevertheless, Luke is not above rephrasing those summaries called speeches in his work, as he has added a definite Lucan stamp to the material in both of his books, and the phrase may be his own, regardless of the type of material in which it is found. Whatever the origin of the expression it is a stock phrase in Luke's program, carrying a meaning that Luke has specially designed for it, as demonstrated in the individual contexts which give rise to his use of it.

D. The Function of Fulness of the Spirit Contrasted with Other Pneumatological Expressions in Luke–Acts

Luke's specialized use of the phrase can be demonstrated statistically as well. If Acts 6:3 and 6:5 are included as uses of fulness of the Spirit in relation to inspired speaking and if fulness in Luke 1:15 and 4:1 are taken to refer to reception of the Holy Spirit, then in Luke–Acts there are 11 instances of fulness of the Spirit to inspired speaking outside of contexts where initial reception of the Holy Spirit is mentioned and 4 instances where it appears in a passage noting initial reception (73% and 27% respectively). It may be that 6:3 and 6:5 should not be included in the data. We have already argued that these should indeed be included as they do refer to empowering to speak, but a significant tendency in Lucan phraseology can be demonstrated without them. If for the moment 6:3 and 6:5 are eliminated from the inspired speaking category and Luke 4:1 is treated as solely referring to reception, then there are 9 instances referring to speaking without reference to initial reception and 4 instances occurring in the context indicating initial reception (67% and 33% respectively). So even with the minimal amount of data in the first category, the differences are significant and are not likely due to chance.

Acts 6:3 and 6:5 should *not*, in my opinion, be excluded from the first category; furthermore, "full of the Holy Spirit" in Luke 4:1, though it does constitute a Lucan commentary on the baptism of Jesus, should be seen primarily in terms of inspired speaking since it prefaces Jesus' victory over the temptation in which his principal weapon was inspired speaking. But putting Luke 4:1 aside, there are 11 instances of fulness without reference to reception and 3 instances of fulness with reference to reception which yield 79% and 21% respectively. This leaves Luke 1:15, Acts 2:4 and 9:17 as the 3 incidents of fulness and initial reception. If the reference to Paul at Damascus (9:17) is included in the first category, then there are 12 instances relating to speaking and 2 to reception, which is 86% and 14% respectively.[20] These expressions may be schematized in Chart I.

A quick glance shows Luke preferred the expressions of fulness of the Holy Spirit to indicate inspired speaking. A comparison of the three possible groupings of "filled with/full of the Holy Spirit" with the amalgamated results of rows 1 through 6 yield the results[21] found in Chart II.

The best explanation for these data is a specialized Lucan use of filled with/full of the Holy Spirit to express inspired speaking. Luke's preferred verb is *pimplēmi* (10 times). Only once does he use *plēroō* to express being filled with the Holy Spirit (Acts 13:52).[22] The general use of *pimplēmi*, *plērēs*, and *plēroō* shows Luke often used the first two words to refer to speaking regardless of the "contents" to which fulness refers.

If rows 1, 2, and 3 in Chart III are expressed in terms of the x^2 test, the results are significant: $x^2 = 18.48$ at one degree of freedom, which means that this arrangement of the three words into categories A and B has less than one chance in a thousand that it is due to chance. Rows 1 and 2 are not compared to each other because *plērēs* is the adjectival form of *pimplēmi* and their use is similar.[23]

CHART I

	A Used for speaking with no reference to reception	B Used to indicate reception of the Holy Spirit (speaking role may be present as well)
1. Baptism in the Holy Spirit	0	3
2. Holy Spirit was upon or came upon, or rejoiced in the Holy Spirit in col. A and Luke 3:22 in col. B	2	4
3. Received the Spirit or the power of the Spirit	0	9
4. Gift of the Holy Spirit including Acts 11:17 in col. B	0	3
5. Promise of the Spirit	0	4
6. Holy Spirit fell on believers	0	3
Subtotals	2	26
7. Filled with the Holy Spirit or full of the Holy Spirit including Luke 4:1 and excluding Acts 6:3,5 in col. A	9	3
8. Filled with the Holy Spirit or full of the Holy Spirit including Luke 4:1 in col. B and excluding Acts 6:3,5 in col. A	8	4
9. Filled with the Holy Spirit or full of the Holy Spirit including Luke 4:1 and Acts 6:3,5 in col. A	11	3

If the smaller numbers for speaking are employed, then the results are still similar: rows 1, 2, 3 = x^2 of 11.99 (less than one chance in a hundred due to chance). Rows 1 and 2 *contra* 3 = x^2 of 11.92.[24] This appears to indicate that Luke had a specialized use of *pimplēmi* and *plērēs*.

CHART II

	x^2 score	Degrees of freedom	Per cent due to chance
Row 7	19.40	1	less than 0.1
Row 8	15.87	1	less than 0.1
Row 9	22.28	1	less than 0.1

CHART III

	A Speaking	B Not speaking	Totals	Per cent speaking
1. pimplēmi	11*	11	22	50
2. plērēs	7**	3	10	70
3. plēroō	1	24	25	4
Totals	19	38	57	33

* includes Luke 1:15 and Acts 9:17.
** includes Luke 4:1 and Acts 6:3,5

E. *Inspired Speaking and the Fulness of the Holy Spirit*
   in the Program of Luke–Acts

In addition to the phrases, "full of the Holy Spirit" and "filled with the Holy Spirit," used in connection with the reception of the Spirit, Luke also employs the latter phrase in situations where inspired speaking occurs but no reference is made to receiving the Spirit as a part of a conversion-initiation process. It is in this interest that the expressions of fulness of the Holy Spirit primarily contribute to the witness motif that dominates the structure and *raison d'être* of Luke–Acts.

1. *Peter's Inspired Speaking and Fulness of the Spirit (Acts 4:8).* Like his sermon on the Day of Pentecost, Peter's response to the rulers and elders is a result of his being "filled with the Holy Spirit" (4:8). Since this is in the narration, it is Luke's own

observation and is characteristic of his use of the expression
and similar phrases in Luke–Acts in general. In keeping with
the Synoptic tradition that the Holy Spirit would aid in the
disciples' defense before rulers, Luke notes the activity of the
Spirit.[25] The expression describing Peter's defense is Luke's
own, one which replaces the more traditional structures, i.e.,
"the Holy Spirit" or "the Spirit of your Father speaking," "the
Holy Spirit teaching," or Jesus giving to the witness "a mouth
of wisdom" (Matt 10:20; Mark 3:11; Luke 12:12; 21:15, respectively). Characteristically, Luke seldom presents actual accounts of legal self-defense in these frequent instances of
believers before authorities (e.g., Acts 4:3–12; 5:26–32; 6:12–
7:53; 23:1–9; 24:10–21; 26:1–21). The notable exception in
these instances is Paul, whose genuine self-defense statements
also provide an opportunity to present the gospel.) Instead, the
context for believers tried before authorities provided in the
Synoptic tradition primarily presents these trials as occasions
for witness (Matt 10:18; Mark 13:9). The context that Luke
provides makes this Synoptic emphasis all the stronger (Luke
12:8–10; 21:12–14). In Acts 4 Peter presents elements parallel
to his Pentecost sermon. Luke again notes that under the
direction of the Holy Spirit Jesus is preached, Scripture is
correctly interpreted, and salvation is proclaimed.[26] Verse 20
makes it clear that the "defense" speech is a witness to Jesus.

2. *Disciples and Inspired Speaking (Acts 4:31)*. The latter part of
Acts 4 provides another example of Holy Spirit-inspired speaking in response to Peter's bold testimony before the rulers
(4:24–31). After noting the relevance of the events to Scripture, the disciples pray that in spite of the authorities they may
speak "with all boldness" (v 29) as the Lord attests the validity
of their speaking through signs and wonders (v 30). As a result
of this prayer, "they were all filled with the Holy Spirit and
spoke the word of God with boldness." Here again the fulness
concept emphasizes speaking,[27] while signs and wonders vali-
date the words spoken by Jesus' followers.

3. *Paul and Spirit-Filled Speech (Acts 13:9)*. We see a similar
example in Paul's ministry. Like so many other characteristics
of Paul's ministry, the references to "filled with the Holy
Spirit" parallel the ones in Peter's ministry. Both Peter's and
Paul's work begins after an initial reference to being filled with

the Holy Spirit. This filling can be seen as corresponding to the initial reception of the Holy Spirit, and in both cases results in preaching (Acts 2:4,14–40; 9:17,20–22). Peter addresses Jerusalem while Paul preaches to Damascus. Elsewhere both Peter and Paul are said to have been filled with the Holy Spirit to speak in special situations. Peter addresses the rulers of the Jews (4:8–20), and Paul, filled with the Holy Spirit, speaks a word of rebuke and condemnation to Elymas the magician and calls down temporary blindness upon the enemy of the gospel (13:9). Not only do these two events have parallels in the apostles' ministries elsewhere but the two events (witnessing before authorities and verbally confronting the powers of evil) correspond to events in Luke's Gospel which are also accomplished by the activity of the Holy Spirit (Luke 4:1; 12:12). Like Jesus, both men preach the good news to audiences in general aided by the presence of the Holy Spirit (in a similar but lesser way to Luke 4:14,18,19).

It cannot be said that Paul was filled with the Holy Spirit only to "fix his gaze upon" Elymas. He was filled primarily for the purpose of speaking and of participating in the Lord's act which caused the blindness as well. The syntax makes this clear. *Atenisas*, the aorist participle, has its meaning completed by *eipen*. Furthermore the aorist active participle *atenisas* appears to be in tandem with *plēstheis pneumatos hagiou*, the aorist passive participial phrase. Certainly the passive participle *plēstheis* in some sense functions attributively, but *plērēs* would fit better as a purely attributive element in this sense as he used it in v 10 to describe the degenerate condition of the magician. (Luke may juxtapose the two contrasting views of the fulness for effect.) Therefore it is probably better to view both aorist participles, active and passive, as functioning adverbially and indicating that two actions occurred prior to the subsequent action of speaking. In this syntactical structure, "gazing intently" (*atenisas*) would not be seen as a subsequent result of being filled with the Holy Spirit, grammatically speaking (although this connection would logically follow). It would instead denote that the speaking of Paul resulted from or after the fact that he was filled with the Holy Spirit and that he "fixed his sight" upon his opponent. The sentence is diagrammed in Chart IV.

CHART IV

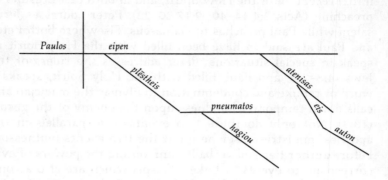

4. *Examples of Parallel Use of "Filled" and "Full" (Acts 4:31; 7:55).* Luke employs similar structure in Stephen's speaking after having been filled with the Holy Spirit prior to his martyrdom (7:55). There are two participial phrases, one beginning with present active *hyparchōn* and the other with the aorist active *atenisas*, which modify two main verbs, *eiden* and *eipen*. The basic structure is diagrammed in Chart V.

CHART V

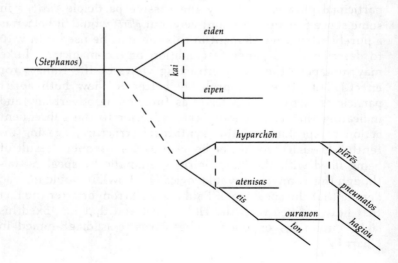

In the Stephen account "being full of the Holy Spirit" and having "gazed into heaven" explain the two consequent actions. The two participial phrases can effect the two main verbs, but the translation should be as follows if the tense of the two participles is observed: "but while or since he was filled with the Holy Spirit, after he looked into heaven he saw . . . and said" or "but being full of the Holy Spirit after having looked into heaven he saw . . . and said" (my translation). Here the tense of the present participle appears to correspond more to the verb of speaking, although technically it could modify both. It may be possible to link only one of the two participial phrases to one of the main verbs since "gazing" and "seeing" are complementary. Thus the sense of the structure would appear as in Chart VI.

CHART VI

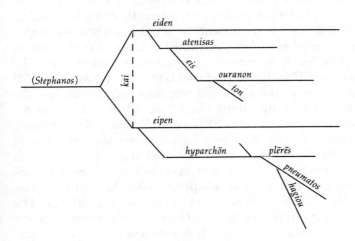

Regardless which diagram is to be preferred, the relationship between the phrase, "full of the Holy Spirit," and speaking is established. The structure of both the passage about Stephen and the one about Paul certainly appear to be Lucan when the participial forms are noted, and when one realizes that *atenizō* and filled with/full of the Holy Spirit (*pimplēmi* and *plērēs*) are

preferred expressions of Luke. (*Atenizō* is used 12 times in
Luke–Acts, nearly always as a participle; 2 elsewhere in NT,
2 Cor 3:7,13. *Pimplēmi* is almost exclusively used in Luke–Acts,
22 out of 24 total in the NT. *Plērēs* is dominated by Luke–Acts in
contrast to other Gospels. Furthermore, Luke often connects
plērēs, plētheis, and the aorist of *pimplēmi* plus a genitival form of
the Holy Spirit with *kai eipen* or similar expressions indicating
speech.)

II. Other Expressions of Spirit-Inspired Speech

Luke does not limit his associations of the Holy Spirit and
inspired speaking to the concept of fulness.[28] In other passages
where authoritative speaking occurs but the Holy Spirit is not
explicitly named as the agent behind the speaking, the work of
the Spirit is often implied by the presence of particular items in
the context. Luke does not feel compelled to preface every
statement of the faithful with a reference to the Holy Spirit.
He is content to let the reader understand that this is implicitly
so. Furthermore he is content to let the summaries which
conclude several preaching accounts indicate that the power
of the Holy Spirit is behind the speakers by mentioning the
activity of the Holy Spirit (Acts 4:31,33; 9:27–29,31; 13:49,52)
or by referring to the signs and wonders that accompany the
words inspired by the Spirit (Acts 2:42–43, as related to the
Pentecost sermon; Acts 4:8–20 as an explanation of the healing
and sermon of Acts 3). Once he mentions the presence of
the Holy Spirit in a speaker, Luke does not repeat this each
time he introduces one of that speaker's speeches. He considers the first reference as adequate unless he wishes to emphasize the Holy Spirit's activity in a special circumstance. The
frequency of references to the Holy Spirit's activity in the
speaking ministry of the church demonstrates that Luke considers it the norm in the progress of the early church.

III. Conclusion

In Luke–Acts "filled with the Holy Spirit" and "full of the
Holy Spirit" usually indicate divine power resting upon an

individual Christian or group of Christians enabling them to speak authoritatively. Even in situations in which these expressions appear to describe an enduring characteristic of a believer or a special one-time dispensation of the Spirit, the contextual emphasis is the same: inspired speaking. In this sense the meanings of "full" and "filled" overlap. The presence of fulness of the Spirit in references to initial reception of the Holy Spirit is also governed by Luke's overriding interest in inspired speaking.

The concept of fulness in the Spirit does not begin with Luke. It has precedents in the OT, perhaps in the sources of Acts and the infancy narratives, and in some degree in the rest of the NT, especially Eph 5:18.[29] Even if Luke acquired the expression from tradition, he quickly transformed it into a specialized tool serving his overall program of attributing the growth of the church to the activity of the Holy Spirit. Luke's pneumatology primarily serves to show how Spirit-inspired preaching started and expanded the kingdom of God.

This study of Luke's pneumatology also sheds light on the Pentecostal-charismatic movements in the church today. First, because of Luke's specialized use of "full of/filled with the Holy Spirit," too much weight should not be put on the expression, especially when it is perhaps used as an indicator of the reception of the Holy Spirit or when it accompanies a description of the initial reception of the Holy Spirit.[30] When Luke's specialized use of the phrase to effect inspired speaking (especially in 4:8,31; 13:9) is taken into consideration, his description of receiving the Holy Spirit does not appear as consistent and normative as is sometimes assumed (cf. n. 30).

Luke was not addressing himself specifically to the same questions that today's church is requiring of him. One could say that in the Lucan accounts about initially receiving the Holy Spirit a pattern *begins* to emerge, but little more than that can be said. The church's pneumatology should be as flexible as Luke's, even with all its unanswered questions and overlapping categories. Let the church recognize the sovereignty and supremacy of the Spirit who is too large to fit in one pneumatology.[31]

For those who reject *a priori* or are wary of much of the phenomena of the Pentecostal-charismatic movements, it should be noted that for Luke, Jesus was not only the one and only *Christos* but he was also the archetype of the Spirit-led man.[32] Luke saw many charismatic phenomena as essential to the church and as flowing in the mainstream of the church's growth since the Day of Pentecost. If Luke's motives for writing are identified and acknowledged and if the specialized uses of his terms are identified, those participating in the on-going discussion about the charismatic movement may find themselves speaking with more agreement and hopefully in the same environment, full of the Holy Spirit!

Luke's specialized pneumatological interest is expressed well in the following prayer for the confirmation of believers in the faith:

> Lord,
> we celebrate the memorial of our redemption
> by which your Son won for us the gift of the Holy Spirit.
> Accept our offerings
> and send us your Holy Spirit
> to make us more like Christ
> in bearing witness to the world.[33]

Notes

1. The unity of Luke's pneumatology weakens H. Conzelmann's suggestion that Luke has created three distinct epochs, cf. his *The Theology of St. Luke* (New York: Harper & Row, 1961). The pneumatology of the infancy narrative is the Achilles' heel of Conzelmann's epochs, cf. P. S. Minear "Luke's Use of the Birth Stories," *Studies in Luke–Acts* (eds. L. E. Keck and J. L. Martyn; London: SPCK, 1968) 111–30.

2. Haenchen suggests that Luke is maintaining two different theologies of the church in using "filled" as a special endowment for a special function and "full of the Holy Spirit" as a durative presence in a person, *Acts*, (ET; 14th ed.; Oxford: Blackwell, 1971) 187,216. If this is the case then Luke utilized traditional phraseology to express his special interest: the Holy Spirit and authoritative speaking.

3. As held by M. Turner in "Spirit Endowment in Luke–Acts: Some Linguistic Considerations," *VoxEv* 12 (1981) 45–63. He is correct in noting that "full of the Holy Spirit" indicates that the church felt the impact of the Spirit "through that person's life" (53–55), but the specialized use of this fulness (i.e., speaking) is not used. Bruce is close to my observation here: "After the initial receiving or filling with the Spirit, individuals may be described in a distinctive sense as being

'full' of the Spirit, like the seven almoners of Acts 6, especially Stephen (6:3,5; 7:55), or like Barnabas (11:24); or they may be 'filled' with the Spirit for a particular purpose, especially for authoritative or oracular utterance," "The Holy Spirit in the Acts of the Apostles," *Int* 27 (1973) 180. Earlier Bruce maintained the iterative nature of "filled" and the durative nature of "full," *Acts* (NICNT; Grand Rapids: Eerdmans, 1954) 99; *Acts, Greek* (Leicester: Inter-Varsity, 1952) 120; cf. also William Neil, *Acts* (NCB; London: Marshall, Morgan and Scott, 1973) 89.

4. I. H. Marshall, *Luke: Historian and Theologian* (Grand Rapids: Zondervan, 1970) 199.

5. The double expression, *plērēs pneumatos kai sophias*, may have a twofold meaning, but it seems likely that this is not an overt reference to the Holy Spirit but a reference to wisdom, the Spirit of wisdom, or "wisdom inspired by the Spirit." See Haenchen for the first two meanings, *Acts*, 262, and Marshall for the last one, *Acts* (TNTC; Leicester: Inter-Varsity, 1978) 126-27. Haenchen notes that wisdom is emphasized in the following context (vv 8,10). He also correctly notes Luke's penchant for such double phrases but also points out that the LXX uses *sophia* in such pairs and uses the expression *pneuma sophias* in Exod 31:3; 35:31 and Wis 1:4; cf. *Acts*, 262, n. 4. J. Kilgallen, *The Stephen Speech: A Literary and Redactional Study of Acts 7,2-53* (AnBib 67; Rome: Pontifical Biblical Institute, 1976) 49, identifies wisdom as a Lucan interest here so that Luke is probably responsible for the expression. *Sophia* is used by Luke often, and it occurs in similar situations in Luke 2:40,52; 21:15. In Stephen's speech wisdom is used to describe Joseph (7:10) and Moses (7:22). Cf. also Ulrich Wilckens, *Die Missionsreden der Apostelgeschichte: Form-und traditionsgeschichtliche Untersuchungen* (WMANT 5; Neukirchen-Vluyn: Neukirchener, 1974) 210, n. 2. Several MSS add *hagiou* after *pneumatos* (A C* H P S vg cop[5a] eth) while the shorter form occurs in others (p[8], p[74], Sinaiticus B D 431 614 2412 syr[h] Chrysostom). Metzger suggests that Christian scribes would naturally provide the reading, "Holy Spirit," *Textual Commentary* (New York: UBS, 1971) 337. It would not be beyond Luke to have inserted the adjective into a traditional description of the major requirement of wisdom for admission into the early diaconate.

6. Technically only Stephen, the preacher whose speeches occupy the following context from 6:10-7:60, is described as full of the *Holy* Spirit. The adjective holy does not occur in 6:3 describing the apostolic guidelines for selection of deacons of which wisdom is paramount (see preceding note). Luke may be responsible for the elaboration of *pneuma* in v 3 into the work of the Holy Spirit in the following context.

7. Leadership, counselling and teaching could be intended in the meaning of the phrases as well; cf. J. D. G. Dunn, *Jesus and the Spirit* (London: SCM, 1975) 176. Luke may intend the wonders to be attestations of the inspired speaking. Stephen is described in terms similar to Barnabas, "full of the Holy Spirit and faith" (11:24). These descriptions accompany the speaking ministries of both men.

8. The traditional background of the Stephen material has often been noted in scholarship. (For a summary of criticism see Haenchen, *Acts*, 264–69; also G. Stanton, "Stephen in Lucan Perspective," *Studia Biblica 1978: Papers on Paul and Other New Testament Authors* [JSNTS 3; ed. E. Livingstone: Sheffield: JSOT, 1980] 345–60.) Harnack saw 6:1–7:50 as a "single connected narrative," *Acts* (London: William & Norgate, 1909) 169–70, while more recent scholarship has acknowledged a source for 6:1 but identifies redactional elements as well, e.g., Martin Dibelius, *Studies in the Acts of the Apostles* (London: SCM, 1956) 11, n. 20. Conzelmann also notes the presence of tradition. "V 1–6 Zugrunde liegt ein Traditionstück, das Lk schriftlich vorgefunden haben muss vgl. die Art und Weise, wie die 'Hellenisten' und 'Hebräer' eingeführt werden." These two categories suggest that it is tradition because "bisher wurde nichts von einem Nebeneinander zweier Gruppen angedeutet"; furthermore, "Konkret Wunder des Stephanus kennt Lk nicht." *Apostelgeschichte* (HNT; Tübingen, Mohr, 1963), 49,51; cf. also his *History of Primitive Christianity* (Nashville: Abingdon, 1973) 35. Kilgallen thinks signs and wonders (v 8) should be linked to the miracles of Moses mentioned in Stephen's speech (7:36), *Stephen Speech*, 81. Nevertheless the main event is the speech. Signs and wonders accompany the word as in 4:31–33. It is also surprising that the apostles assign the deacons mundane tasks, so that they will have time to minister the word of God, only to have the deacon Stephen to be described as a preacher. Luke has apparently telescoped the ministry of Stephen presenting its beginning, middle, and end as one section. The tradition concerning the deacons gives Luke another opportunity to present another big step in the church's expanding mission. J. Lienhard suggests that Luke learned the names of the deacons and the fact that they were appointed to wait tables from his source. He also questions that the source would have especially noted that they were filled with the Holy Spirit for this mundane purpose (230). This observation is more in keeping with the ability to preach and do missions, in that "Preaching flies in the face of the traditional view of *diakonia*" (234). He also notes the extensive Lucan vocabulary in vv 1–6 (232–34). Lienhard notes Luke's motive for his restructuring of the "Stephen Cycle" in 6:1–6, "The final redactor of Acts (i.e., Luke) intended to associate 6:1–6 with the narrative about Stephen which follows it," cf. "Acts 6:1–6: A Redactional View," *CBQ* 37 (1975) 228–38. M. Scharlemann also considers the deacon's "gift of the Spirit (6:3)" as an indicator that Stephen (in anticipation of his speech) was "obedient to the Spirit of God and had a Messianic understanding of the Old Testament." *Stephen: A Singular Saint* (AnBib 34; Pontifical Biblical Institute, 1968) 12. Kilgallen also notes that Stephen was enabled to present a proper exegesis of the OT, *Stephen Speech*, 5. If Dunn's suggestion is correct that "the description of various individuals as 'full' (*plērēs*) of the Holy Spirit" was acquired by Luke "from a special and primitive source (6:3,5,8; 7:55; 11:24)," then we may be face to face with an early church concept of the enduring

quality of the Holy Spirit as the means of "sureness of insight and conviction of speech," *Jesus and the Spirit*, 171. Cf. also Haenchen who identifies this as a "Hellenistic Christian view," *Acts*, 187. It is of interest that the dominant context of the passages with "full of the Spirit" is inspired speech. It is equally valid to view the associations of "fulness" with inspired speaking as Luke's own contribution as he uses traditional descriptions of persons (e.g., full of wisdom or spirit of wisdom for deacons) as an opportunity to emphasize the role of the Spirit in the kerygmatic mission of the early church. Luke may indeed be indebted (at least in part) to a source for the designation of deacons as "full of the Spirit" since it seems unlikely that Luke would describe deacons as continually full of the Spirit to speak while the apostles were filled to speak only on occasion. Certainly in his use of "filled with/full of the Spirit" to designate authoritative speaking, the differences in iterative and durative meanings are minimized.

9. Bezae provides an interesting alternate reading, "who could not withstand the wisdom that was in him and the Holy Spirit with which he spoke, because they were confuted by him with all boldness. Being unable therefore to confront the truth . . ." (in slightly different forms in D E vg[mss] syr[hmg] cop[G67] and Bohemian version), cf. Metzger, *Textual Commentary*, 340. This reading certainly follows the Lucan pattern of associating the Holy Spirit with inspired speaking and the pairing of Spirit with virtues in 6:1–8. This could be a part of Luke's overall activity in chapter 6 of expanding the meaning of traditional descriptions of fulness, wisdom, and spirit among the early church characters to present his reconstruction of the sermons that are the mainstay of his account of the ever-expanding church. Bruce (*Acts, Greek*, 157) notes that *autophthalmein* (to confront) only occurs in rest of NT in Acts 27:15. He also notes the parallel sense for this in Luke 21:15. Bezae often mentions the Holy Spirit in reference to speaking especially when "anti-Judaic" or "pro-Gentile" views are presented, cf. Eldon Jay Epp, *The Theological Tendency of Codex Bezae Cantabrigiensis in Acts* (SNTSMS 3; Cambridge: University, 1966) 116–18,132,135. Scribal abbreviation could account for the shorter forms, but admittedly Bezae's tendency to expand the texts mitigates against anything but a cautious suggestion that the longer form is Lucan. The description of Stephen as having a "face of an angel" prior to his address perhaps stands to remind us of his supernatural empowering to speak (6:3,5,8,10) and to reveal his vision of Christ (7:55).

10. Marshall, *Acts*, 148. Haenchen, *Acts*, 292, n. 1.

11. BDF, 456.1.

12. Note also that rejoicing is mentioned here (v 23) in relation to the Holy Spirit. This is similar to Luke's presentation of Jesus rejoicing in the Holy Spirit in Luke 10:21.

13. The word ecstatic has often been used to describe the events at Pentecost. It often carries a pejorative nuance. What happened at Pentecost, although supernatural, was a well-ordered evangelization complete with translation. To describe it as "ecstatic" is often a value

judgment with "ecstatic" approaching something of a theological "dirty word."

14. These assumptions seem to suppose that the abuse and excesses that Paul tries to correct in 1 Corinthians 12–14 were the norm in such phenomena in the early church.

15. The context and general practice of Luke make it clear that Peter addressed the onlookers (2:14) as a result of being filled with the Holy Spirit with the other believers in 2:4. Luke's choice of word to describe Peter's speaking also reinforces this observation. *Apophthengomai* can refer to oracular or prophetic speech in classical and Hellenistic Greek, and in the LXX. It occurs 3 times in the NT, all in Acts: in 26:25, here, and in 2:4 (cf. BAGD, 101). Wilckens considers the connection between the "Spirit-outpouring" of 2:4 and Peter's speech at 2:14 as a *fait accompli*. He reasons that the reader is not surprised by this since he has been prepared for it beforehand (Luke 24:49; Acts 1:5; 2:4), *Missionsreden*, 56. The following scholars also take *apophthengomai* to indicate that Peter's address is indeed inspired utterance, several of whom explicitly link it with the earlier aspect of the Pentecost event (2:4): H. J. Cadbury and K. Lake, *Acts*, BC 4:21; Haenchen, *Acts*, 178; Marshall, *Acts*, 72–73; Bruce, *Acts, Greek*, 88; Neil, *Acts*, 75; R. Zehnle, *Peter's Pentecost Discourse: Tradition and Lukan Reinterpretation in Peter's Speeches of Acts 2 and 3* (SBLSBS 15; Nashville: Abingdon, 1971) 37,117.

16. "We are probably meant to understand that in receiving the gift of the Holy Spirit, Paul experienced the Pentecostal ecstacy," Neil, *Acts*, 131; but note also H. M. Ervin, *These are Not Drunken, As Ye Suppose* (Plainfield, New Jersey: Logos, 1968) 56,61. Others simply note that reception of the Spirit is meant, e.g., Dunn, *Jesus and the Spirit*, 193, and *Baptism in the Holy Spirit* (London: SCM, 1970) 78; Conzelmann, *Acts*, 66; Haenchen, *Acts*, 325; D. Guthrie, *New Testament Theology* (Leicester: Inter-Varsity, 1981) 543; Marshall, *Acts*, 172. (Inevitably discussion arises as to whether the laying on of hands or baptism causes the reception of the Holy Spirit, but it is doubtful that Luke makes any overall fixed connection between the Spirit and these events.)

17. As evident in the use of *sōzō* in Luke 17:11–19. See G. Montague, *Holy Spirit: Growth of a Biblical Tradition* (New York: Paulist, 1976) 255–57.

18. The reference to the filling with the Holy Spirit may refer to "the prophetic gift." "Paul was to bear witness before the Gentile Emperors and the Sons of Israel, and therefore he must receive the Spirit for 'the testimony of Jesus is the spirit of prophecy' (cf. also Mk. xiii. 11)," Lake and Cadbury, *Acts*, BC 4:104. Bruce links the phrase with the preaching as well: "Such filling was necessary for the prophetic service indicated in ver. 15," *Acts, Greek*, 202; cf. also Barrett, *The Holy Spirit and the Gospel Tradition*, (2nd ed.; London: SPCK, 1966) 1, and Dunn, *Baptism*, 71.

19. For more of Luke's pneumatological adjustment of the Baptist traditions see J. Shelton, *Filled with the Holy Spirit: Redactional Motif in Luke's Gospel* (Ph.D. thesis, University of Stirling, Scotland, 1982) 24–132.

20. There is reason to consider even Luke 1:15 as primarily in a speaking category, which would leave only Acts 2:4 in the category of reception. Some may contend that Acts 6:3,5 and Luke 4:1 should be included in group "B" in the following chart. But even if this is done the resulting ratio of 7 to 5 is significantly different from 2 to 26. Therefore, my thesis still stands. In doing so, however, the overriding contextual use of "fulness" must be minimized.

21. The x^2 contingency score expresses the possibility that a given sample could randomly arise. Alone it cannot automatically be used to determine chance or premeditated selection of a sample group. But *with* the theological tendency already noted it becomes a very strong indicator of Luke's redactional activity.

22. Perhaps this use of *plēroō* here is due to traditional language even though Luke is responsible for the summary statement here.

23. If *plērēs* and *pimplēmi* were compared then the x^2 score would be .05 (not significant, which is what should be expected if they are used similarly). However, when *plērēs* and *plēroō* are analyzed together it is significant ($x^2 = 17.4$). Even if the smaller numbers for fulness and speaking were used it still is significant.

24. With the smaller numbers allowed for speaking, then row 1 *contra* row 2 = x^2 of .05, again not significant. If Luke's other uses of *plērēs* not referring to speaking were to be seen as mitigating its inclusion in the chart, then *pimplēmi* alone becomes a specialized word for Luke.

25. Haenchen, *Acts*, 187,216; Marshall, *Acts*, 69,100. Marshall argues that Luke considers it possible "that a person already filled with the Spirit can receive a fresh filling for a specific task or a continuous filling." E. Schweizer presents a similar view, *The Holy Spirit* (London: SCM, 1980) 75. Cf. also Dunn, *Baptism*, 71; Bruce, *Acts, Greek*, 120; Lake and Cadbury, *Acts*, BC 4:23.

26. The juxtaposing of the healing at the Gate Beautiful, the preaching of Peter and his courtroom "defense" is characteristic of Luke's holistic approach to salvation.

27. Clearly this is divine enabling for speaking and not a reference to initial reception of the Holy Spirit, cf. Lake and Cadbury, *Acts*, BC 4:47, who link *parrēsias* with the words used in v 13 which is related to Peter's Spirit-inspired address before the rulers (vv 8–12); so too Marshall, *Acts*, 107; Haenchen, *Acts*, 228; Dunn, *Baptism*, 70; Schweizer, *Holy Spirit*, 76. Although this passage does have parallels to the Pentecost events of chapter 2, it is not an alternative version of Pentecost as Harnack suggests, *Acts*, 183. The strength of the immediate context dispels such a notion. Likewise attempts to identify 4:31 and following as the initial reception of the Holy Spirit for the

converts who joined the church as a result of Peter's first sermon come to ruin under the weight of the immediate context (*pace*, Ervin, *These are Not Drunken*, 62–67). First, the apostles who already had received the Holy Spirit (2:4) apparently "took part in the prayer of 4:24–30" and were filled with the Holy Spirit along with the other Christians (Dunn, *Baptism*, 70–72). This is corroborated by the reference to the apostles' witness in the summary in v 33 as well. Second, the immediate context demands that Luke use the filling with the Spirit to note the means whereby the disciples "spoke the word of God with boldness." As Dunn observes, "As for the formula *plēstheis pneumatos hagiou eipen*, when an aorist participle is used with *eipen*, it always describes an action or event which had taken place immediately prior to or which leads into the act of speaking (e.g., Acts 1.15; 3.4; 5.19; 6.2; 9.17,40; 10.34; 16.18; 18.6; 21.11)," *Baptism*, 71; cf. Zehnle, *Peter's Pentecost Discourse*, 37, 117.

When it is recognized that the Lucan association of fulness of the Spirit with inspired speaking is the primary significance for the expression and that its association with receiving the Holy Spirit is governed by this interest too, then a major link in classical Pentecostal theology slips. It is critical that "full of/filled with the Holy Spirit" be seen as a term for receiving the Spirit, if the events of Acts 2:4 are considered somewhat normative for reception of the Spirit. When the specialized and dominant function for fulness of the Spirit is recognized, then tongues as the initial evidence of receiving the Holy Spirit cannot be viewed as explicitly normative. Tongues can only be seen as perhaps a frequent attestation of receiving the Holy Spirit (see also n. 30).

28. For an analysis of other pneumatological expressions used by Luke to indicate divinely inspired witness see Shelton, *Filled with the Holy Spirit*, 70–132,173–405.

29. Note that Eph 5:18 has *plēroō* plus *en pneumati*. With only one exception Luke prefers *pimplēmi* over *plēroō* in the use of the expression. Note also the brief prepositional phrase (no genitive and no modifiers for "Spirit"). It is unlikely that this expression in Ephesians owes its existence to Lucan influence. This weakens R. Martin's suggestion that Luke was responsible for the final form of the Ephesian Epistle based on linguistic affinities between Luke–Acts and the Prison epistle, cf. "An Epistle in Search of a Life-Setting," *ExpTim* 79 (1968) 296–302; and also in *New Testament Foundations* (Grand Rapids: Eerdmans, 1978) 230–3.

30. It is here that the classical Pentecostal position is overstated. Luke does not directly address himself to the question, What phenomena accompany initial reception of the Holy Spirit? Furthermore, Luke does not use the expressions, "filled with/full of the Holy Spirit," primarily as an indication of initial reception of the Holy Spirit. The dominant redactional function of Luke's pneumatology, i.e., inspired witness, must not be blurred by asking questions of Luke that are

peripheral to his greater program and expecting universally applicable answers. *Nevertheless,* one can and should conclude that tongues often accompanies initial reception of the Holy Spirit in Luke–Acts. An undeniable pattern begins to emerge in Luke–Acts, albeit not a universal one. The Pentecostal position is also correct in asserting that pneumatic empowerment is often subsequent to conversion. By insisting on these two points in Lucan exegesis the distinguished honoree of this festschrift, Dr. Stanley Horton, has performed an invaluable service to the church and the Spirit that empowers her; cf. *What the Bible Says About the Holy Spirit* (Springfield, Missouri: Gospel Publishing House, 1976). Another scholarly presentation of the classical position is in Ervin's *These Are Not Drunken (Spirit Baptism. A Biblical Investigation* [Peabody, Mass.: Hendrickson, 1987]). Often attempts to minimize these two distinctive Lucan patterns are a result of imposing Paul's pneumatology found in Romans—which primarily addresses soteriological questions—upon Luke–Acts—which addresses different questions to the Holy Spirit. These attempts reflect a misunderstanding on the part of biblical scholarship in general for which the recent redaction-critical school also provides a corrective.

31. When one does not appreciate the precise functions of pneumatology in the NT inevitably interpreters from all sides of the current debate begin to interpret with abandon Luke's pneumatology in terms of Paul's or vice versa or Luke's with John's, etc. Unbridled attempts at harmonization, though well-intentioned, only cloud the issue at hand because they fail to recognize that the NT writers often have a specific use of pneumatology. Thus the wrong questions about the Holy Spirit are being addressed to Luke, John, and Paul!

32. Shelton, *Filled with the Holy Spirit*, 133–201, passim.

33. *The Sunday Missal*, ed. Harold Winstone (London: Collins, 1977) 787.

7

NEW DIRECTIONS IN LUCAN THEOLOGY: REFLECTIONS ON LUKE 3:21-22 AND SOME IMPLICATIONS

Ben Aker

I N THE SPIRIT OF THE PERSON to whom this volume is dedicated, I want to reflect upon Jesus' baptism as described in Luke 3:21-22 and to make some observations about Pentecostal hermeneutics and theology. It is my contention that scholars have, in general, overlooked the significance of Jesus' baptism in Luke for Lucan theology and for contemporary church life. It is possible that Luke's treatment of his materials at this point may have more significance than previously realized.

Howard Ervin, for example, has offered a rebuttal to James Dunn's earlier work, *Baptism in the Holy Spirit*, and has discussed Luke 3:21-22. Ervin has reached different conclusions from those developed in Dunn's thesis, has contributed to our understanding of the pentecostal spirit of Luke's writings, but still has not uncovered the full significance of Jesus' baptism in Luke.[1] Another scholar, Gordon Fee, while a participant in the evangelical pentecostal tradition, does not think that Pentecostals have a precedent in Acts for their experience.[2] A mere recording of history, if this is Luke's intention, does not establish a theological precedent for similar charismatic experience today. While Fee does allow for Luke's charismatic interests, which go beyond mere historical motives, his criticism of the traditional pentecostal interpretation has stimulated further discussion about the relation of hermeneutics, theology, and experiences as evidenced by the response of William Menzies.[3]

James Dunn, in a serious attempt to understand Luke's theology, works with some diligence on Luke 3:21–22, devoting an entire chapter to the passage, and concludes that Jesus' baptism in Luke denotes the pivotal point in salvation history.[4] He incorporates an interpretation of the passage into his overall thesis that the main "pentecostal" events in Acts represent the end point of a conversion-initiation process. The charismatic nature of these events is more unique than suggestive of a precedent. Two evangelical scholars have reached about the same conclusions. George Ladd, in his NT theology, is strangely silent about the Spirit.[5] Donald Guthrie relies far too heavily on Dunn's model of conversion-initiation and makes little effort to deal with critical passages aside from this model.[6] Re Luke 3:21–22, Guthrie notes the anointing of Jesus by the Spirit for his messianic office and public ministry.[7] On this passage the Catholic scholar, Robert O'Toole, states that

> The Spirit in Luke should never be separated from Christian baptism which initiates Christians into the community and imitates Christ's own baptism. As the Spirit introduced Jesus' ministry, so he introduces the Christians to theirs.[8]

Aside from a restrictive and non-Lucan emphasis on a union of water baptism and the Spirit,[9] an emphasis not shared by Dunn or Guthrie, O'Toole's valuable contribution towards doing theology in Luke–Acts lies in his concern for the unity of these two books. This is a trend to which evangelicals have not been sensitive. Even before O'Toole, Charles Talbert was breaking ground with his studies on the genre of Luke–Acts which took their unity seriously.[10]

The purpose of this article, then, is to propose some new directions for Lucan hermeneutics and, consequently, theology. We will examine the unique elements in Luke's baptism account of Jesus, then the unique elements of Luke's immediate context, and, finally, the greater context of Luke–Acts.

The Unique Elements of Luke 3:21–22

Many have noted the unique elements in Luke 3:21–22, but have not followed their implications to proper conclusions.[11] It is clear, however, that Luke intends to emphasize the coming of the Spirit upon Jesus. Both Matthew and Mark have his baptism as the main point of their accounts, both in terms of the amount of material and coordinate sentence structure. For example, Matthew 3:13, the introduction to the baptism paragraph, reads, "Then Jesus came from Galilee to Jordan to John to be baptized by him." The infinitive construction denotes Jesus' purpose in coming to Jordan. Likewise, in Mark 1:9, "In those days Jesus came from Nazareth to Galilee to be baptized in Jordan by John." The same purpose clause exits in Mark. In contrast, Luke places Jesus' "baptism" in a subordinate clause and separates it from the baptism of the "people."[12] He also drops the name of John from the baptism account. Luke then uses three infinitives as the main verbs in three coordinate clauses, which form the main thrust of what he intends to convey: *aneōchthēnai . . . kai katabēnai . . . kai . . . genesthai.* The flexible use of the infinitive is Lucan style.[13] He is unique in saying that heaven opened and the Spirit descended while Jesus was praying (*proseuchomenou*). Luke also is the only writer to concretize the descent of the Spirit by adding "in bodily form."[14]

Up to this point, the evidence is clear—Luke emphasizes the coming of the Spirit upon Jesus.[15] But what of the voice from heaven? Does it refer to Jesus' adoption, or does it refer to a significant point in the history of salvation when Jesus enters the new epoch, or is this experience here merely anticipatory?[16] What is the function of the voice that accompanies Jesus' baptism? I think that it is clearly demonstrated by others that this is the time when Jesus is declared to be God's Messiah and when Jesus is prepared to enter into this ministry. Keck, for instance, believes that "sonship" here means anointing for Luke, who has in view the semitic understanding of the son of God—Luke is not thinking in metaphysical terms.[17] In others words, there is no view of adoptionism here. Bretscher gives ample evidence that this is the case. He notes, for example, that *agapētos, monogenēs, ekletos,* and *prōtotokos* are all synonyms, and are all used in reference to sonship.[18] Bretscher, consequently, believes that this refers to "anointing" (i.e., for messianic ministry) but, in contrast to Keck, he believes that it also refers to incarnation. Collins too (with Guthrie and most

NT theologies) opts for anointing for ministry.[19] Rice accepts an alternate rendering of the statement of the voice and says that this reading quotes directly Psalm 2:7, which refers to the anointing of the messianic king.[20] The context bears out that this coming of the Spirit refers to Jesus' anointing for messianic ministry. For example, in Luke 1:35 the angel announces that, when the Holy Spirit comes upon Mary and she has a child, he will be called the *Son* of God. That is, Jesus is Son at conception. Later to the shepherds, the angel says that this one that is born is their savior—he is the *Messiah* Lord.[21] This is also supported in 2:26 where Simeon was told that he would see the Lord's *Messiah* before he died. Thus, son equals messiah in Luke's birth narratives. And certainly just before our passage at 3:15f, Luke places the account of the people who were wondering whether John was the Messiah or not. The point of this paragraph in this regard is that John is not God's messiah—Jesus is. This is significant, as we shall see later, for Luke distinguishes sharply between John the Baptist and Jesus.

The Unique Elements in the Context of Luke 3:21-22

The way Luke arranges and selects his material around the immediate context supports his emphasis on the anointing of Jesus in his baptism account. In order to see what Luke's concerns are, it is helpful and necessary to compare his narrative with those of the other Gospels. We should take seriously the historical interest in Jesus' words and deeds and we must recognize that each moment in history will reflect different situations. To "flatten" out biblical revelation by ignoring this important fact, then, is to question with unnecessary skepticism the historicity of events, both the particular Jesus-event a writer uses and the situation of the writer's church.

The baptism of Jesus occurs in all four Gospel accounts, emphasizing different aspects of his baptism. In Matthew's account this difference (i.e., Matthean material) is largely in 3:14-15, where John hesitates to baptize Jesus and where Jesus responds to this hesitancy by saying that he, Jesus, should be baptized, for, "it is fitting for us to fulfill all righteousness." The meaning of "to fulfill all righteousness" is the key to understanding the function of the baptism account in Matthew. I suggest that "baptism" here should be understood in terms of "to identify with." Though Jesus was born in the Abrahamic and Davidic lineage (1:1–17) and thus partook of normal Jewish nature (humanity), he was still considered to be distinct in one regard: he was without sin. Mary's child is "from the Holy Spirit" (1:20). It is true that Matthew does not emphasize the holiness of the child as Luke does. In Luke 1:35 "holy" is an attribute of the child (cf. Acts 3:14; 4:27,30). But both Matthew and Luke draw upon similar traditions. At least similar terms and emphases in the infancy narratives suggest similar sources. Both emphasize the miraculous birth and are concerned with the legitimacy of that birth. Both are interested in the Davidic, messianic elements of Jesus' ministry. How then does Jesus become "fully" Jewish (human)? By identifying with "Israel" in their sins. Already it had been announced that Jesus' task was to "save his people from their sins" (Matt 1:21). This is the functional motif of the infancy narratives in Matthew. Jesus identifies with his people in their journeys and trials but comes out victorious through God's divine intervention. Even in his temptation he responds as the pious Israelite would—he is totally under the word of God and obedient to his Lord.[22] This is even brought out in the baptism of Jesus— he does not confess his sins as all the others who had come to John,[23] a circumstance that is suggested by John's hesitancy to baptize Jesus. It is still appropriate, however, to see an anointing for Jesus' mission of salvation in Matthew; he simply does not emphasize it.

In contrast, Mark uses the baptism account to introduce Jesus and to distinguish between Jesus and John. Mark only has the OT quote about the messenger preceding the way of the Lord (1:3). Moreover, the first thirteen verses are a literary unit. Several words demonstrate this unity: wilderness (3,4,12) and Spirit (8,10,12). It is significant that "Spirit" occurs rarely in Mark—three of them here in the prologue.[24] Furthermore, scholars disagree about what "beginning" in v 1 means. I suggest that it means "introduction," not so much in the literary as in the theological sense.[25] In support of this view, it is to be noted that "the gospel" in v 1 does not occur again until v 14, where for the first time Jesus announces the arrival of the kingdom of God. The kingdom arrives with the announcement of "the gospel of God." At v 14 an adverbial, infinitive clause (strictly Marcan) makes sure that the reader knows that it was *after* John's imprisonment and Jesus' preparation that Jesus came proclaiming the kingdom of God. (Only in Matthew's Gospel do we find John the Baptist and Jesus proclaiming the kingdom of God.) Thus, Mark wants us to know that Jesus' preparation (i.e., his anointing) was not closely linked to the *time* of his ministry. Jesus' temptation and baptism, along with John's ministry, belong to the same salvation moment, but not with Jesus' proclamation of the kingdom.

John's Gospel, on the other hand, is the most distinct. Strictly speaking, John has no baptism account. There are two references to the Spirit coming upon Jesus, both in regards to the Spirit's coming from heaven at Jesus' baptism, but both have reference to John's knowledge of Jesus' identity:

1:31   And I would not have known him (pluperfect tense)
1:33   And I would not have known him (identical words in Greek).

To the last reference, however, John adds that God told him that this is how he would know Jesus: "Upon whomever you see the Spirit descending and *remaining*, this is the one who baptizes with the Holy Spirit." This is important for John's theology. The evangelist is struggling with a group of Jewish "believers" who are unwilling to accept Jesus for who he is and for what he does. These "believers" simply have faith in a Jewish messiah, one who is not divine and who does not negate the Jewish way of being the people of God. In the argument between these groups in John, the question naturally arises—who, then, are the true people of God? "The natural sons of Abraham," the Jewish "believers" would say. "No," says the fourth evangelist, "those who have the Spirit of God remaining upon them are—just as the Spirit remained upon Jesus." This fact is also significant in 1 John. The ones who departed from that community went out because they were not of the true believers—they were not born of the Spirit nor did they *remain*. John's function, then, is to bear witness to Jesus.[26]

Luke emphasizes the Spirit in the mission of Jesus, and this mission is inaugurated at his baptism. In the immediate and preceding context of Luke 3:21–22, several unique Lucan elements occur, which support my position. These elements, by the way, are Lucan themes and go with his emphasis. In 3:5 Luke adds to the Isaiah quote, in 3:6, the matter about "all flesh shall see the salvation of God." Further, in vv 10 to 14, Luke has "crowds" instead of the Matthean "Pharisees" and "Sadducees." He also uses different material at that point— material which is Lucan. He shows his ethical concerns for the proper handling of money and goods.[27]

After this baptism account, only Luke has "And Jesus full of the Holy Spirit" to begin the temptation account. Then in 4:14–15 Luke has a summary, and a highly condensed one at that, about Jesus returning from the temptation in the power of the Spirit and ministering in Galilee. This is immediately followed by the sermon at Nazareth, which, as many scholars correctly say, is Luke's programmatic essay for his work.[28] In this sermon, Jesus quotes from two places in Isaiah (61:2; 58:6), a quote missing from both Mark and Matthew. This quote begins with, "The Spirit of the Lord is upon me, because he has anointed me." The effect of this, then, is to emphasize Jesus' anointing for ministry. Jesus is anointed at his baptism, remains full of the Spirit to and from his temptation, which is part of his ministry, and quickly establishes what his ministry will be and some of its results. The summary at 4:14–15 serves two purposes. It brings forward Jesus' empowerment of the Spirit and quickly moves over a part of Jesus' ministry to bring him to his programmatic sermon—all to emphasize the anointing with the Spirit for ministry.

The Greater Context of Luke-Acts

Why, then, did Jesus need this power for ministry, if Jesus' baptism in Luke is where he is anointed for ministry? Can the answer to this question be found in Luke's Christology? I think that it can and that it supports my thesis regarding Luke 3:21-22.

If Luke wanted to emphasize the divinity of Jesus, there would have been less need for him to have Jesus relying upon the power of Another, as in the case, say, of John's Gospel. There are some texts, then, in which Jesus' humanity is clearly emphasized. Luke 2:52 is one of these. There, only Luke among the Gospel writers, refers to Jesus' physical, mental, social, and spiritual growth.

Another place which emphasizes the humanity of Jesus is in Acts 2:22, where Peter, after being filled with the Spirit and after preaching from the book of Joel, addresses the Israelites saying, "Jesus of Nazareth, a man (*andra*) who was set forth by God with miracles, wonders, and signs. . . ."

Likewise, the two who walked on the road to Emmaus and conversed with Jesus (Luke 24:19), not knowing it was he, called Jesus a man (*anēr*) from Nazareth, "a prophet mighty in deed and word before God and all the people."

Similarly, in Peter's speech in Acts 3:12ff, Jesus is a "prophet raised up from among your brothers like unto me (Moses)" (v 22). Peter brackets this speech at vv 13—a reference to Isa 52:13 and 53:11—and 26 by calling Jesus God's servant (*paida*). This is evidence that *pais theou* was an early, Palestinian title for Jesus that signified humility and servanthood, and even his humanity. This title was perhaps best preserved in the liturgical reflections of the early church,[29] where Luke possibly found it and then used it in his writings. *Pais* originally meant "servant" and later "child of God."[30] Further, Jeremias suggests that "To the Gentile Church it was offensive from the very first because it did not seem to bring out the full significance of the majesty of the glorified Lord."[31]

Pais theou was also used with David (cf. the juxtaposition of David and Jesus in Acts 4:25,27,30). We have already mentioned that both Matthew and Luke connect Jesus with the son of David messianology. In this respect more support is given to Luke's emphasis upon Jesus' humanity. In contrast to Matthew, who portrays Jesus as the royal, kingly messiah who inherits David's throne, Luke paints a suffering, humble servant as David's son who identifies with all humanity (thus Jesus' identity with Adam in the genealogy).

This brief survey will suffice to demonstrate my point about Jesus' humanity and his anointing for Luke. But one other major consideration exists, one which remains untouched but which can lead to a new understanding of Luke-Acts. This concern is about Luke's community and the followers of John the Baptist. We have noted earlier that John's name (even his presence or influence) is missing from the account of Jesus' anointing and baptism in Luke 3:21-22. We must now explore, in a limited way, why this is so.

In terms of the name "John," Luke-Acts has the most occurrences: thirty-three in all. And among the Gospels Luke has more than the others: 33 > 23, 16, 20 re Matthew, Mark and John, respectively. Although many in Luke are parallel to the other Gospels, Luke adds significantly to other Synoptic traditions. Outside the Gospel accounts, only Acts mentions John (the name, John the Baptist, occurs more in Matthew, less in Mark, and only in Luke in two parallels which come from Q, cf. Luke 7:18-35/Matt 11:2-19; Luke 9:18-27/Matt 16:13-28).

While all Gospel accounts make some sort of distinction between John and Jesus, a distinction which seems to indicate some sort of trouble with John's followers in all their communities, it is particularly Luke who draws a line between John and Jesus (and, I must add, so does the fourth Gospel, to a great extent). It must also be noted, however, that what Conzelmann observed in his Lucan theology regarding John the Baptist, and in which he believed Luke to have three epochs of history,[32] must be modified. Scholars now see a closer relationship between Jesus and John, and rightly so. We must see that John does provide some sort of continuity between the old and the new era of Jesus. In fact, Luke provides a witness to the ongoing dynamic of the Spirit which had been noted in the OT.[33] Or one might even say, Luke "recaptures" the dynamic of the Spirit noted during certain epochs in the OT. But one cannot help seeing that Luke does make a difference between John and Jesus. What Conzelmann noted was true, his epochal explanation, however, was not.[34] We must try to answer this and, in so doing, find if it is a clue to understanding Luke 3:21-22 and Jesus' anointing.

Only Luke deals with the birth of John, and at some length. This should give us a clue regarding the importance of John the Baptist traditions, for in them Luke gives the role of the

Baptist. And while John has many miraculous things surrounding his birth, he is contrasted with Jesus and subjugated to him. For instance, John, like some in the OT, has divine help in being conceived. Jesus is similarly conceived, i.e., in the same tradition of these OT examples, but upon closer inspection, a distinction exists. The Holy Spirit overshadows Mary. Also, John is filled with the Spirit in his mother's womb, Jesus is filled later with the Spirit. More importantly, Jesus is the one who gives the Spirit. This is brought out in John's contrast of himself with Jesus in Luke 3:15–16, in the same paragraph where the question about Jesus being the Messiah arises, and in Peter's sermon in Acts 2:33.

Moreover, John just introduces Jesus. John "shall be great before the Lord" (Luke 1:15) but only because he will prepare the way for a far greater One. Jesus, too, "shall be great," but because "he shall be called the *Son* of the Most High" (1:32). The Baptist will simply be called "John" (1:13,60)—he shall be called a *prophet* of the Most High.

When Luke introduces the birth of each, he places John in a local Judean setting (1:5) but Jesus in a universal context: Joseph had to go to Bethlehem to register because Caesar Augustus had decreed a census for the entire Roman world (2:1f). Furthermore, John grew and became strong in spirit, but he was in the wilderness until the time of his manifestation to Israel (1:80). But of Jesus' childhood it is said that he grew in wisdom, in stature, and in favor with God and man (2:52).[35]

One significant fact has to do with the imprisonment of John. Luke mentions that Herod put him there before Jesus' ministry began, just before Jesus' anointing, as a matter of fact (3:19–20). The impression this leaves, that is, John being in prison just before Jesus' anointing and the passive verb (3:21) describing Jesus' baptism, is that John has nothing to do with the baptism. In the Lucan material of 3:15–17, there is a question about who the Messiah is. The people think that John may be (3:15). The effect, then, is that Jesus stands alone as the Messiah—Jesus' anointing with the Spirit not only identifies him as the Messiah but prepares him for the Messiah's work.

The effect of Luke's placing John's imprisonment here, then, is increased when we compare the location of John's imprisonment in Mark's Gospel. Mark places the account of John's imprisonment and beheading in 6:14f. The time of this, however, is alluded to in 1:14 where John is imprisoned and then Jesus comes preaching and presenting the kingdom of God. But the reference to John's imprisonment occurs after Jesus' baptism. It is true that the Gospel writers do not handle Jesus' life in a strict chronological fashion, and that is why it is more accurate to define the Gospel genre as "sermonic."[36] And this is the issue, Luke makes a theological point with his material to handle a problem in his community.

Even Matthew refers to John's imprisonment at a different place, at 4:12f, just after Jesus' temptation. Matthew 4:12 is roughly parallel with Mark 1:14 and Luke 4:14, and we have already seen how these verses fit into the writers' plans. In a similar way, the fourth Gospel places John's imprisonment during Jesus' ministry and, thus, after Jesus' anointing. Chapter 3, vv 22f, say that Jesus and his disciples were baptizing at the same time John was. Particularly, v 24 reads, "For John had not yet been thrown into prison."

We can glean more important information about John from Luke 11:1–13, a passage containing the Lord's Prayer. Besides having a slightly different version of this prayer, Luke has other differences as well. He places several small parables after it, emphasizing perseverance in asking in prayer. Furthermore, Luke has in a *qal wahomer* in v 13 the children asking their heavenly Father for the Holy Spirit:

> If you, then being evil know to give good gifts to your children, how much more the heavenly father will give the Holy Spirit to those who ask him.

The Lord's Prayer in Matt 6:9–13 is oriented towards restoring and maintaining relationships among believers (i.e, forgiveness), and the exhortation to ask, seek, and knock, along with the *qal wahomer* in 7:7–12, though occurring in a later chapter, still addresses the same issue of relationships. The children in Matthew ask for "good gifts" and in Luke, for the "Holy Spirit." In similar fashion as a prayer in Judaism, the *qaddish*, which contains some of the same elements and used for a variety of reasons, the Lord's Prayer was used in different contexts for different reasons. And Jesus himself intended it to be used for a variety of needs. And since the context of this saying in both Gospels has *children* asking, it is for those who are already believers. The prayer is for Jesus' disciples, not for unbelievers! So, the request in Luke for the Spirit as a subsequent gift for the *Christian* fits, not only concerns in Luke's Gospel, but those in Acts. Believers need the Spirit for ministry and are so urged to pray for him.

Another Lucan contribution to our matter at hand involves his introduction to the Lord's Prayer. There one of the disciples asks Jesus to teach *them* to pray just as (*kathōs*) John taught his disciples. But it is obvious that Jesus' disciples operate in a different eschatological age than that of John's disciples. The Lord's Prayer becomes a model explicating the normal life for all Christian disciples. Especially is this noteworthy for all believers now to know that they need, by praying fervently if necessary, the gift of the Holy Spirit, now available from Jesus himself (Acts 2:33). Furthermore, in Luke 5:33f, John's and the Pharisees' disciples fast but Jesus' disciples do not. Following this, the sayings about the bridegroom and the new wine and wineskins illustrate the distinction between John's age and that of Jesus. In the Lord's Prayer, moreover, concerns are given for all of life, including those for food. John's praying, then, is not a good model for Jesus' followers. This certainly suggests that John's disciples were affecting Christians in Luke's day.

Another item needs to be mentioned regarding the Lord's Prayer in Luke's Gospel. Praying for the Spirit serves as a prelude to Acts. Receiving the Spirit, then, comes through prayer, and this is especially the case in Acts 2 where the disciples are praying when the Spirit comes upon them. In the parables following the Lord's Prayer in Luke, there is a suggestion that it may take much prayer, persistent prayer, to receive the Spirit. This further supports that this does not refer to the Spirit's work in regeneration, for, when Jesus gives life at salvation, one does not have to "persist." This encouragement to persist dovetails with Jesus' exhortation to the disciples in Acts 1:4 not to leave Jerusalem until they receive the Spirit. Indeed the disciples do remain in Jerusalem and are filled with the Spirit (Acts 2). But the context of Luke 11 addresses more than just this particular episode in

Acts 2. It is important to notice, however, that John's baptism of water is contrasted with the baptism with the Spirit in Acts 1:5.[37]

In other places Acts contrasts John and Jesus. Peter in his speech at 10:37–38 places distance between John and Jesus by saying that Jesus began his work after (*meta*) the baptism which John preached and that God anointed him with the Holy Spirit and power. Peter then lists several miraculous deeds that Jesus performed with this power. This is probably a later "interpretation" (i.e., a reference to) of Jesus' encounter with the Spirit in Luke 3:21–22. Peter says that this *is Jesus' anointing with power for his ministry.* He says nothing about inaugurating a new epoch, although that happened too. A similar contrast between Jesus and John occurs in Acts 11:16 and 13:24–25.

This section of Acts centers on Ephesus where John has a number of disciples. One of them, Apollos, comes to Ephesus. This man knows the Scripture and the way of Jesus well, but he needs to know the way of God better. And Priscilla and Aquila take him aside and instruct him in that way more adequately. We are not told specifically what Apollos lacks. But we do know that he knows Jesus well. Furthermore, he never "professes faith in Christ," nor "receives the Spirit." After he is thus prepared, he moves on to other places. But Ephesus still is the focal point in Acts 19 and Paul is the main person involved there. Immediately Paul confronts John's disciples and asks them about the Spirit. At this point, scholars usually argue whether or not this baptism in the Spirit refers to initiation into the body of Christ or to an additional work of the Spirit for ministry.

Several points need to be made. First, the result of Paul's laying his hands on these disciples is that they speak in tongues and prophesy (19:6). These are rather uncommon phenomena for a salvation experience, even though these miraculous phenomena are emphasized in Luke–Acts.

Furthermore, by superficially reading 19:1f, it appears that these disciples have never heard of the Holy Spirit, something unheard of in the world of Judaism, especially from those who probably heard John speak about the Messiah and the Spirit. This reference to being unaware of the Spirit then, I submit,

pertains to this subsequent experience of the Spirit. To understand this text, we must pay attention to more than superficial
components of grammar, though important. We need to listen
to the deeper structure of Acts to see what is meant. This can
be done simply by looking at the context. Also, a sociological
observation can help us here. Luke's world was one in which
supernatural activity was expected. This is not the case for
"modern" European and American societies. The third world is
closer in such attitudes to the NT world. Interpretive models
based upon appropriate Christian congregations can help us
understand these phenomena. Choosing a model may involve
setting aside one's ethnocentricity, and, of course, models can
be bad ones, so that care has to be taken.[38] This text in Acts
does not trouble pentecostals and third world people the way it
does Westerners.

What I suggest is, these disciples knew full well about the
Spirit. What they were "ignorant" of was the anointing of the
Spirit for ministry subsequent to salvation. We must notice
the immediate context of our text. Apollos came to Ephesus
while having heard only the baptism of John, but he knew
Jesus well. Other persons strongly influenced by the John-the-
Baptist tradition (like Apollos) are there too, namely the disciples in our text. It would be strange indeed if they had not
heard about Jesus. They had heard and believed in him, just
like Apollos had.

A good reconstruction of the situation in Ephesus would find
a community of John's disciples there—this is what brought
Apollos to that city. And he was preaching the way of Jesus,
just as John did. These observations and ideas find support in
the larger context of Luke–Acts and move us over the question
about the relationship between the participle and main verb
at 19:2 (i.e., is "believing" before or during "receiving the
Spirit"?). Of course John's disciples were believers already—
the context makes this clear. But they had not received the
work of the Spirit to be better prepared to minister in a new
Christian manner which Luke accepted as appropriate to the
new age. The point is that Luke's audience has trouble with
John's disciples and they need to know that John's ministry
was a passing one, a ministry which pointed to a greater one.

And Luke has shown this to be the case in many episodes which have been mentioned in this discussion.

This conclusion is different from the one that many reach, of which Wink's is characteristic. He believes that

> Luke redirects the passage to speak to the problem of apostolic authority as it touches upon the essential marks of a Christian: baptism and the conferring of the gift of the Spirit.[39]

Wink does not see any reference to John the Baptist here.[40] And though he correctly notes the function of this text, he is not right about the reason for the exercise of authority. Paul corrects the situation in the same way that Apollos had been corrected earlier. These disciples had not received the Spirit for ministry. Luke has shown that apostolic oversight was important and that on occasion they had to correct certain abuses: for example, in Samaria (Acts 8) and in Jerusalem (Acts 5). What Luke is saying, then, is that a new Christian experience for the church was a subsequent reception of the Spirit for ministry.

We can now perceive better one of the reasons for Luke–Acts. John's disciples were influencing Luke's community wrongly—they did not believe in a subsequent experience and they apparently were convincing the church to believe likewise. At least, Luke–Acts attributes the influence of John's disciples to others not receiving this baptism. Another reason, and it could be related to the effect of John's disciples, is that people did not believe that a subsequent experience existed beyond salvation. One's theology plays a major role in one's experience. For example, if one does not believe in salvation by regeneration of the Spirit, he or she will consequently not be reborn. It is the same regarding the Spirit baptism for ministry. This is the emphasis in Luke 11 and the context of the Lord's Prayer. There, John's model was not to be followed. Rather, one believes that such an experience exists, he prays and, then, receives the Spirit from the Father.

Conclusion

I have attempted to show that in interpreting Luke–Acts, we need, indeed, we must, assume the unity of the two accounts.

It is not legitimate to have one hermeneutic for Luke's Gospel and another for Acts, as we have noted earlier that Fee suggests. We have seen how Luke has chosen and interpreted his material to minister to the needs of his community. Of course, it is much more difficult in interpreting Acts, for we do not have parallel accounts to help us to see and thus sharpen Luke's perspective there as we do in his Gospel. Therefore, we must analyze closely what Luke says in his Gospel and then work through Acts carefully. To work through the text this way, then, influences one's theology and, consequently, one's experience. For example, it not only places those who do not believe in a subsequent experience in the category of being John's disciples, it influences the pentecostal authority of taking Acts 2 (and consequently, the book of Acts) as establishing some sort of precedent theology—it removes the theological precedent of the disciples' experience in Jerusalem in Acts 2 and places it at Jordan and upon Jesus' anointing with the Spirit. What happened to the disciples on the Day of Pentecost, then, was patterned after Jesus' experience at Jordan. Other apostolic experiences in Acts are similarly patterned after Jesus'. This trend among scholars, e.g., Talbert and O'Toole, etc., of observing parallels between Jesus and the apostles should be applied to hermeneutics. When reading Luke–Acts together, then, we find theological precedents for pentecostal experiences today.

But this raises another question, though certainly not an insurmountable one. Acts 2:33 says that Jesus received the promise from the Father after he ascended to heaven. Is this a reference to Jesus' anointing? Scholars have discussed this and have, by and large, related it to texts other than to Luke 3:21f.[41] Haenchen, however, rightly understands it: "The Spirit bestowed on the Exalted was not an endowment of which he had need: it was given him only for distribution!"[42] And this is what Acts 2:33b means: Jesus, the Lord of the church, pours out the Holy Spirit—and the effects of that is what everyone saw and heard.

One other thing, too, this affects. If Acts 2 by itself is no longer a precedent text, how can those who believe that speaking in tongues is the initial evidence for this baptism support their theology? Jesus certainly did not speak in tongues—not even at Jordan. One reply can be this, however. While Luke identifies Jesus with us in our humanity and, consequently, in our need of this anointing, he also notes a distinction between Jesus and believers. It was Jesus who inaugurated this new era and who was its Lord. Believers, then, differ in their experience from Jesus in that they may speak in tongues in accord with the lordship of Jesus.[43]

Notes

1. Cf. Howard M. Ervin, *Conversion-Initiation and the Baptism in the Holy Spirit* (Peabody, Massachusetts: Hendrickson, 1985).

2. Fee's view has substantially remained the same over the years as found in Gordon D. Fee and Douglas Stuart, *How to Read the Bible For All Its Worth* (Grand Rapids: Zondervan, 1982) 87–102.

3. William Menzies, "The Methodology of Pentecostal Theology: An Essay in Hermeneutics," in *Essays on Apostolic Themes* (ed. Paul Elbert; Peabody, Massachusetts: Hendrickson, 1985) 1–14.

4. Cf. J. D. G. Dunn, *Baptism in the Holy Spirit* (SBT; London: SCM, 1970) 23–27; cf. also his *Jesus and the Spirit* (Philadelphia: Westminster, 1975).

5. George E. Ladd, *A Theology of the New Testament* (Grand Rapids: Eerdmans, 1974).

6. Donald E. Guthrie, *New Testament Theology* (Downers Grove, Illinois: Inter-Varsity, 1981) 510f,308f,815.

7. Guthrie, *Theology*, 518.

8. Robert O'Toole, *The Unity of Luke's Theology* (Wilmington: Glazier, 1984) 29.

9. For a critique of this emphasis, cf. Paul Elbert, "The Charismatic Movement in the Church of England: An Overview," *JSPS* 6/1 (1984) 38–43.

10. E.g., cf. Charles H. Talbert, *Literary Patterns, Theological Themes and the Genre of Luke–Acts* (Missoula, Montana: Society of Biblical Literature, 1984); *Reading Luke: A Literary and Theological Commentary on the Third Gospel* (New York: Crossroad, 1982) and a review by William S. Kurz, *Int* 38 (1984) 415–17.

11. M. Ramsey, *Holy Spirit* (Grand Rapids: Eerdmans, 1970) 20f; L. Keck, "Jesus' Entrance Upon His Mission: Luke 3:1–4:30," *RevExp* 64 (1967) 465–83; L. Morris, *The Gospel According to Luke* (Grand Rapids: Eerdmans, 1974) 99; I. Howard Marshall, *Luke* (NIGTC; Grand Rapids: Eerdmans, 1978) 177f; F. Danker, *Jesus and the New Age: A Commentary on the Third Gospel* (St. Louis: Clayton, 1974) 51; N. Perrin, *The New Testament: An Introduction* (New York: Harcourt Brace Jovanovich, [1]1974)

13-14 (cf. p. 312 of ²1982 edition); even Dunn, *Baptism*, 23-27, recognizes an emphasis on the Spirit here, but he interprets its significance differently.

12. Well noted by Marshall, *Luke*, 150; B. E. Beck, *Reading the New Testament Today: An Introduction to the Study of the New Testament* (Atlanta: Knox, 1978) 101, observes "In contrast to Mark, Luke reduces the reference to the actual baptism in 3:21f to a bare minimum, and lays all the stress upon the coming of the Spirit and the voice from heaven."

13. A. T. Robertson, *A Grammar of the Greek New Testament in the Light of Historical Research* (Nashville: Broadman, 1914) 1055,1056; Danker, *Jesus and the New Age*, 51, thinks the syntax is thereby strained, but this strain is unlikely to have been detected by a first-century Greek reader; rather, it would be taken in stride as a matter of style.

14. Cf. Keck, "Jesus' Entrance," 473; C. G. Dennison, "How is Jesus the Son of God? Luke's Baptism Narrative and Christology," *CalTheoJ* 17 (1982) 13,20.

15. Luke only has "Holy Spirit," the name he prefers.

16. Dennison, "How is Jesus the Son of God?" 22, opts for both adoption and anticipation, although in an unusual sense. G. W. H. Lampe, *The Seal of the Spirit* (London/New York: Longmans, 1951) 38,45, connects this with the servant role of Jesus and says that this proleptic experience was fulfilled at Calvary.

17. Keck, "Jesus' Entrance," 474f.

18. P. G. Bretscher, "Exodus 4:22-23 and the Voice from Heaven," *JBL* 87 (1968) 301-11. Cf. R. N. Suder, "Epiphany Texts and the Akedah," *Lutheran Theological Seminary Bulletin* (St. Louis) 62 (1982) 3-7, for the rabbinic background, which he thinks is based upon the model/type found in the Abraham/Isaac situation. He does not opt for anointing, however.

19. R. F. Collins, "Luke 3:21-22, Baptism or Anointing," *The Bible Today* 84 (1976) 821-31. Marshall, *Luke*, 151, also believes that this anointing refers to equipping Jesus for his task.

20. G. E. Rice, "Luke 3:22-28 in Codex Bezae: The Messianic King," *AUSS* 17 (1979) 203-8. Dunn, *Jesus and the Spirit*, 336; chap. 2, n. 73, accepts this reading.

21. This variant is by far to be preferred over the others. However, in 2:26 we have the Lord's messiah, the reason for some of these variants at 2:11. J. W. Bowman, "Eschatology of the NT," *IDB* 2:137, notes that "It is generally agreed that the 'voice' which spoke to Jesus at his baptism quotes from Ps 2:7; Isa 42:1—passages relating respectively to the coronation of the contemporary messiah and to the call or ordination of the (suffering) servant of the Lord."

22. J. Ramsey Michaels, *Servant and Son* (Atlanta: Knox, 1981) 46-51.

23. Robert H. Gundry, *Matthew: A Commentary on His Literary and Theological Art* (Grand Rapids: Eerdmans, 1982) 51.

24. William L. Lane, *Commentary on the Gospel of Mark* (NICNT; Grand Rapids: Eerdmans, 1974) 40, observes that "The fact that the Spirit is introduced into the record only rarely beyond the prologue suggests that Mark has consciously unified his opening statement by a threefold reference to the Spirit."

25. Ibid., 703.

26. I think that a major problem which the fourth Gospel addresses is friction between these two parties.

27. At this point it will be well to address a matter of contention between interpreters of Luke and Paul. Some have noted a difference between Paul's usage of the Spirit and Luke's, pointing out that Paul's interest is in the ethical dimension of the Spirit while Luke's interest lies in power for ministry. This is only true to a certain degree. Luke, who is interested in the power of the Spirit, also pays attention to certain ethical concerns. He devotes much attention to foreigners, women, and the poor, for example. Paul's concerns are more in the areas of sanctification and the inner life, and although power is not explicitly mentioned in Rom 8:13b, for example, there is little doubt of Paul's intention.

28. E.g., Marshall, *Luke*, 177f; Danker, *Jesus and the New Age*, 58; O'Toole, *Unity of Luke's Theology*, 35; Malcolm Tolbert, "Leading Ideas of the Gospel of Luke," *RevExp* 64 (1967) 442f; Keck, "Jesus' Entrance," 468.

29. Graham N. Stanton, *Jesus of Nazareth in New Testament Preaching* (SNTSMS 27; Cambridge: University Press, 1974) 190, rightly concludes that the church's traditions about Jesus "were very probably more influential on early reflection about the significance of Jesus than is often supposed."

30. Joachim Jeremias, *TDNT*, 5:677–704.

31. Ibid., 703.

32. Hans Conzelmann, *The Theology of St. Luke* (ET; London: Faber, 1960). Conzelmann's epochal theory was not new, but built on that of Heinrich von Baer, *Der Heilige Geist in den Lukasschriften* (BWANT 39; Stuttgart: Kohlhammer, 1926).

33. E.g., cf. C. Westermann, "Geist im Alten Testament," *EvT* 41 (1981) 223–30.

34. Cf. Keck, "Jesus' Entrance," 465–83; J. R. Meier, "John the Baptist in Matthew's Gospel," *JBL* 99 (1980) 384–85, makes a similar criticism of Conzelmann's epochal hypothesis re Luke's handling of John. John, according to Meier, bestrides like a colossus the time of the law and prophets and the time of Jesus as far as Luke is concerned.

35. Harold S. Songer, "Luke's Portrayal of the Origins of Jesus," *RevExp* 64 (1967) 453–63, in an excellent article lists seven episodes in which Luke deliberately contrasts John and Jesus. Walter Wink, *John the Baptist in the Synoptic Tradition* (London: University Press, 1968) 70, denies any reference to the presence of a Baptist group in Luke's time. However, the clues Luke leaves us in his text do not support Wink's view.

36. A genre with historical intentionality, cf. Donald A. Hagner, "Interpreting the Gospels: The Landscape and the Quest," *JETS* 24 (1981) 23–37.

37. It is reasonable to expect that, for Luke, the context of Luke 11 relates to episodes other than those during Jesus' earthly ministry (i.e., Acts 2 and 19, e.g.), but the context of Luke 11 relates especially to the need which exists in Luke's community. Acts 1:5 also speaks to this need to place Jesus and John in proper perspective and encourage reception of the gift of the Spirit from Jesus.

38. Cf. Derek Tidball, *The Social Context of the New Testament: A Sociological Analysis* (Grand Rapids: Zondervan, 1984) chap. 1.

39. Wink, *John the Baptist*, 85.

40. Ibid., 85, n. 1.

41. J. Dupont, "Ascension du Christ et don de l'Esprit d'apres Actes 2:33," *Christ and Spirit in the New Testament* (eds. B. Lindars and S. Smalley; London: University Press, 1973) 219–28.

42. E. Haenchen, *The Acts of the Apostles* (ET; Philadelphia: Westminster, 1972) 182.

43. On the other hand, a Lucan theology which does not insist upon tongues (as far as Luke would be concerned) as initial evidence for a subsequent Lucan anointing/baptism, but which admits other experiences of the Holy Spirit mentioned in Luke's writings, obviously has no problem with the suggestion made here of diminishing or removing Acts 2 as a precedent text in Luke's thought.

8

EPHESIANS 4:7-16:
THE PAULINE PERSPECTIVE OF PENTECOST

David G. Clark

Introduction

F ACES OF RENEWAL is indeed an appropriate title for a collection
of essays honoring an educator who has contributed so
much from within the Pentecostal tradition. But it is also
an apt description for the times in which we are privileged to
live. Although the 20th century is not yet history, religious
"happenings" have already characterized this century as the
era of Charismatic or Pentecostal renewal. The baptism in the
Spirit, together with the charisms or gifts of the Spirit, were
once nearly exclusively limited to the little storefront church.
Now, they are found in major denominations around the
world, including those usually regarded as much more liturgical
than spontaneous.

One of the results of the modern renewal of the church has
been a great interest in (and reassessment of) those biblical
passages (such as Acts 2) which provide insight into the Pentecostal experience. One such passage, however, is generally
overlooked: Ephesians 4:7-16. The most relevant parts, vv 7-
8,11 read as follows:

> But grace was given to each of us according to the measure of Christ's
> gift. Therefore it is said, "When he ascended on high he led a host of
> captives, and he gave gifts to men." . . . And his gifts were that some
> should be apostles, some prophets, some evangelists, some pastors and
> teachers. (RSV)

The purpose of this article is to emphasize the importance of
the *historical* aspect of Eph 4:7-16. All too often commentators
devote the major part of their efforts to the theology of this

passage, while overlooking or understating its historical significance. Obviously, Paul is referring to the ascension of Christ when he says "when he ascended on high," but what time does he have in mind when he states that Christ "gave gifts to men" (v 8)? I intend, then, to fix more precisely this time of giving and to explore the implications of this passage for our understanding of Pentecost. Before dealing with the text directly, I wish to make several introductory observations that will recall the wider context of the passage to be studied.

In the first three chapters of Ephesians, Paul has been explaining the means by which God has accomplished his saving purpose for the world through Jesus Christ; with that, we all are familiar, but sometimes we fail to appreciate the enormity of the divine purpose as Paul understands and explains it in this epistle. Perhaps a brief summation of his teaching will help us gain a sense of perspective.

(1) God's redemptive plan for the world, including both Jew and Gentile, has not been revealed before now. (2) This mystery does not stop at the atoning death of Christ nor the salvation of the Gentiles, but comprises as well the revelation that all of redeemed humanity stand in special relation to each other and to God by virtue of their new life in Christ. This relation is called the church, the body of Christ, 2:19–22. (3) The church is where Christ dwells in his fulness (1:20–23) and where God reveals to creation the ultimate expression of his wisdom as far as the earth is concerned (2:10). (4) The culmination of God's redemptive mystery—the church—was not revealed to humanity by Jesus during his earthly ministry but to the leaders of the church for the first time (3:5). (5) Finally, the passage which is the focus for this study, 4:7–16, contains ecclesiastical truth not found anywhere else in Scripture, namely, the *source*, *time* (both inception and duration), and *form* of church government.

The Time-Inception

A brief reference to the *source* of the ministries will suffice, since vv 7–11 clearly ascribe the establishment of the governmental offices to the risen Christ. As Markus Barth says, "The apostle used the psalm to show that the exalted Christ is the source of the spiritual gifts."[1] But the *time* of this establishing deserves a closer look. The key words, found in v 8, are "when he ascended" (or, more clearly, *"after* he ascended," since the aorist tense of the participial form for "he ascended" indicates here that he gave *after* he ascended), a quotation of Ps 68:18.[2] Paul pauses in his discourse to comment on the words "he ascended" so that he may help the reader understand that the Psalm prophetically refers to the ascension of Christ, an event which took place some 40 days after the resurrection, according to Luke (Acts 1:3).

But I believe that Paul has a specific time in mind when he writes "after he ascended." To begin with, the reference to the ascension makes sense only if the time of when "he gave" is fairly close to the time of the ascension. Otherwise, why associate "he gave" with the ascension? The most reasonable inference is that Paul means the Day of Pentecost. This is the first (and only) logical time, for the Spirit *is* the gift of the risen Christ and his entering into the disciples marks the birth of the church and the emergence of its leaders. This association also appears in Acts 2:33, where "having been exalted . . . he has poured out this . . ." is much the same as "after he ascended on high . . . he gave gifts. . . ."[3]

The use of Psalm 68 in this passage may also have some bearing on this matter. As Bruce indicates, Psalm 68 was associated in the synagogue calendar with the Feast of Pentecost.[4] Caution must be used here since our knowledge of institutions in NT times is limited, but it is worth noting that this liturgical use of the Psalm could explain why Paul cited this unusual text and why he did not need to make more explicit its association with Pentecost.

The above considerations notwithstanding, most commentators explore the "what" of "he gave" instead of the "when." Although Eadie clearly has the Day of Pentecost in mind when he interprets Eph 4:8-11 by saying "It is of the gifts of the Spirit, especially in the administration of the church, that the apostle speaks in this paragraph,"[5] he stands nearly alone.[6] More importantly, even those who do associate this text with Pentecost fail to follow through with the implications raised thereby.

In sum, few if any of the major treatments of Ephesians written during the last one hundred years have explained to any degree the implications of this passage for Pentecost, a significant oversight in light of today's renewal.

I say "significant" because modern Pentecostal and Charismatic groups tend to place a high value upon the Scriptures as the authoritative source for faith and practice; in particular for their understanding of themselves in comparison to the church of the NT. But since Eph 4:7-16 is seldom associated with the events of Pentecost, modern views of Pentecost are largely derived from passages like Acts 2 and 1 Corinthians 12 and 14. Pentecost thus comes to mean a church with power to witness and charisms of the Spirit, but missing is the realization that from its conception the church was furnished with a structure of ministry and administration through the offices of apostles, prophets, evangelists, and pastor-teachers.

This is not to imply that Luke is unaware of these offices, for they are present in the Acts. In 13:1-2 he mentions prophets and teachers, in 14:14 apostles, and in 21:8 Philip the evangelist. But Luke does not specify how these offices began; for the most part his concern is not the inner organization and practices of the church but the impact of the church upon its world.

Likewise, in the Gospels, not even Jesus prepares us for the church, much less how it is to be governed. True, there are hints, there are warnings of an impending change in the identity of God's people—"the vineyard shall be taken from you and given to another nation"—but even years after Pentecost the disciples do not fully grasp what God is doing in and through the church. Indeed, some of Paul's contemporaries never do accept his message of God's grace apart from the Law. This brings us full circle; Paul emerges in the Scriptures as the one to whom and through whom this mystery of grace culminating in the church is principally revealed.

To summarize up to this point, Paul traces the origin of the church offices to Christ, and the time of their inception is after his ascension. Given this same association with the ascension in Eph 4:8 as in Acts 2:33, I conclude with Eadie that when Paul says "after he ascended . . . he gave" he is referring to the Day of Pentecost. Also, Paul's words in Ephesians remind us that the church is not God's contingency plan hastily drawn up after his efforts to establish his kingdom in Israel were thwarted. Rather, it is a mystery, the masterpiece God has been saving until last, an ultimate showcase of wisdom wherein God displays the grace that breaks down the dividing wall between Jew and Gentile and between humanity and himself. And from its inception, Paul teaches, the church comes equipped with a variety of offices sent by Jesus through the Holy Spirit.

The Form and Duration of the Offices

An adequate treatment of the nature and functions of each of the offices mentioned in Eph 4:11 is beyond the scope of this preliminary discussion. But I would like to set the stage for further research by making a few observations which I hope will bring this subject into clearer focus.

I begin with the obvious: if Paul is taken literally (and I see no reason not to), the ministries of the church were from the beginning specified and appointed by God, not elected by any human organization. It may well be that the synagogue had some influence upon the governing of the local church (elders and deacons), but the ministries of Eph 4:11 are significantly different from those within Judaism. Indeed, the most recent consensus is that nothing in the intertestamental period offers much help in understanding the origin and meaning of the NT apostolate.[7]

Even the office of prophet, the office with the most obvious associations with Judaism, now, among other differences, functions in the context of collegiality. That is, a prophet functions in conjunction with the other ministries and is dependent upon the church for the recognition of this ministry. In sum, Judaism provides only a few clues at best; we must look elsewhere for the source of this list of ministries just as we must for the nine categories of gifts or manifestations of the Spirit in 1 Cor 12:8–10. Paul claims to have received his gospel by divine revelation. Perhaps we should take this claim literally and understand that at Pentecost, Jesus did something new and without precedent. While I am stressing the obvious, I would also like to point out that these offices are not only depicted as divinely established, they are also described as permanent or at least of lasting value "until we come to the unity of the faith" (4:13).

Markus Barth makes this point most emphatically:

> In 4:11 it is assumed that the church at all times needs the witness of "apostles" and "prophets." The author of this epistle did not anticipate that the inspired and enthusiastic ministry was to be absorbed by, and "disappear" into, offices and officers bare of the Holy Spirit and resentful of any reference to spiritual things. Eph 4 does not contain the faintest hint that the charismatic character of all church ministries was restricted to a certain period of church history and was later to die out.[8]

But the offices of the apostles and the prophet seem to have been anything but permanent. Yet, both here in Ephesians and in the ministry list of 1 Cor 12:28 they are the highest ranking offices. If—using Paul as a guide—the apostle could found and oversee churches, even appointing bishops to oversee the local churches, how is it that such an important office could disappear? Or are these functions still being discharged, but by ministries which are now called by different titles?

Some do not find it strange that apostles are not seen today because they associate this office chiefly with the Twelve, regarding Paul as a replacement for Judas or perhaps as having earned the title of apostle through his unique force of character and undeniable success in ministry. But, of course, Matthias was Judas' successor and the Twelve were chosen by Jesus to minister to Israel. Only in this context, as a symbol of the hope of Israel's restoration, is the number twelve significant. But as Paul sees the apostolate in Ephesians, the office is inaugurated *after* the ascension, not during Jesus' ministry on earth. And a glance at a concordance will reveal that several other people besides the Twelve are called apostles in the NT.

But this is a complex issue that needs more explanation than is possible here. Apostleship was a fluid conception in the early church and meant different things to different people.[9] For now, I must be content to point out that the reason for the Spirit's coming at Pentecost is because Jesus no longer walks with his followers as before. Now, the physical limitations of his humanity are gone and through the Spirit he can call into the offices people from every place and time. Perhaps Paul himself was the first example of this, for he did not see the

"historical" (i.e., pre-ascension) Jesus. Thus, some did not recognize his apostleship (1 Cor 9:2), perhaps feeling that, as with
the Twelve, a direct commission was necessary.

Perhaps the danger here is in thinking that the events that
got the church off to a strong start are normative in every
respect. Modern Pentecostals believe that Acts 2 is valid for
today but no one would question someone's experience just
because the Holy Spirit did not come with the sound of a
mighty wind and the appearance of tongues of fire. Rather, the
validity of such an experience is judged by the changes it
produces in the believer's life. Likewise, why should Jesus
appear throughout history to appoint leaders when he has
already sent the Spirit to accomplish this? Paul refers to his
encounter with the risen Lord because this is what his oppo-
nents think is so important. But as he tells the Corinthians,
they themselves are the real proof (literally *seal*) of his apostleship (1 Cor 9:2; cf. 2 Cor 12:12).

But the controversy over apostleship should not cause us to
overlook the fact that the office of the prophet has also disappeared from mainstream Christianity. Too often, commentators practice theology through history; i.e., since prophets no
longer exist, this office must have been given only for the
church of the first century, when it was most needed! In response, I would argue that the church lost the prophetic office
when it lost its Pentecostal character.[10] At any rate, there is
nothing in Ephesians or the rest of the NT to suggest that the
prophetic office was given only to the early church.

Conclusion

I believe that Eph 4:7–16 has provided us with several valuable
insights into a complex and difficult subject. The renewals of
our day have brought about a reassessment of passages like
Acts 2. Rather than serving only as reminders of how things
used to be in the beginning, such texts are viewed as possible
patterns for today's church as well. But to Luke's conception
of Pentecost we must add Paul's . Only then do we realize that
at Pentecost Christ equipped his church not only with power
to witness and with the gifts of the Spirit but with a divine

pattern of government as well. But Paul does not stop here. He describes all of the offices (not just the last three) as normative and vital to the life and growth of the church. Only through them can the believer attain to the stature of Christ and be prepared to carry out the Great Commission. The implications of this are far-reaching indeed. Paul is telling us that from the very beginning Christ established the church with a governmental structure. When this is overlooked, disunity results. Consider some of the ways denominations refer to themselves: Episcopalian, Congregational, Presbyterian—names which are memorials to long-standing disagreements over what form church government should take. I am convinced that as the church struggles toward a new unity through fellowship of the Spirit, that unity will be possible only when there is agreement upon how authority is to be exercised within the church. Paul has described that structure—God's structure: now it is up to us to "build the tabernacle according to the pattern shown us upon the mountain."

Notes

1. Markus Barth, *Ephesians: Translation and Commentary on Chapters 4-6* (AB 34A; Garden City: Doubleday, 1960) 476.
2. Paul's quotation of Ps 68:18 differs significantly from the MT; on this difficulty see Barth, *Ephesians*, 475; Gary V. Smith, "Paul's Use of Psalm 68:18 in Ephesians 4:8," *JETS* 18 (1975) 181-89; and Richard Rubinkiewicz, "Ps LXVIII 19 (= Eph 4:8): Another textual tradition or Targum?" *NovT* 18 (1975) 219-24.
3. John Eadie, among others, understands Eph 4:8 and Acts 2:33 to refer to the same events, cf. his *Commentary on the Greek Text of the Epistle of Paul to the Ephesians* (2nd ed.; London: Griffin & Bohm, 1861) 297.
4. F. F. Bruce, *The Epistle to the Ephesians* (London: Pickering & Inglis, 1961) 82; also, J. C. Kirby, *Ephesians: Baptism and Pentecost* (London: SPCK, 1968) 145.
5. Eadie, *Commentary on Ephesians*, 282. Others who briefly allude to the connection between the ministry gifts of Christ and the coming of the Spirit in Acts 2 are: Francis Foulkes. *The Epistle of Paul to the Ephesians* (TNTC; London: Tyndale, 1963) 114; Barth, *Ephesians*, 476; and B. F. Westcott, *Saint Paul's Epistle to the Ephesians* (London: Macmillan, 1906) 60.

6. Some of the commentaries on Ephesians that largely ignore the historical implications of "after he ascended" are: Charles Hodge, *Commentary ont he Epistle to the Ephesians* (New York: Hodder & Stoughton, 1856); Charles J. Ellicott, *A Critical and Grammatical Commentary on St. Paul's Epistle to the Ephesians* (Andover: Draper, 1880); Heinrich August Wilhelm Meyer, *Critical and Exegetical Hand-Book to the Epistle to the Ephesians* (ET; MeyerK 13; New York: Funk and Wagnalls, 1884); T. K. Abbott, *A Critical and Exegetical Commentary on the Epistles to the Ephesians and to the Colossians* (ICC; Edinburgh: T & T. Clark, 1897); J. Armitage Robinson, *Commentary on Ephesians* (London: Clarke, n.d.); H. C. G. Moule, *Studies in Ephesians* (London: Pickering & Inglis, 1934); E. F. Scott, *The Epistles of Paul to the Colossians, to Philemon and to the Ephesians* (MNTC 11; New York: Harper & Brothers, n.d.); E. K. Simpson, *Commentary on the Epistle to the Ephesians* (NICNT; Grand Rapids: Eerdmans, 1957); William Hendriksen, *Exposition of Ephesians* (New Testament Commentary; Grand Rapids: Baker, 1967); Fritz Rienecker, *Der Brief des Paulus an die Epheser* (Wuppertaler Studienbibel; Wuppertal: Brockhaus, 1971). Even Schmithals' very thorough study of apostleship fails to explore this subject (*The Office of Apostle in the Early Church* [New York: Abingdon, 1969]).

7. J. Andrew Kirk, "Apostleship Since Rengstorf: Towards a Synthesis," *NTS* 21 (1973) 250.

8. Markus Barth, *Ephesians*, 437. I note with interest that Barth's position is finding growing support. For example, Kirk, "Apostleship," *NTS*, 264, and J. E. Young, "That Some Should Be Apostles," *EQ* 48 (1976) 103.

9. Some recent studies are: Jacques Dupont, "L'apôtre comme intermediare du salut dans les Acts des Apôtres" *RTP* 112 (1980) 342-58; Ronald Y. K. Fung, "Charismatic versus Organized Ministry?" *EQ* 52 (1980) 195-214; Kevin Giles, "Is Luke an Exponent of 'Early Protestantism'? Church Order in the Lukan Writings," *EQ* 55 (1983) 3-20; K. H. Schelkle, "Charisma und Amt," *TQ* 159 (1979) 243-54, J. Mühlsteiger, "Zum Verfassungsrecht des Frühkuche" *ZKT* 99 (1977) 129-55. I have already cited Kirk's study above; another good survey of recent discussion on church ministries has been done by A. Lemaire: "The Ministries in the New Testament," *Biblical Theological Bulletin* 3 (1973) 133-66.

10. See too, David Aune, *Prophecy in Early Christianity and the Ancient Mediterranean World* (Grand Rapids: Eerdmans, 1983) 338, although it should be noted that charisma and institution need not at all be in antithesis.

9

THE SOCIAL AND POLITICAL IMPLICATIONS
OF THE MIRACULOUS IN ACTS

J. Massyngberde Ford

ACTS PORTRAYS THE BEGINNING of Christianity as an enthusiastic, Spirit-filled movement.[1] The preaching of the Good News is complemented by signs and wonders that are even more dramatic and diverse than those portrayed in the Gospels.[2] They include resurrection of the dead, healings and exorcisms, curses, nature miracles, and liberation miracles.[3] However, from a redactional point of view it is obvious that Luke has imposed upon his sources (which at points appear fairly primitive) an extremely vital and arresting social message having provocative repercussions for the witness and history of Christianity in the ancient world.

Before examining the phenomena which are often named the Jerusalem Pentecost (Acts 2), the Samaritan Pentecost (Acts 8), the Gentile Pentecost (Acts 10–11:18), and the Ephesian Pentecost (Acts 19:1–7)—all of which are landmarks in the theology of Acts—I should like to make some general remarks about the miraculous in Acts. Firstly, if one studies the miracles in Acts attentively one sees that, although the miraculous (both benevolent and malevolent) has a prominent place in Acts, in actual fact there are only seven major miracles, namely:

1. The Healing of the Lame Man by Peter (Acts 3:1–10)
2. The Healing of Aeneas (Acts 9:32–35)
3. The Raising of Dorcas (Acts 9:36–42)
4. Peter's Escape from Prison (Acts 12:3–17)
5. The Healing of the Lame Man at Lystra (Acts 14:8–10)

)

6. The Escape from Prison of Paul and Silas (Acts 16:25-34)
7. The Raising of Eutychus (Acts 20:7-12)

Four are performed with reference to Peter and three with reference to Paul. I am uncertain whether one should include the miraculous escape from prison in Acts 5:17-21[4] and the great sea voyage, since these do not have the same literary structure as the other miracles. I omit general references: Acts 2:43; 5:12,15,16; 6:8; 8:6-13; 14:3; 19:11-12; 28:9. I shall deal with the malevolent miracles later in this paper.

Secondly, a closer examination of these seven pericopes reveals that they are signs rather than wonders,[5] two of which are followed by important discourses: that is, Acts 3:11-26 and 4:8-12, after Peter cures the lame man; and Acts 14:15-17, after the cure of the lame man by Paul. Thus the miracles have a certain similarity to the signs in the Gospel of John. The miraculous is a mere springboard for Luke to show the fruits of the Spirit in a deeper way.[6]

We may distinguish the gifts of the Spirit from the fruits of the Spirit in the following way. The gifts[7] are a revelation of supernatural activity which assist in extending the church and in building up its members. The fruits,[8] on the other hand, are a revelation of divine essence or personality. They are indispensable, both for the individual Christian and for the church at all times, and they can never be counterfeit.

The Major Miracles in Acts

1. The Healing of the Lame Man by Peter (Acts 3:1-10)

The healing of the lame man at the Gate Beautiful is told in much more detail than the other healing miracles in Acts. It is referred to as a sign (*sēmeion*) in Acts 4:10 and 22 (cf., *iasin kai sēmeia kai terata* in v 30). Yet the actual miracle pales in significance before the great christological revelation given by Peter and John in Peter's second speech (Acts 3:12b-26) and in the apostles' defense before the council in Acts 4:8-12. In other words the miracle becomes the vehicle of a dramatic christological statement. It is the proclamation of Jesus as the *pais*, the Suffering Servant of Yahweh. In him God vindicates the weak, the persecuted, and those accounted accursed by human beings. The apostles repeat this publicly before the council, a Lucan technique by which he repeats important doctrines and events (cf., the double report of Cornelius' conversion [Acts 10–11:18] and the three accounts of Paul's conversion [Acts 9; 22; 28]). Peter's christological statement is linked closely to the miracle by the presence of the healed person at the defense of Peter and John (Acts 4:10b and 22, again a double reference). Yet, even this does not exhaust the theological implications of the miracle and its discourse.

(a) The apostles emphasize that the power within them is possible only through the name of Jesus. This becomes the foundation of Luke's assertions elsewhere in Acts, namely, that Jesus' name has power far superior to Jewish and pagan magical practices. This will become clearer as one progresses through Acts. It is noticeable that faith[9] is not mentioned in connection with the miracle itself, but only after the apostles are imprisoned (Acts 4:4); it is faith in the resurrection of Jesus, rather than in the miracle itself, that is required. It is also noticeable that the complaint about teaching concerning the resurrection seems to be dropped, perhaps because Pharisees as well as Sadducees were present at the council (cf., the presence of Gamaliel in Acts 5:34). The real accusation is found in 4:7, namely, "by what power and by what name have you done this?"

The emphasis on the name or personality of Jesus in this incident is found repeatedly in Acts 3 and 4 (Acts 3:6,16 [twice]; 4:7,10,13,17,18,30); that is, nine times in this pericope. The pivotal verse is;

> And there is salvation in one one else, for there is no other name under heaven given among men (sic) by which we must be saved (Acts 4:12).

In order to understand the importance of this assertion one must realize how important names were in the ancient world, especially in exorcisms, magic, and prophylactic formulas. Names of angels, of gods and goddesses, and of God himself were used in incantations and similar practices.[10]

(b) The Lukan emphasis on lack of wealth is also thrown into prominence in this pericope. Peter and John declare that they have no silver or gold.[11] When they are before the council the comment is made that they are "uneducated, common men" (Acts 4:13).

In fact in these two details, the use of Jesus' name and the emphasis on poverty, Luke may wish the reader to see some affinity between Jesus as *pais* (servant) and the apostles in a similar status. The main point, as seen from the whole structure of Acts, would seem to be that the apostles and Christian community in early Acts (not necessarily in the Pauline communities)[12] are from a different social class from the people with whom they will be contrasted, e.g., Simon Magus (Acts 8); the owners of the slave girl (Acts 16); the sons of Sceva, who was a Jewish high priest (Acts 19); the people who burnt their magical books, which were so valuable (Acts 19:19); and the silversmiths (Acts 19). Thus the first miracle establishes the fact that the apostles are not mercenary magicians with empty power but disciples of the Resurrected One.

It may also be significant that this whole episode is concluded by a mini-Pentecost (Acts 4:31) which forms a kind of *inclusio* with the Jerusalem Pentecost. We should probably be correct in thinking that Luke wished his readers to see the whole section containing the Jerusalem Pentecost to extend to Acts 5:42.

Thus the first miracle really sets the stage for an understanding of the whole of Acts. We are to look now for a community of *anawin* who have no pretensions towards the status of "divine people" (*theioi andres*) and pecuniary gain, a people who are prepared to suffer and to preach the gospel with boldness.

2. The Healing of Aeneas (Acts 9:32–35)

The second miracle, the healing of Aeneas (Acts 9:32–35), may appear to be insignificant. It is extremely succinct. Lydda (the ancient "Lod" in the Hebrew Scriptures) lies in a strategic position where the road from Jerusalem to Joppa crosses the north-south highway of the plains of Sharon and Philistia. The healing leads to the conversion of all the residents in Lydda and Sharon (*ton Sarona*)—that is, the coastal plain north from Joppa to Caesarea, extending about 10 miles wide and 45 miles long. The news of the miracle, therefore, was not confined to the towns. This short pericope might be seen as an appendix or conclusion to the preceding section, which reports the spread of the gospel in the regions of Judaea and in Samaria (cf., Acts 1:8). Just as Peter's first speech was, as it were, confirmed or complemented by the healing of a lame man, so the Judaean and Samaritan missions are also confirmed by the healing of a lame man. In this way Acts 9:31 corresponds to Acts 2:43–47, both of which are followed by healings of the lame. It must also be the prelude to the conversion of Cornelius, as Peter is shown working in areas in which he would meet many Gentiles.

3. The Raising of Dorcas (Acts 9:36–43)

This miracle is of great significance. Joppa is 10 miles from Lydda, and doubtless the news of the healing of Aeneas had spread to Joppa and had given the widows the hope of Peter's raising Dorcas. Luke has carefully and closely linked the passage to the Gentile Pentecost. We are told that all Joppa turned to the Lord after the raising of Dorcas and that Peter remained in the city for some days lodging with Simon, a tanner. The angel of God reveals this information to Cornelius (Acts 10:6). It is at Joppa that Peter receives his important and controversial vision, which is intended to show him that all peoples are ritually pure.

Moreover, in the Dorcas pericope there are two details which may cast light on the social status[13] of the early Christian communities. Firstly, Dorcas apparently belongs to a group of widows; she is a seamstress but does not seem to be in a business like Lydia (Acts 16:14). She seems to be helping the poor. Marshall[14] suggests that the other widows may be wearing the tunics that they show to Peter. Most important of all is that she is called a disciple (v 36 *mathētria*, the only feminine occurrence of the word in the NT). It would not be improper to assert that what we have here is a house church, perhaps comprising only women, for Peter does not stay with Dorcas as he stays with Lydia (Acts 16:15). This house church is the scene of a resurrection from the dead.

Secondly, Peter lodges with a tanner by the sea. This is an interesting detail because it gives further insight into the social status of the early Christians. A tanner was not only an artisan but belonged to one of the despised trades.[15] Cornelius is given this information by the angel (Acts 10:6), perhaps as a rather startling piece of information, because Cornelius would not expect a Torah-abiding Jew to stay with a tanner[16]—just as when the disciples (cf., his reluctance to eat unclean animals) were told by Jesus where they would find a place in which to prepare the Passover, they are told that they will see a man carrying a pitcher of water (they would expect a woman to be carrying water).

Thus from a sociological point of view the third miracle tells us:

(a) Peter is shown working outside Jerusalem, and he is engaged in both preaching and miraculous activity; (b) he is probably working in Judaea, Galilee, and Samaria (Acts 9:31), in which areas he would meet, but not necessarily baptize, pagans; (c) he consorts with people of moderate economic status; (d) a house church may already be established at Joppa with Dorcas and her fellow widows, and there is possibly one at the house of Simon, the tanner; and (e) Peter performs a miracle which is akin to that of Elijah (cf. 1 Kgs 17:19) and of Elisha (2 Kgs 4:21).

4. The Fourth Miracle, Peter's Escape from Prison (Acts 12:6–23)

This fourth miracle obviously falls into a different category from the healing miracles. It is a legend with theological significance. Strobel[17] seems to have recognized the full impact of this miracle in seeing in it the Exodus/Passover motif.

He observes this motif in:

(a) The reference to the time, "during the days of Unleavened Bread" (v 4); (b) Herod's intent to bring him out after Passover (v 4); (c) that the escape appears to take place on the night of Passover (v 6 "the very night"); (d) the delivery is effected by an angel of the Lord (v 7); and (e) the command for Peter to dress himself and, most importantly, to put on his sandals and his mantle (v 8), which is consonant with the Passover theme, because participants at the Passover were to be dressed in preparation for a journey (Exod 12:11).

God performs an Exodus miracle for Peter in response to the earnest prayer of the church (vv 5 and 12). In v 17 Peter says that it is "the Lord" who had brought (*exēgagen*) him out of prison. The Passover ritual emphasizes that God, not an angel or a seraph, brought the children of Israel out of Egypt.

This pericope includes the mysterious disappearance of Peter from the story of Acts. He goes to another place (Acts 12:17). Yet he is present at the council reported in Acts 15. Would it be farcical to say that Peter, like Moses, does not enter into the promised land, that promised land of the full Gentile mission? It is Paul and Barnabas who go to Antioch and are appointed by the Holy Spirit to accomplish the first missionary journey, which includes Paul's declaration to turn to the Gentiles (Acts 13:46).

This miracle cannot be separated from the incident of Herod's withdrawal to Caesarea and his subsequent demise. It is to be noted that it is both the angel of the Lord who rescues Peter and the angel of the Lord to whom is attributed the death of Herod (v 23). The malevolent miracles will be discussed later. Suffice it to say here that such is the power of Christianity that political leaders must succumb to it. In this pericope, too, one has another glimpse of a house church apparently belonging to a woman, Mary, the mother of John Mark (v 12).

5. *The Healing of the Lame Man at Lystra (Acts 14:8–20)*

The healing of the congenitally lame man at Lystra is succinctly told in three verses, but again it is strategically placed. It occurs on the first missionary journey of Paul and Barnabas. It is reported after Paul's long speech at Antioch of Pisidia, just as Peter cured the lame man after his Pentecost speech. This miracle is, of course, parallel to Paul's healing. Whereas Peter's miracle is followed by a speech addressed to the Jews, Paul's is followed by a speech to the pagans; the content of this will be discussed later. The miracle and speech, both in the case of Peter and Paul, are followed by hostility from the Jews (Acts 4:1–22; cf. 14:19–20). As in the case of the healing of the man at the Gate Beautiful, the miracle itself is merely a starting point for a theological (here not christological) statement, by both Barnabas (mentioned first) and Paul. There is no reference to Christ or Jesus in the statement.

6. The Escape from Prison of Paul and Silas (Acts 16:16-40)

This miracle is, of course, parallel to Peter's escape from prison in Acts 12:6-25. The story falls into the genre of legend (cf., pagan sources).[18] The reason for the imprisonment is base and mercenary, although perhaps less capricious than the motive of Herold when he imprisoned Peter because the death of James pleased the Jews (Acts 12:3). Here again a comparison and contrast with the Petrine pericope is instructive. In the account of Peter's escape we have observed two important points: (a) The Exodus/Passover motif; (b) the political consequence, namely, the death of Herod.

The Pauline pericope is set in a pagan environment, therefore Luke has used pagan (classical) material from which to compose his legend; this replaces the OT/Exodus background to the Petrine pericope. The Pauline pericope ends with or reaches a climax in the apology made by the Roman magistrates. This forms a sharp contrast with the death of the Jewish leader, Herod. Luke wishes to elevate the Roman authorities in the mind of his readers (hearers). This, in all probability, is the explanation of the double reason given for complaint against Paul and Silas—namely, the loss of profit which motivated the owners of the slave girl, and then their accusation that the apostles preached customs unacceptable to people who lived according to Roman law.

Seen in this light Luke strongly implies the culpability of Herod and his subsequent unavoidable punishment. But he may be contrasting this with the responsible reaction of the Roman magistrates to their mistake about Paul and Silas (who, apparently, holds Roman citizenship as well). Luke's purpose is clear: the Romans, unlike Herod, do not impede but rather protect Christian missionaries. Luke's emphasis on the apology and the main thrust of the pericope may explain why there is such apparent neglect of the slave girl, who is not converted, and of the fellow prisoners whom both the apostles and the jailer and his family appear to ignore. These points would be irrelevant because this is not a conversion legend/pericope.

Once again one has an interesting insight into the social stance of the early Christians. Up till now the missionaries have been led by "uneducated and common" men; but now the two leaders, Paul and Silas, are both Roman citizens who command respect from the authorities.

When one considers that the first Gentile convert, albeit a worshipper of God, was an important official in the Roman army,[19] a centurion, one is able to discern an interesting progression of thought vis-à-vis Roman and Christian relationships. First, Cornelius was converted; now the apology on the part of the Roman magistrates (Acts 16) is described; later the conduct of Gallio in Acts 18:12-17 will be seen as complimentary. In Acts 19:35-40 the town clerk reminds the people that there were (Roman) courts for trying differences between the people, such as, those between Paul and Silas and the silversmiths. These courts were usually under a Roman provincial governor. Roman law and order is also emphasized by the commander who takes control during the riot in the temple (Acts 21:37ff); it is also evident in the prompt action of the tribune who, on hearing that Paul was a Roman citizen, immediately consulted his superior. It is demonstrated again in the elaborate security given to Paul when he was sent to Felix (Acts 23:23-35). However, neither Felix or Porcius Festus are the subject of laudatory comments by Luke.[20]

7. The Raising of Eutychus (Acts 20:7-12)

This miracle is parallel to the raising of Dorcas. The raising of Dorcas is a prelude to the conversion of Cornelius. From a theological point of view the raising of Eutychus may be a prelude to the Roman ministry that brings the gospel to the end of the earth, thus, completing the conversion of the Gentiles which began after the resurrection of Dorcas with the Roman military officer Cornelius and his household. One notes also that, just as the raising of Dorcas took place in a house church comprised of nonaffluent people, the raising of Eutychus occurs in a house church which appears to be situated in a tenement house, which denotes a nonaffluent neighborhood.[21]

The raising of Eutychus is immediately followed by the poignant farewell by Paul to the elders at Miletus, where Paul protests his abstention from making religion the source of gain (Acts 20:33–35). The raising of Eutychus is an element of hope in the tragedy of Paul's journey and the shipwreck.

The Pentecosts in Acts

There are, in reality, four Pentecosts in Acts, that is, four occasions upon which the Holy Spirit comes with external manifestation to a group of people. These Pentecosts are: the Jerusalem Pentecost (Acts 2), the Samaritan Pentecost (Acts 8), the Gentile Pentecost (Acts 10–11:18), and the Ephesian Pentecost (Acts 19:1–7). The first three, at least, involve important and challenging social and religious upheaval. However, this aspect has often been overlooked, and interpreters of the NT have spent more time discussing the phenomena of glossolalia than considering the social message. It is instructive that these Pentecosts are consonant with Jesus' words in Acts 1:8; namely, that the apostles will be his witnesses in Jerusalem, Judea, Samaria, and the "ends of the earth" (that is, Rome, which symbolizes the Gentile world). The Pentecostal phenomena may come as God's seal of approval on each important advance in missionary work, and on the acceptance of people who were normally regarded as ritually impure and hence unacceptable. Yet we must discuss the miraculous element which is equally understood to be glossolalia or speaking in tongues.

Bruner[22] makes an important distinction between glossolalia in 1 Corinthians 12–14 and glossolalia in Acts. He says:

> In Acts, on the three occasions where tongues occur, they come to an entire group at once, sometimes with prophecy, bringing complete Christian initiation, and they occur in all three cases, (that is the Jerusalem Pentecost, the Ephesian Pentecost and the Gentile Pentecost—tongues are not mentioned in Samaria) apart from recorded effort on the part of the recipients. Speaking in tongues in Acts is on all three occasions a corporate, church-founding, group conversion phenomenon. . . .

If Acts is written later than 1 Corinthians, could this be a "correction" on the part of Luke? For him, glossolalia and other external signs of the Spirit are not important per se, they are more a confirmation of faith than that which elicits or originates faith. Dunn[23] remarks, "In all this string of signs and wonders (in Acts) and striking miracles, only *twice* is faith mentioned. . . . " On the other hand, on a number of occasions Luke makes clear the faith-producing effect of miracles (5:14; 9:42; 13:13; 19:18). This is the aspect of the miracle/faith relations which apparently interests Luke—the publicity, propagandist value of miracle—that which elsewhere in the NT is disparaged.

On the occasion of each of the Pentecosts a novel or controversial step is taken in missionary activity, then God gives a novel and visible sign to confirm this. The sign is, however, a crowd phenomenon. We must bear in mind that glossolalia and Pentecost are not identical. The gift at the Jerusalem Pentecost may be interpretation, and one is not certain which external sign was manifested in Samaria.

We may somewhat advance Bruner's hypothesis. Glossolalia, or whatever external sign attends the Pentecost, not only marks the approval of God upon some new missionary endeavor from a geographical point of view, but it also emphasizes a significant social/racial triumph.

1. The Jerusalem Pentecost (Acts 2)

The Jerusalem Pentecost is novel on the following points: (a) Peter announces that the Spirit has been poured upon "all flesh." The immediate context of the phrase is, of course, the quotation from Joel, but the wording itself perhaps takes one back to the story in the first eleven chapters of Genesis. There the phrases "one flesh" occurs several times and means all humankind, sometimes all living creatures. This is an interesting point, because theologically it suggests a biblical basis of the Gentile mission, for which Peter laid the foundation and which was fully implemented by Paul and his companions. (b) This Pentecost is a reversal of the story of the tower of Babel, in that it is the dismantling of the communication barrier; (c) The peoples listed in Acts 2 correspond to the table of nations in Genesis 10.[24] (d) The emergence from the upper room of the apostles and/or the 120 endowed with the power of being understood by people speaking diverse languages must be seen in the light of Peter's speech, in which he asserts that the cursed and crucified one has been vindicated and raised to divine status by the resurrection.

All of these points have important social implications. The passage from Joel which Peter sees as fulfilled at Pentecost speaks of the Spirit coming to all classes of people—young and old, slave and free, men and women, saint and repentant sinner. This text was also used in Jewish tradition, and interpreters pointed out that whereas the Spirit had only come on leaders of the community of Sinai—because of the sin of the golden calf—in messianic times the Spirit would come to all, small and great, not only to anointed prophets and kings.

2. The Samaritan Pentecost (Acts 8)

Here it appears that we have two important social and/or racial aspects. With regard to the first we may again quote from Bruner:[25]

> It is evidently not the divine plan, according to Luke's understanding, that the first church outside Jerusalem should arise entirely without apostolic contact. For this to have occurred could have indicated indifference to the apostolic tradition—viz., of the history of Jesus Christ and of the unity of the church. Both tradition and the union were preserved through the apostolic visitation. The Samaritans were not left to become an isolated sect with no bonds of union with the apostolic church in Jerusalem. If a Samaritan church and Jewish church had arisen independently, side by side, without the dramatic removal of the ancient and bitter barriers of prejudice between the two, particularly at the level of ultimate authority, the young church of God would have been in schism from the inception of its mission. The drama of the Samaritan affair in Acts 8 included among its purposes the vivid and visual dismantling of the wall of enmity between Jew and Samaritan and the preservation of the precious unity of the church of God through the unique divine "interception" and then prompt presentation of the Spirit in the presence of the apostles.

This assertion has merit, but it must be seen against the whole history of Samaritan-Jewish relationships, particularly the Samaritan-Jewish conflict in the first century C.E., especially the Samaritan relationship to the Romans and to Herod, the incident of the bones placed in the temple, and the domestic war over the killing of the Galilean(s) at Ginae.[26] This major achievement is thrown into sharper relief when seen in the light of the absence of favorable references to Samaritans in any of the NT books except John and Luke, and the prohibition against entering a Samaritan village or town in Matt 10:5.

However, the second social aspect is also of importance, especially against the background of the whole structure of Acts. It is the message which Luke means to convey by the narration of the episode concerning Simon Magus' request to buy from Peter and John the power of transmitting the Spirit. This narrative enables Luke to make a very bold and clear statement about the position of mercenary practitioners of magic, who were prevalent in the days of the early church and in ours as well. Barrett[27] gives important background in this matter: for example, the statement of Celsus, who compared the miracles in the Gospels to "works of sorcerers who profess to do wonderful miracles, and the accomplishments of those who are taught by the Egyptians, who for a few obols make known their sacred lore in the middle of the market place . . ." (*Contra Celsum* 1, 68); the assertion of Juvenal that Jewish magicians were met frequently and charged little (cf. Juvenal, *Satires* 6.546f); the prohibition forbidding Christians to become magi (*Did.* 2:2; 5:1; cf. 3:4; *Barn.* 20:1; Justin, *Apology* 1:14). Barrett also quotes from the *Acts of Thomas* 20 (cf., sections 101, 152 therein as well):

> We think that because of his miracles he is a *magos* yet his compassions and his cures, which are done by him freely (*dōrean*), and moreover his simplicity and kindness and his faith, declare that he is a righteous man or an apostle of the new God whom he preaches.

Christianity is not just another magi movement with pecuniary interests (cf. Acts 5, Acts 16, Acts 19).

3. The Gentile Pentecost

The importance of the Petrine Gentile mission is accentuated by the precise structure of Acts and by the fact that Luke tells this episode three times: Acts 10, 11:1–18 (twice), and 15:6–11 (note too the three accounts of Paul's conversion). With regard to the structure, from Acts 1:8 we see that the mission is foreshadowed in the prediction of the resurrected Lord and can be included in the phrase "ends of the earth."

It is closely linked to the persecution by the conversion of
Paul. He keeps the clothes of those who stone Stephen. In fact,
the Gentile Pentecost is placed between the first account of the
conversion of Paul, and the spread of the missionary work
outside Palestine owing to the persecution of Stephen (Acts
11:19). Stephen may have been a Hellenist associated with
Samaria.[28]

However, the most important point is that it is the foundation stone of Paul's fully fledged mission to the Gentiles in
Greece, Asia, and Europe. However, it would appear that those
whom Paul converted later were purely pagan, not Jewish
proselytes. Cornelius appears to be a proselyte; he is called a
worshipper of God, *phoboumenos ton theon* (Acts 10:22).

Moreover, there is no doubt that Peter's step is innovative,
startling, controversial, and of great consequence. It is, I think,
the basis or impetus for the Petrine/Pauline parallels which are
so clear in Acts.[29] So it is Peter's action rather than Paul's
which is attended by glossolalia. Perhaps an external, miraculous sign was not needed to seal divine approval of Paul's
mission because it had already been given on the occasion of
the Cornelius' conversion. In fact, given this interpretation, it
would be difficult to find a Gentile Pentecost as such in the
Pauline mission, unless it would be the Ephesian Pentecost.[30]
Another social/political aspect lies in the fact that the first non-
Jewish convert is a Roman in high standing in the army. In this
pericope Luke shows that the Roman may offer acceptable
prayers and alms to God and be elected by God for the gift of
the Spirit.

4. *The Ephesian Pentecost*

It is more difficult to see a social implication in the Ephesian
Pentecost, but as it is placed almost immediately before the
incident of the sons of Sceva,[31] Luke probably meant to show
again, this time in Asia Minor, that in no way could the new
movement be associated with the ordinary *magi*, Jewish or
pagan. The bestowal of the Spirit of Jesus brings gifts, the
misuse of the Spirit brings misfortune.

The Cursing Miracles in Acts

Integral to the understanding of the benevolent miracles (discussed above) are the cursing miracles in Acts. They are arresting in their contrast to the avoidance of destructive miracles in Luke's Gospel; he even omits the cursing of the fig tree from the Jerusalem ministry. Yet the cursing miracles are closely associated with the activity of the Spirit, both from a theological and structure point of view in Luke's second volume.

These malevolent miracles have proved a source of embarrassment to the Christian exegete. Of the many interpretations I think that Barrett's thesis mentioned above[32] is the most persuasive. His essay concerns Simon Magus, whom he sees against the background of the pagan and Jewish magi in the ancient world; but he has occasion to make some perspicacious remarks about similar pericopes which deal with magic and charlatanry, e.g., Ananias and Sapphira and Elymas-Barjesus.

One could extend Barrett's thesis by placing all these pericopes within the heart of the structure of Acts. Luke appears to have planned the following structure to show the difference between the activities of the Holy Spirit and the pagan supernatural forces.

Spirit of Truth	*Spirit of Perversity*
Jerusalem Pentecost	The lying spirit in Ananias and Sapphira
Samaritan Pentecost	The refutation of Simon Magus
Gentile Pentecost	The death of Herod due to blasphemy
Cure at Lystra	Repudiation of *theios anēr*

In other words, each manifestation of the Holy Spirit is balanced by an example of the false use of supernatural power.

In this way Luke shows the dramatic and lethal result of lying to the Spirit in contrast to the proclamation of the truth in Acts 2 (cf., Acts 2:36). Marshall[33] observes that Ananias and Sapphira took greater credit than they deserved by misrepresenting the amount of the sale, and that they were tempting the Spirit as the Israelites did in the desert.[34] The lying spirit and the Person of the Lie are now well known from Qumran.[35]

The reception of the Spirit by the Samaritans is complemented by the reprimand to Simon Magus: the gift of the Spirit is not to be bought. Simon is actually a magician whom Peter discredits. He wanted the Spirit for illegitimate use, that is, the practice of magic. The Gentile Pentecost is balanced by the death of Herod. Josephus gives an account of this incident in *Ant.* 19:343–350. However, Luke imputes the death of the king to his presumption to divine honors when the assembly cried: "This is the voice of a god not a man." The angel of the Lord struck Herod at once because he did not ascribe the honor to God, and he died eaten by worms (Acts 12:22).

Luke nonchalantly adds: "Meanwhile the word of the Lord continued to spread and increase" (12:24). Acts 13:1–3 reports the commission of Paul and Barnabas by the Holy Spirit for the first mission. They are clearly numbered among the teachers and prophets. In Acts 13:4–12 Paul brings down a curse of temporary blindness upon Elymas, a Jewish false prophet at the court of Sergius Paulus. The curse is implemented and the man is blind for a time. Elymas appears to be a practicing magician and a false prophet (cf., prophets mentioned in 13:1). He may have been afraid of losing his position in favor of Paul in the court of the proconsul. Luke must have intended the reader to contrast him with Paul and Barnabas, who are said to be prophets and/or teachers in Acts 13:1. The account of the first mission also describes the repudiation of the gods of the Lystronians which occurs after the cure of the lame man at Lystra (Acts 8:18). Just as Peter gave his exposition of the power of Jesus' name after the cure of the lame man at the Gate Beautiful, so Paul and Barnabas preach to the Lystronians but repudiate the roles of *theioi andres*. The scene is vivid and contains subtle humor. In Acts 16:6–10 Paul, Timothy, and Silas (apparently) are directed by the Holy Spirit not to go to Phrygia and Galatia, but in a dream a man from Macedonia asks for help. This spiritual guidance can be contrasted with popular superstition in the Greek world by the "exorcism" of the slave girl (16:16–19). She is possessed by a python spirit (a spirit of divination). She may be a ventriloquist and/or a fortune-teller.

Acts 19:1–7, the Ephesian Pentecost, where the followers of John the Baptist receive the Spirit with the gifts of prophecy and tongues, is balanced by the incident of the sons of Sceva. Here it is particularly important that the proper use of the name of Jesus is emphasized: "fear came upon all, and the name of the Lord Jesus came to be held in great reverence" (Acts 19:17). This Lucan polemic against non-Christian magic seems to us to come to a climax with the burning of the magical texts in Acts 19. Magical books were known as "Ephesian Letters." The value of those burned amounted to the salary of 50,000 workers' daily wage, that is, 50,000 silver pieces. This incident may be seen not only as a climax in Luke's polemic against magic but also against making "godliness the source of gain." Christianity triumphs vis-à-vis pagan magic and mercenary religious practices.

Through the six cursing miracles and the incident of the apostles being taken for gods at Lystra, Luke shows that Christianity is to have no part in:

Lying to the Spirit
Simony
Blasphemy
False Prophecy
Idolatry
Ventriloquism
False Exorcism
Magical Books

Finally, readers will notice the omission of the reference to the blinding by God or Jesus on the road to Damascus. Stanley[36] has shown that the blindness of Paul may be associated with the curse of blindness in Deut 28:28–29, where disobedience to the Law is threatened with the following curse:

The Lord will smite you with madness and blindness and confusion of mind; and you shall grope at noonday, as the blind grope in darkness.

If one is to include this among the cursing miracles, a total of seven is attained, making a parallel with the seven major miracles. We are now in a position to investigate a further aspect of the miraculous which has social implication for the world into which Peter and Paul and their companions (both men and women) took Christianity.

Polemic Against Pagan Magical Practices

The ancient world appears to have been rife with magical practices and with what, in our eyes, appears pure superstition. Scholars have already remarked upon Mark's possible effort to prevent his readers from seeing the apostles as "divine men." If the problem was acute for Mark, how much more would it be for the writer of Acts?

We have already commented on the problem of admitting non-pure-blooded Jews, especially the Samaritans, into the Christian community. Barrett addresses the problem of sources and of historicity in Acts 8.[37] Pertinent to our investigation, Barrett argues that the pre-Lucan tradition did not link the figures of Simon and Philip.[38] The location in Samaria is associated with Simon rather than Philip. Barrett observes the phenomenon of Jewish magicians who plied their trade at a very modest price (cf. Juvenal, *Satires.* 6:546f). Christians were not permitted to be *magoi* (*Did.* 2:2; 5:1; cf. 3:4; *Barn.* 20:1; Justin, *Apology* 1:14), although they were sometimes confused with such people; see the quotation from the *Acts of Thomas* cited above from Barrett. Now Simon was a *magus* who wanted to buy the power to confer the Spirit and, as Barrett observes, was certain to charge when he transmitted it. Luke is interested in the improper use of monies. Barrett points out that the sin of Ananias and Sapphira was not in keeping the property but in lying; Elymas-Barjesus was a false prophet accused of "sharp practice." Pseudo-miraculous power as a source of financial gain is also condemned by Paul by his act of exorcizing the slave girl with the gift of divination. The sons of Sceva may also have been making money from their exorcisms. This may explain why Luke condemns the use of the name by non-Christians for exorcisms. The same issue of improper monies is behind the riot at Ephesus and the burning of the magical books.

Luke does not mention the Great Collection and shows Paul emphasizing that he did not do missionary work for financial gain. The same principle is behind the Simon incident. There must be no financial interchange when the Holy Spirit is at work. The apostles are not *theoi andres*, and they are poor. "It is this desire of Simon's that Peter denounces, partly because this is not the way a Christian minister should approach his work, partly because it implies a misunderstanding of such spiritual gifts as glossolalia, but mainly because it would put the Holy Spirit under the control of one whose motives were mainly those of profit-making."[39]

Thus one sees a thread running through Acts. Firstly, one hears that Peter has neither silver nor gold; the early Jewish-Christian community shares its possessions, meals and prayer; Ananias and Sapphira are cursed because they lied in the matter of property. In the structure of Acts this incident occurs near the end of the Jerusalem ministry. Elymas is cursed at the beginning of the mission of Paul and Barnabas (13:4–12); this false prophet may have been tenacious about the lucrative advantages of his position at Sergius Paulus' court. The slave girl is "exorcized" at the beginning of the mission of Paul and Silas. The sons of Sceva episode occurs in the second missionary journey, and the burning of the books (19:19–20) and the riot in Ephesus occur as the climax of this.

Thus these pericopes are strategically and meaningfully placed in the structure of Acts. It is interesting that there is no overt magic in the Jerusalem ministry—unless we count Ananias and Sapphira.

Acts and the Inclusive Community

Luke has not only carefully structured Acts to form a juxtaposition—both from a literary and a theological point of view—between enthusiastic ministry and social/political revolution, but Acts also shows an evolution of the charismatic

Christian community which differs strikingly from the usual evolution of such communities.

I should like to make a comparison and contrast with the *Rule of the Community* from Qumran (hereafter cited as 1QS) as redacted by Murphy-O'Connor,[40] who had divided the *Rule* into four stages.

Qumran Community, Stage 1: 1QS 8:1–16a and 9:3–10:8a

The retreat into the desert has not taken place. The community is contemplating the withdrawal and using the time for study of the Torah. It is under the guidance of twelve or fifteen men and the role of the *maskil*, the man of understanding, is important. The community would appear to be flexible and not encumbered with too many rules or penalties for deviant behavior. The manifesto of the community is expressed in 1QS 8:5–10:

> ... the Council of the Community shall be established in truth as an everlasting planting.
> It is the House of holiness for Israel and the Company of infinite holiness for Aaron; they are the witnesses of truth into Judgment and the chosen of Loving-kindness appointed to offer expiation for the earth and to bring down punishment upon the wicked. It is a tried wall, the precious cornerstone; its foundations shall not tremble nor flee from their place. It is the Dwelling of infinite holiness for Aaron in (eternal) Knowledge unto the Covenant of justice and to make offerings of sweet savor; (it is) the House of perfection and truth in Israel to establish the Covenant according to the everlasting precepts.
> And they shall be accepted as expiation for the earth and to decree the judgment of wickedness with no perversity remaining.[41]

Qumran Community Stage 2: 1QS 8:16b–19 and 8:20–9:2

The *Sitz im Leben* is different from the first stage. They have retired into the desert to form a separate community and have introduced the principle of temporary exclusion and reintegration into the community for certain transgressions; but willful breaking of the biblical law merits expulsion.

Qumran Community Stage 3: 1 QS 5:1–13a and 5:15b–7:25

This stage begins with a solemn opening: "And this is the rule for the members of the Community ..." (1QS 5:1). In this stage the members appear to be required to give firmer obedience to the *Rule*. There is an oath of admission into the congregation. Classification of members has been introduced and also the practice of mutual reproof. Common life seems to have grown in importance and there are rules concerning the assemblies. The penal code is much more developed.

At this stage the community is fully conscious of the true response to God. To become a member of the community is to become a true member of the covenant. In Stage 1 the covenanters sought pardon for the country, but now the idea is to expiate for all those who have volunteered to enter the holiness of Aaron and the house of Israel.

Qumran Community Stage 4

This stage is more complex. One must distinguish between the interpolations in 1–3 and additions made at the beginning and end of the document. The content of this stage is diverse but the underlying aim appears to be to rekindle a dwindling fervor in the community. This section contains the aim and ideal of the community and the ceremony for entry into the covenant. The instruction of the two spirits (1QS 3:13–4:26), the spirit of truth and spirit of perversity, seems to divide the people into two opposing camps. At the beginning of 1QS 5 is found the liturgy of entry into the community. Now 1:16–2:25a was most probably separate before it was included in the *Rule*, the maledictions seeming to suggest that some members have fallen short of the idea of the community. Following these, 2:25b–3:12 comprises a catechetical section. The final hymn is found in 1QS 10:9–11:22—it contains an introduction, promises, declaration of salvation; reflections of the misery of people; words of confidence and a doxology. It can be compared to the hymn scroll of the community (1QH).

The Christian Community According to Acts

I do not wish to say that Luke was influenced directly by this or other Jewish communities (e.g., the Essenes) akin to it. I am merely using the *Rule* as a "control" group to measure the nature of the communities of Christians as seen in Acts. The following points may be of interest.

(1) The Christian community begins as a Jewish community. There is sharing of property, and meals together with prayer, but these principles are relinquished; perhaps because of table fellowship problems, perhaps merely because of practical reasons and the growth in numbers.

(2) The community is scattered by persecution and spreads to Samaria; it embraces a people who for many centuries were hostile to the Jewish peoples. Qumran retired to the desert to be more exclusive; the Christians of necessity—or rather by divine providence—were scattered to become a more inclusive community.

(3) Peter brings Cornelius and his household into the church, that is, the church admitted uncircumcised Jewish proselytes into her community. Cornelius is a *Roman Centurion*.

(4) The council establishes the least onerous obligations— ritual ones (then ethical)[42]—for the converts.

(5) Paul takes the gospel to the pagans per se (Acts 13:46), and through his ministry they become equal and fully empowered members.

Thus the Christian community developed in a way opposite to the average charismatic community in becoming more and more inclusive.[43] In his second volume to Theophilus, Luke presents a religion which eschews magic and money making, and seeks to embrace all humanity and bring it to its bountiful and merciful Lord and God.

Notes

1. J. D. G. Dunn, *Jesus and the Spirit* (London: SCM, 1975) 158–63.

2. Cf. John 14:12, where Jesus indicates that the person who believes in him will do greater works than he; but, of course, the interpretation of *erga* is open for discussion.

3. F. Neirynck, "The Miracle Stories," *Les Actes des Apôtres* (BETL 48; ed. J. Kremer, Gembloux: Duculot, 1979) 169–213.

4. From a form-critical point of view, Acts 5:17–21 does not appear to fall into the category of miracle, certainly not when compared with the other liberation miracles in Acts 12–16.

5. Luke uses *teras*, *sēmeion* and *dynamis* for wonders and miracles but none of the major miracles are called *teras*.

6. Such as listed in Gal 5:22–23.

7. Such as those listed in 1 Corinthians 12, Romans 12 and Ephesians 4; cf. discussion of those in the first two texts by F. A. Sullivan, *Charisms and Charismatic Renewal: A Biblical and Theological Study* (Ann Arbor, Michigan/Dublin: Servant/Gill and Macmillan, 1982) 27–46,121–68.

8. G. Campbell Morgan, in a sermon from the Westminster pulpit, defined the fruits of the Spirit as follows:

Joy is Love's Consciousness;
Peace is Love's Confidence;
Patience is Love's Habit;
Kindness is Love's Activity;
Faithfulness is Love's Quantity;
Meekness is Love's Tone;
Temperance is Love's Victory.

See the sensitive pastoral discussion by E. D. O'Connor, "Love in This World," *ThRen* 10 (October 1978) 23–29.

9. Dunn, *Jesus*, 167–69, discusses the relationship between faith and miracles in Acts.

10. For an example of the use of names in magic see the use of the names of angels to ward away particular demons in the *Testament of Solomon*, conveniently printed in D. C. Duling, in *Old Testament Pseudepigrapha* (2 vols., ed. J. H. Charlesworth; New York: Doubleday, 1983) 1:935–87.

11. C. K. Barrett, "Light on the Holy Spirit from Simon Magus (Acts 8, 4–25)," *Les Actes*, 288–89.

12. For a study of the Pauline communities see Wayne Meeks, *The First Urban Christians: The Social World of the Apostle Paul* (New Haven: Yale University, 1983), as well as R. F. Hock, "Paul's Tentmaking and His Social Class," *JBL* 97 (1978) 555–64; G. Clark, "The Social Status of Paul," *ExpTim* 96 (1985) 110–11.

13. It would appear that here we are still dealing with purely Jewish communities, but those surrounded by Gentiles.

14. I. H. Marshall, *The Acts of the Apostles* (TNTC; Leicester/Grand Rapids: Inter-Varsity/Eerdmans, 1980) 179.

15. For despised trades see J. Jeremias, *Jerusalem in the Time of Jesus* (London: SCM, 1969) 304.

16. *Pace* Marshall, *Acts*, 180.

17. A. Strobel, "Passa-Symbolik und Passa-Wunder in Apg. 12.3 ff," *NTS* 4 (1957–58) 200–5.

18. V. K. Robbins, "By Land and By Sea: The We passages and Ancient Sea Voyages," *Perspectives on Luke-Acts* (ed. C. Tablert; Danville, Virginia/Edinburgh: Association of Baptist Professors of Religion/T. & T. Clark, 1978) 215–42.

19. It is difficult to know the precise connotation of such phrases as *phoboumenos ton theon* in this text and *sebomenē ton theon* used of Lydia in Acts 16:14. They certainly denote some degree of allegiance to Judaism.

20. For further information about Luke's pro-Roman proclivity, see P. W. Walasky, *"And so we came to Rome"*: *The Political Perspective of Saint Luke* (SNTSMS 49; Cambridge: Cambridge University, 1983).

21. Marshall, *Acts*, 326.

22. F. D. Bruner, *A Theology of the Holy Spirit* (Grand Rapids: Eerdmans, 1970) 192; for a different view of Luke's intention in Acts, see our honoree, S. M. Horton, *What the Bible Says About the Holy Spirit* (Springfield, Missouri: Gospel Publishing House 1976) 135–66.

23. Dunn, *Jesus*, 168.

24. M. D. Goulder, *Type and History of Acts* (London: SPCK, 1964) 152–59.

25. Bruner, *Theology*, 176; see also Horton, *What*, 153–55.

26. For a sketch of the conflicts between the Samaritans and the Jews into the first century A.D., see by book, *My Enemy is My Guest* (Maryknoll, New York: Orbis, 1983) 79–85.

27. Barrett, "Light," *Les Actes*, 287–88.

28. See G. Schneider, "Stephanus, die Hellenisten und Samaria," *Les Actes*, 215–40.

29. For the Peter and Paul parallels see W. W. Gasque, *A History of the Criticism of the Acts of the Apostles* (Grand Rapids/Tübingen: Eerdmans/Mohr, 1975).

30. C. K. Barrett, "Apollos and the Twelve Disciples of Ephesus," *The New Testament Age: Essays in Honor of Bo Reicke* (2 vols. ed. W. C. Weinrich; Macon, Georgia: Mercer University, 1984) 1:38–39, suggests that Luke insists that Paul's version of the faith was normative and victorious, and that he desires to show that Paul was not only a great evangelist but also the great unifying agent in the church.

31. For the cultural and social setting of these scenes in first-century Asia see B. A. Mastin, "Scaeva the Chief Priest," *JTS* (1976) 405–12.

32. Barrett, "Light," *Les Actes*, 284–85.

33. Marshall, *Acts*, 112.

34. Ibid., 113.

35. Cf. the Person of the Lie and the Spirit of Perversity in the Qumran scrolls.

36. See D. Stanley, "Why Three Accounts," *CBQ* 15 (1953) 315–38.

37. Barrett, "Light," *Les Actes*, 283.

38. Ibid., 284.

39. Ibid., 292.

40. J. Murphy-O'Connor, "La Genese Litterarie de la Regle de la Communate," *RB* 76 (1969) 528–49.

41. A. Dupont-Sommer, *The Essene Writings from Qumran* (tr. G. Vermes; Cleveland: World, 1962) 91.

42. Acts 15:20 appears to have comprised ritual requirements, but later with the omission of "strangled things" to have interpreted in a moralistic way.

43. Exclusive motifs are noted, e.g., in J. R. Williams, *The Gift of the Spirit Today* (Plainfield, N. J.: Logos, 1980) 149–50.

PART II:
HISTORICAL STUDIES

10

WILLIAM TYNDALE: A THEOLOGIAN OF RENEWAL

Donald Dean Smeeton

IN A.D. 393 AUGUSTINE, as yet an obscure presbyter and a priest of only two years, addressed a council of bishops appealing for the formulation of a biblical doctrine of the Holy Spirit. From that speech, Augustine attempted to fill this need in Christian theology by considering not only the Spirit's person and procession but also his place in Christian experience. Swete judged Augustine's pneumatological understanding of conversion to be a bulwark against Pelagianism.[1] More than a thousand years later an Augustinian monk, Martin Luther, appealed for reformation in church life and thought, buttressing his call by appealing to Augustine.

Through the intervening years, pneumatology had been endangered by the twin evils of scholasticism and mysticism. In the first case, the Holy Spirit had been reduced to an impersonal yet divine force complementing the orthodox doctrine of the Trinity, but having little to do with the individual except in and through the sacraments. On the other side, late medieval mysticism saw the Holy Spirit as the direct link between God and humanity—a link by which the individual could directly experience the supernatural without the mediation of the religious externals. The mystic's concern was to achieve the possibility of being like Christ through an ineffable spiritual experience. Both these options were rejected by the Reformers. Their constant emphasis was that the Holy Spirit always worked by the Word in conjunction with faith in the incarnate

Christ, never as an intellectual or spiritual exercise of humanity's unaided powers.[2]

It should not be surprising that the renewal of religion in the 16th century was also a rediscovery of a dynamic pneumatology, for the Reformation cannot be fully understood as only the rending of ecclesiastical organization or merely a restructuring of theology. The early 16th century was, among other things, a period of profound spiritual renewal.[3] Regin Prenter claimed that pneumatology was not merely a significant topic of Luther's thought, but the dominant factor. Luther's work, according to Prenter, could best be understood by the "spiritus creator" motif because it was an articulate summary of Luther's theology, that is, the Spirit's miraculous work of creating out of nothing.[4] Calvin, likewise, contributed to pneumatology by indicating the work of the Spirit throughout the length of his *Institutes*.[5] It is, however, a mistake to assume that everything of significance in the 16th century happened in Geneva or Wittenberg. There were at least two other rapidly budding theological branches on the Protestant tree, namely, Anabaptist thought and early English theology.

In a recent study of charismatic motifs in the Anabaptist movement, Davis draws parallels between Anabaptism in the age of Reformation and Pentecostalism today. His conclusion is that Anabaptism was, in fact, a charismatic movement.[6] Because much of Pentecostalism is, perhaps unconsciously, Anabaptistic, at least in ecclesiology, one might want to address the proposition: "Pentecostalism as an Anabaptist movement." It is, however, the second aspect of this neglected field which now demands attention.

For convenience this investigation will be restricted to the first Anglo-Saxon Reformer, William Tyndale. This delimiting is justified by the fact that John Wesley, who stressed the role of religious experience in conversion and sanctification, is often seen as the parent of Pentecostalism. This son of the Epworth rectory, however, did not create the Wesleyan renewal and theology *de novo*, but rather he built on an "evangelical" tradition that had already been established in English Christianity. Tyndale's internalization of pneumatology and his concern for "feeling" faith were part of that tradition. Nor did Tyndale construct his theology without earlier foundation.[7] However, the pneumatology of William Tyndale can provide some insights into a better understanding of the Spirit's role in religious conversion, assurance, and ethics today. Although Tyndale's name is used to identify specific evangelical enterprises (commentaries, publishing houses, etc.), few know much about the man apart from the fact that he was a Bible translator and martyr. He is treated in the histories of translation, but seldom if ever in the histories of theology. Tyndale the translator overshadows Tyndale the theologian. He attended none of the theological debates, colloquies, or councils of his age. He led no movement nor founded any organization. For the ten years that followed the publication of his English NT, however, he was hounded by the authorities, both civil and religious, in his native England and on the Continent. During much of this time, Tyndale based his work of translating, editing, and writing in the Flemish port of Antwerp. Under pseudocolophons, he produced an amazing array of theological, polemical, and expository writings which were, like his biblical translations, smuggled back into England. In these writings one can see his approach to renewal, especially as it related to the work of the Holy Spirit.[8]

Like other theologians in the Augustinian tradition, Tyndale depicted unregenerate humanity as helpless and hopeless before God's total righteousness. Neither wit nor will could achieve reconciliation with God. Rejecting any hint of Thomistic confidence, Tyndale claimed "a natural man . . . led of his blind reason only, can never ascend to the capacity of the Spirit" (I, 111).[9] Humanity's efforts, even through the sacraments, were without profit. Externals such as holy water, bells, fire, bread, salt, and wax were mere superstitions which could never bring the Holy Spirit. Tyndale found a path between the mystic and the scholastic by placing the Spirit's capability over against humankind's inability.

In opposition to those who presumed the efficacy of the sacraments, Tyndale did not assume that the Spirit was active simply because the sacraments were being observed. When the opposition cited John 3:5 ("born of water and the Spirit") as a reference to baptism, Tyndale countered with Gal 3:2 ("Did you receive the Spirit by observing the law or by believing what you heard?"). He agreed, "So now if baptism preach me the washing in Christ's blood, so doth the Holy Ghost accompany it; and that deed of preaching through faith doth away my sins. For the Holy Ghost is no dumb God, nor a God that goeth a mumming" (I, 423f). In a similar way, the Eucharist was considered. Tyndale pointedly described, and rejected, both the Catholic and Lutheran interpretations. The Eucharist, for Tyndale, was like baptism in that it must "preach" to those present as they think of Christ's death. The key phrase for Tyndale was not "This is my body" but rather "do this in remembrance of me" and "you do show the Lord's death." The Eucharist, like all the sacraments, was a memorial which called to mind the thing signified. They were but signs on the outside of the taverns which indicated to the thirsty where drink might be obtained (II, 184). For Tyndale, a sacrament which did not preach the promises of Christ was "dumb," superstitious, and magical.

Following the Augustinian tradition, Tyndale acknowledged election without making it central to his understanding of salvation. It was clear, however, that God, not humanity, must initiate the application of salvation.

> No man can prevent (go before) the Spirit in doing good. The Spirit must first come, and wake him out of his sleep with the thunder of the law, and fear him, and show him his miserable estate and wretchedness; and make him abhor himself, and to desire help; and then comfort him again with the pleasant rain of the gospel, that is to say, with the sweet promises of God in Christ, and stir up faith in him to believe the promises. (I, 498)

It was the work of the Holy Spirit to convict before the law, to reveal one's helpless condition without grace, and then to apply the "sweet promises of God in Christ."

Exactly how does the Spirit apply this marvelous salvation? Tyndale's answer is repeated often in his works, namely, by faith in the biblical message as it is preached. "When this testament is preached and believed, the Spirit entereth the heart, and quickeneth it, and giveth her life, and justifieth her" (I, 417).

Tyndale was careful, however, not to reduce the mystery of soteriology to the mechanics of homiletics. Although the preacher must prepare and preach, he cannot apply the message to the heart of the hearer. Tyndale confessed that the preacher "cannot make his preaching spring in the heart, no more than a sower can make his corn grow, nor can say, 'This man shall receive the word, and this not'; but soweth the word only, and committeth the growing to God, whose Spirit breatheth where he listeth" (II, 181).

Like the Lollards, Tyndale assumed that the vernacular Scripture could be understood in its literal sense without the benefit of scholastic glosses. Scripture in the word of the preacher and in the hand of the reader would produce faith. "Faith cometh by hearing." If one's heart is inclined toward the truth, the spiritual work of the Word is to "stir up faith in him to believe the promises." The publishing of the vernacular Scriptures would produce a great light among the people and the reading of the Word would produce growth in grace. Tyndale could have this confidence because, as he said, "God is Spirit, and all his words are spiritual. His literal sense is spiritual, and all his words are spiritual " (I, 309). Faith activates the Spirit.

> All our justifying then cometh of faith, and faith and the Spirit come of God, and not of us. When we say, faith bringeth the Spirit, it is not to be understood, that faith deserveth the Spirit, or that the Spirit is not present in us before faith; for the Spirit is ever in us, and faith is the gift and working of the Spirit: but through preaching the Spirit beginneth to work in us. (I, 488)

As the believer embraces the merciful promises, God demonstrates his faithfulness and by his Spirit gives a love for his law as well as a strength for his work. The Spirit, coming by preaching, brought salvation. "As soon as thou believest in Christ, the Holy Ghost cometh, sin falleth away, and devils fly" (I, 225f).

The expectation that at faith "sin falleth away" should not escape notice. Although some have charged Luther with preaching a forensic justification stripped of ethical implications, this accusation could never be brought against Tyndale. Tyndale's focus was not what takes place in the legal transactions of heaven, but rather in the heart of the sinner. True faith is "feeling" faith. As there was not faith without the work of the Holy Spirit, there could be no faith without feeling. "Where the Spirit is," Tyndale argued, "there is feeling; for the Spirit maketh us feel all things. Where the Spirit is not, there is no feeling; but a vain opinion or imagination" (I, 78). This is the "experience" of salvation.

Although Tyndale appealed to internal "feeling" for assurance of salvation, he offered both positive and negative guidance in order to avoid subjectivism. The negative witness is an acknowledging of sin: "weeping in mine heart, because I cannot do the will of God, and thirst after strength; (then) I am sure that the Spirit of God is in me, and his favour upon me" (I, 76). As a positive witness, the Spirit provokes a desire, or in Tyndale's word "lust," to do good. The application of salvation is the internalization of the preached Word so that the experience of salvation, with the resulting assurance, is ascribed to the direct work of the Holy Spirit. For Tyndale, the active role of the Holy Spirit in the individual's decision to choose good was evidence of one's right standing before God. Thus assurance was grounded in desire. Tyndale's soteriology had a unique character among the Reformation theologies in that he emphasized the inner change that justification effected in the behavior by reorienting the believer toward the law. Tyndale described the Christian's relation to law as "lust," "consent," and even "love."

> The Spirit also maketh the law a lively thing in the heart; so that a man bringeth forth good works of his own accord, without compulsion of the law, without fear of threatenings or cursings, yea, and without all manner of respect or love unto any temporal pleasure, but of the very power of the Spirit, received through faith. (I, 417)

Elsewhere Tyndale argued,

> When a man feeleth that his heart consenteth unto the law of God and feeleth himself meek, patient, courteous, and merciful to his neighbor, altered and fashioned like unto Christ; why should he doubt but that God hath forgiven him, and chosen him, and put his Spirit in him? (I, 263f)

Although Tyndale could use the terminology of Luther in his appeal to "faith alone," the English Reformer could not conceive of a faith which was alone. Faith resulted in "consenting unto the law," "feeling oneself meek, patient, courteous, and merciful," and, of course, "fashioned like unto Christ." Faith was not passive, but active. It was always actively doing good and, thus, it gave assurance to the believer. The Spirit of God brought desire and ability to do God's law, so works were an essential consequence of "feeling faith."

Security in salvation was also linked to the Holy Spirit." For the Spirit of God is in his (the individual's) heart, and comforteth him, and holdest him fast to the rock of the merits of Christ's blood, in whom he is elect" (I, 78). Security was possible because faith was the fruit tree which produced love and good works. The fruit of traditional Catholicism was judged to be evil because its root and stock were evil. Tyndale observed, "Where the Spirit is, there it is always summer, and there are always good fruits, that is to say, good works" but, on the contrary, "where God's Spirit is not, there can be no good works, even as where an apple-tree is not, there can grow no apples; but there is unbelief, the devil's spirit, and evil works" (I, 499). Tyndale claimed that as the flow of living waters, all good works would spring from the Christian naturally. "Thou needest not to wrest good works out of him, as a man would wring verjuice out of crabs: nay, they flow naturally out of him as springs out of rocks' (I, 417).[10]

Tyndale, however, went far beyond the assumed acts of charity and kindness to family and neighbor. Love was to embrace everyone, even one's enemies which in the early 16th century meant the dreaded Turk. Even as the crescent cast its shadow of terror across Christendom and Luther called for armed resistance against the Islamic invaders, Tyndale said, "I am bound to love the Turk with all my might and power; yea, and above my power, even from the ground of my heart, after the ensample that Christ loved me; neither to spare goods, body, or life, to win him to Christ" (I, 96). Unlike the major continental Reformers, Tyndale saw the implications of his faith for the evangelization of pagans and for Christian mission. He appealed for Christians to walk "in the plain and single faith and feeling of the Spirit . . . and to walk worthy of the gospel, and as it becometh Christ; and with the ensample of pure living to draw all to Christ" (I, 97). The Christian had a sober and serious responsibility to combat sin. The Spirit set the believer free, but "we are not so free from sin through faith, that we should henceforth go up and down, idle, careless, and sure of ourselves, as though there were no more sin in us" (I, 500).

What later came to be understood as sanctification was not an elective. Although it was not total, progress was possible.

> Though the gifts of the Spirit increase in us daily, and have not yet their full perfection, yea, and though there remain in us yet evil lusts and sin, which fight against the Spirit . . . yet . . . we are counted for full whole, and perfect before God. (I, 492)

Luther, Calvin, and Tyndale all acknowledged their debt to Augustine and made distinctive contributions to a theology of renewal. The Englishman, however, went beyond the others by tying the work of the Spirit to sensation, security, service, and sanctification. Because salvation was effected by the Spirit there were no grounds for boasting, and because the Christian's good works were motivated by the Spirit there was no cause for pride. Spirituality was not a matter of form, but of feeling. Tyndale's focus, of course, was on soteriology for that was the controversy of his age, but by so doing he can contribute to the understanding of the contemporary renewal.

Notes

1. H. B. Swete. *The Holy Spirit in the Ancient Church: A Study of Christian Teaching in the Age of the Fathers* (London: Macmillian 1912) 322–38,405f.

2. George Smeaton, *The Doctrine of the Holy Spirit* (rpt. 1889, Edinburgh: Banner of Truth, 1974) 343.

3. Smeaton, *Doctrine*, 345, notes that "It may be said that the mystic element, though insufficient of itself to give rise to a general reformation, stands connected with almost every true revival or great religious movement that has ever taken place."

4. Cf. Regin Prenter, *Spiritus Creator* (ET; Philadelphia: Muhlenburg, 1953) passim. A similar conclusion is drawn by Arnold E. Carlson, "Luther and the Doctrine of the Holy Spirit," *LQ* 11 (1959) 46.

5. Cf. Paul Elbert, "Calvin and the Spiritual Gifts," *Essays on Apostolic Themes* (ed. Paul Elbert; Peabody, Massachusetts: Hendrickson, 1985) 115–43; Peter F. Jensen, "Calvin, Charismatics and Miracles," *EQ* 51 (1979) 131–44.

6. K. Davis, "Anabaptism as a Charismatic Movement," *Mennonite Quarterly Review* 53 (1959) 219–34.

7. For an extensive comparison of the theologies of Tyndale and the Lollards, cf. the author's *Lollard Themes in the Reformation Theology of*

William Tyndale (Kirksville, Missouri: Sixteenth Century Journal Publishers, 1986).

8. Mozley's study of Tyndale's life and thought, although first published in 1937, has not been surpassed, cf. J. F. Mozley, *William Tyndale* (rpt. 1937; Westport, Connecticut: Greenwood, 1971). Rupp's essay is also of interest, cf. Gordon Rupp, *Six Makers of English Religion* (London: Hodder & Stoughton, 1957) 13–33.

9. Also, cf. *PS* II, 183. The notations throughout the remainder of this paper refer to the first two of the three volumes of Tyndale's works edited by Henry Walker and published by the Parker Society *(PS)* In collaboration with Cambridge University. (These works have been reprinted by the Johnson Reprint Corporation, 111 Fifth Avenue, New York, New York 10003.) Volume I designates *Doctrinal Treatises and Introductions to Different Portions of the Holy Scriptures* (1848) and volume II, *Expositions and Notes on Sundry Portions of the Holy Scriptures Together with the Practice of Prelates* (1849).

10. Tyndale's concern for the positive expressions of faith by good works releases ethics from the narrow traces of legalism. For the missiological implications of these themes, the author's "William Tyndale's Suggestions for a Protestant Missiology," *Missiology* 14 (1986) 173–84.

11

THE BLACK FACE OF CHURCH RENEWAL: THE MEANING OF A CHARISMATIC EXPLOSION, 1901–1985

Douglas J. Nelson

> *Everyone was utterly amazed and did not know what to make of it. Indeed, they kept saying to each other, "What on earth can this mean?"*
> (Acts 2:12, PHILLIPS)

THE PENTECOSTAL-CHARISMATIC RENEWAL MOVEMENT has emerged within our own 20th century as a surprising if not amazing global phenomenon, rivaling or surpassing in scope, intensity, and sheer numbers the many earlier great renewal movements of Christian history. Today, after a historically brief 85 years of growth, it totals well over 114 million adult persons worldwide, including 59 million practicing members of Pentecostal denominations, 17 million active in the older more traditional churches, and over 38 million others nonaffiliated, according to comprehensive statistics for 1985 supplied by Barrett.[1]

Virtually every nation upon earth has been affected, as well as almost all Christian faith groups. In 1982 *Time* magazine reported the remarkable news that Pentecostals have become the largest distinctive group of Protestants globally, not counting those of similar persuasion within older Protestant denominations, Orthodoxy, and Roman Catholicism.[2] Understandably, this renewal has been called "The most powerful force within the Church at this moment."[3]

In the United States alone, 19% of all adults—29 million persons 18 year of age and older—identified with this renewal in 1980, according to a special Gallup Poll commissioned by *Christianity Today* magazine.[4] Latest official figures from the National Council of Churches reveal that the fourth largest Protestant American denomination is now the Church of God in Christ, a Pentecostal and predominantly black organization with almost 4 million members.[5]

As the 20th century draws to a close, it may be helpful to attempt a fresh assessment of the meaning of this renewal based upon its fountainhead at Los Angeles. The historic roots of Pentecostalism present questions relevant for the future: After a hesitant start from 1901 to 1905 under white leadership, why did the renewal explode with such dramatic force around the world from Los Angeles between 1906 and 1909 under black leadership? What can this history teach us? What is the meaning of the black face at the source of this explosive renewal?

Two visionary American clergymen share primary responsibility for launching and shaping this renewal: Charles Fox Parham (1873–1929) and William Joseph Seymour (1870–1922). The fascinating story of these two pioneering leaders provides valuable lessons for the future of renewal. These lessons hang upon the deceptively simple fact that Parham was a white man and Seymour a black man. This basic difference has already had far-reaching consequences for past renewal, yet still offers new possibilities for future renewal.

The highlights of Parham's leadership are relatively well known. Seymour's leadership has been obscured by time and the treatment historically accorded those of his race. Parham's formative influence upon modern Pentecostalism emerged at Topeka, Kansas in the early hours of January 1, 1901, the precise dawning of the 20th century, 1900 having been the last year of the 19th century.[6] When glossolalia appeared among Parham and his students during a Bible school he was conducting, they believed this to be scriptural evidence of Pentecostal Spirit-baptism. Despite momentary enthusiasm at the beginning, and some lively press coverage, Parham struggled with a seriously faltering ministry until by winter of 1904–1905 his health had broken under the strain. He left the Midwest snows to rest and recover with friends in the warm sunny Houston Gulf Coast area. As his strength improved he began preaching there on Easter Sunday of 1905. His message generated some enthusiasm, encouraging him to continue his Texas ministry and open a short-term Bible school in Houston that December to train evangelists.

Seymour, based in Houston as a widely travelled evangelist for several years, attended the school by sitting in segregated isolation outside the classroom door purposely left ajar for him by Parham.[7] This began a brief but friendly and productive association between the two men which lasted just less than a year until the autumn of 1906.

In January of 1906, with Parham's Houston Bible school still in session, Seymour withdrew before receiving the baptism in the Holy Spirit he was seeking. He departed for Los Angeles to accept an invitation to pastor a mission congregation there.[8] Only one week after arriving he met unexpected rejection from the congregational founder and lay leader who disapproved of his Pentecostal emphasis.

Seymour then formed a small predominantly black home prayer group of loyal followers. They met together regularly until Easter of that year when during three climactic days of Holy Week, April 9–12 amid a ten day fast, Seymour and the others found what they were seeking: more of God—glossolalia and other charismatic phenomena burst forth with unusual intensity and evident sincerity.

Within days huge crowds of interested persons and curious onlookers—mostly white—descended upon the little group, forcing a move to larger quarters. Seymour leased a ramshackle barnlike former church building on Azusa Street in the old downtown black ghetto. It had a dirt floor and had been used as a livery stable, but cost only $8.00 per month and could hold as many as 900 persons. Services soon expanded to morning, afternoon, and night sessions, sometimes continuing without break from morning to the next day. All kinds and types of people came, some to scoff but many to pray, and some who scoffed stayed to pray. Within the first week, a prominent Jewish rabbi even announced his full support. Astounding healings and dramatic conversions were reported. Azusa attracted scores of the varied racial and ethnic groups from cosmopolitan Los Angeles, adding to the colorful atmosphere. At one communion and foot washing service lasting until dawn, 20 nationalities participated.

News of the renewal spread rapidly across the USA and internationally. Within weeks an ever growing stream of ardent missionaries began leaving for virtually all points on the compass at home, and to every major continent abroad. Some were seasoned missionaries brought into the movement, others simply former domestic servants or washerwomen. Cecil Polhill, a prominent Cambridge graduate and veteran of the China Inland Mission, who joined the movement from his station in Tibet, observed in 1910,

> The Lord is in this blessed Pentecostal Movement. . . . Nothing has in so short a time sent so many eager souls out . . . to witness for the Lord. Some have gone unprepared, and some have not been very steady, but these are, we believe, comparatively few out of a host of earnest Pentecostal Missionaries.[9]

Seymour's newspaper appeared in September with an initial printing of 5,000 copies followed by later editions growing to 50,000 copies. The papers often passed from hand to hand until they fell apart. Visitors began arriving daily from all over the USA and other nations as far away as China, usually returning home with glowing reports. The Azusa Street Mission became a pilgrimage center, a legend in its own time, being likened by its admirers to the humble stable of old in Bethlehem.

By 1908, only two years later, the surging movement had taken root in over 50 nations.[10] Activities at Azusa peaked in 1909 but the widespread and far-flung renewal continued to grow and flourish. The first scholarly historian of the movement—by no means a sympathetic booster—reported that by 1912 it was publishing literature in 35 languages from Iceland to Tasmania, and it was thought to have penetrated every American town of 3,000 or more population.[11]

Meanwhile, Parham visited Seymour at Azusa Street in the fall of 1906. He received a warm welcome, but the exuberant and distinctive form of worship deeply offended him. There were two main reasons for this: (1) First, he observed various charisms being demonstrated too openly by the congregation to suit him. For example some worshippers were falling to the ground in apparent trance, believing themselves to be under unusual manifestations of divine spiritual power. One report described Azusa as sometimes resembling a forest of fallen trees. Parham emphatically disapproved of such demonstrations.

Seymour defended this phenomenon as following the precedent set by Saul of Tarsus, later St. Paul, who fell to the ground along the road to Damascus during his own spiritual transformation.[12] Parham remained determined to avoid the slightest "holy roller" accusation at all costs. Seymour disagreed, maintaining the risk to be acceptable in view of the principle involved and the spiritual benefits at stake.

(2) Second, Parham saw unusual social and racial integration at Azusa Mission. This struck him as even more unacceptable. Parham admired the Ku Klux Klan, and he especially objected to racial mixing or mingling during the worship and at the altar.[13] At Houston, Parham followed such strict segregation that black worshippers were not only seated at the rear but also excluded from the altar calls following the services. Some believed this to have been simple obedience to Southern law but if so, there was no such rigid requirement in Los Angeles especially in a black church. In fact, Parham abhorred the unrestricted coming together of the races, in agreement with the overwhelming majority of whites at that time. He believed the besetting sin of humanity to have been racial mixing, for which divine judgment was thought to have fallen with the flood of Noah's day, Noah having been chosen to survive supposedly because of his "pedigree without mixed blood."[14]

By contrast Seymour felt just as strongly in favor of what he believed to be an essential and crucial element not only of the Azusa renewal but of true Christianity itself; namely, that there needs to be a great coming together in the church as at Pentecost, beyond the barriers or race, color, gender, nation, class or status, to demonstrate that God is no respecter of persons, and that all believers are truly one in Christ. Consequently, Parham and Seymour found themselves irreconcilably poles apart on this pivotal and far-reaching issue.

It is noteworthy that Seymour accomplished his leadership of a renewal marked by interracial equality, harmony, and unity at the exact epicenter of the most severely segregated time in American history, and among the most resistant social groups. Synan called attention to the fact that this "striking interracial phenomenon" occurred not only "in the very years of America's most racist period, those from 1890 to 1920," but even more significantly, "among the very groups that have traditionally been most at odds, the poor whites and the poor blacks.[15] A. A. Boddy, a leading English clergyman who travelled to Azusa to see for himself what was happening, related the surprising overcoming of racial prejudice among Southerners, saying,

> When the Holy Spirit was poured out at Los Angeles in 1906, it was specially poured out first among negro Christians. One of the remarkable things was that preachers of the Southern states were willing and eager to go over to those negro people at Los Angeles and have fellowship with them, and through their prayers receive the same blessing. The most wonderful thing was that when these white preachers came back to the Southern States, they were not ashamed to say before their own congregations that they had been worshipping with negroes, and had received some of the same wonderful blessings that had been poured out on them.[16]

Frank Bartleman, a frequent participant at Azusa worship, eloquently summarized this distinctive feature of the renewal, writing, "The 'color line' was washed away in the blood."[17]

Parham reacted viscerally to Seymour's unique Azusa community and form of worship. When his efforts to assert his own brand of leadership proved unsuccessful, he scheduled a competing campaign from the fashionable Woman's Christian Temperance Union Building, causing the first schism among Pentecostals. Parham's rivalry in Los Angeles failed to take root permanently but for the rest of his life he denounced Seymour and the Azusa meetings in harsh terms.

After leaving Los Angeles Parham lost influence with his base of followers and co-workers in Texas, and fell back upon an independent ministry largely in the Midwest until his death in 1929. His enduring contribution to the movement lay in his championing of glossolalia and his recruiting of Seymour, through whom he indirectly influenced the beginning of the Azusa revival.

Synan cites the consensus describing Seymour's Azusa Mission as "the beginning of the modern Pentecostal Movement," going on to point out that "Directly or indirectly all of the pentecostal groups in existence can trace their lineage to the Azusa Mission."[18] J. Roswell Flower stated,

> The great impetus to the spread of the Pentecostal message world-wide came from Los Angeles. It was from Los Angeles the good news spread abroad, by word of mouth and the printed page, and it was to Los Angeles that hundreds of ministers came, received the Holy Ghost in Pentecostal fullness, and scattered out to all parts of the U.S.A. and Canada.[19]

Seymour's rare leadership launched the global Pentecostal movement from his small prayer group and humble mission building. But wait. By a curious turn of events, the meaning of Seymour's life and leadership was overlooked or distorted and demeaned by early historical reports. These first reports usually reflected conscious or unconscious racism from unappreciative or hostile critics both inside and outside the movement. For example Alma White, a Christian leader in Denver who later became an ideologist for the Ku Klux Klan, libeled Seymour with an influential but vituperative and heinous attack more than sufficient to make the very angels blush with shame.[20] The mere handful of other references to Seymour in the well-known early literature likewise suffered from obvious biases and prejudices of the authors and their times, rendering any meaningful or even fair treatment of Seymour and his leadership quite impossible.[21] The historical memory of Seymour's crucial leadership disappeared, and Seymour himself remained visible to history only in caricature form. Later scholarly attempts to describe and understand these early black roots of the renewal have been seriously hindered by this unfortunate legacy from racist elements in our past.

The fact remains that the Pentecostal-Charismatic renewal movement began among the black people under the leadership of a black man. Furthermore, Seymour attracted, welcomed, inspired, managed and sent forth all kinds and races of people successfully for over three years of decisive beginnings.

This truth soon proved embarrassing to white Pentecostals struggling to survive and prevail within an era dominated by the social pressures of deeply ingrained assumptions of white superiority and white supremacy. Something had to give. And so it happened that Seymour and his accomplishment became unappreciated, ignored, and forgotten in his own lifetime, while being supressed by history. The integrated movement separated along racial lines. Hollenweger observed,

> The miracle of the Spirit, where "the 'color line' was washed away in the blood" was not only forgotten but sometimes even shamefully hidden away. . . . The Pentecostal Revival was a contribution from the Black community to the white one. This has never been denied by white Pentecostals—it has only been forgotten. The reason for this "forgetting" was due to the fact that between 1908 and 1914 the Pentecostal

revival was—in opposition to what was declared the beginning of the revival—divided into two parts, one Black and one white. However, most Black denominations included white members and in some white denominations a few Black members remained. . . . The main reason for this segregation was the very heavy criticism of the traditional white denominations against the Pentecostals who disqualified Pentecostalism by pointing to its humble Black beginnings. It would therefore be unfair . . . to put the blame for this development wholly on the white Pentecostals. They just adapted themselves to what was considered decent American Protestantism. . . .[22]

George Orwell's novel *1984* coined the term *unperson* to describe the fate of those unwanted and rejected individuals whom the ones in power ordered to be stripped of all status and forgotten. The so-called Ministry of Truth operated a "memory hole," actually an opening to the central furnace down which embarrassing facts and supporting documents simply disappeared forever to oblivion.[23] Similarly Seymour, because of his black face, became an *unperson* without status, historically remembered if at all more by distortion and falsehood than truth. His instrumental leadership with its visionary dream of bringing everyone together in the church as on the Day of Pentecost, just disappeared down the "memory hole" operated by a racially biased culture.

But thankfully this did not happen until after Seymour's leadership and dream had already ignited and launched the major historic Christian renewal movement of our century. And fortunately, many of the original Seymour writings and historical materials were not destroyed permanently down any such "memory hole." Instead, they remained in large measure simply forgotten but awaiting recovery.[24]

Also, because of the tremendous power and appeal generated under Seymour's leadership at Azusa Mission, history could not completely forget. We can be grateful for the perceptive contemporary historians who have probed beyond the inadequacy of early historical treatment of Pentecostal origins, among whom are Anderson, Bloch-Hoell, Brumback, Conn, Golder, Hollenweger, Kendrick, Lovett, Menzies, Nichol, Synan, and Tinney. These studies enabled Sydney Ahlstrom, professor of church history at Yale, to transcend the historical caricature of Seymour, citing him as the very embodiment of black piety, and most influential black church leader in American religious

history, who overcame the color line to make possible the
blessings of Pentecost for everyone, not only in the USA but
all over the world.[25]

The greatness of Seymour's leadership may be seen by the
fact that he launched the movement in such a way that it could
go right on after forgetting him. Gerlach and Hine have explained this rare type of leadership.[26] It dispenses with the
more usual or authoritarian approach in favor of enabling
everyone, including the humblest individual believers, to fulfill
their own usually undreamed of potential for leadership.

Furthermore, as the movement turned away from Seymour
it began to separate along racial lines sometimes camouflaged
by administrative or doctrinal disagreements. This process provided a powerful if unintended tribute to the meaning of his
leadership, which had held the movement together through the
first critical years.

This development also reveals why Seymour was shunned as
an *unperson*: not because of any lack of ability on his part, but
on the contrary, precisely because of his rare ability to bring
together and to hold together all races. This ability was all too
soon perceived as a liability in view of the surrounding and
threatening racist society to which glossolalia did not appear
nearly so dangerous as the revolutionary Christian fellowship.

Seymour's life and leadership brought to modern Pentecost
a Christian perspective and dream forged in the fiery furnace
of 300 long years under bitter slavery and brutal repression.
Black-American Christians had long embraced the faith under
a system so cruel that it left them with an enduring discernment for sham and hypocrisy, and a profound understanding
of the gospel. Their widely acclaimed music bears eloquent
testimony to the power of this truth. As a result, Seymour
could grasp the meaning of Pentecost with a depth unattained
and probably unattainable by any white leader of his time.

Simply put, Seymour found in the Pentecostal experience a
new spirituality not only expressed by glossolalia, but even
more remarkably characterized by the overcoming of the color
line and other lesser barriers. The glossolalia was considered
integral, but not primarily a mark of individual spiritual attain-
ment. Rather it was seen as a kind of energy to be released and
directed to break the barriers blocking full Christian fellowship

Bishop William J. Seymour, c. 1922.

in the new spiritual community, thereby providing the most tremendous power of all, that of Pentecostal togetherness. H. Richard Niebuhr noted that early Christianity overcame the racial problem in the distinctive fellowship between Jews and Gentiles but this unusual feature soon disappeared from history, the principle if not the fact falling down the "memory hole" until modern times.[27]

The "third race" or human race beyond Jew or Gentile that early Christians considered themselves to be, has remained unrecovered by modern Christianity. Not only did the glossolalia of early Christian practice disappear from history but also the transracial fellowship. With this in mind, the entire development of Black-American Christianity may be seen in a new light.

All black Christianity in general, and Pentecostalism in particular, began with the hope of liberating black Christians— but white too-from American white racism and all its effects. Because of this historically new thrust, and the fact that black culture more closely approximates that of the ancient biblical lands rather than that of white America or Western civilization, Barrett and Hollenweger find among black Christians, and especially Pentecostals, "a new expression of Christianity."[28] This new version of Christianity should not mistakenly be confused with Protestantism but rather considered as unique and closely akin to scriptural faith.

It is impossible to exaggerate the damage that racism with its color line has inflicted upon the USA and Western civilization. Historically, for obvious reasons, black Americans have seen more clearly than whites the seriousness of the color line problem. In 1900 W. E. B. DuBois began writing prophetically, "The problem of the twentieth century is the problem of the color line."[29] In 1925 he traced the reasons for World War I to the struggle for racist domination of Africa.[30] When the racism of Hitler and the Nazi philosophy finally stood revealed for what it was, following World War II, many white Americans began to realize for the fist time the true horrors of racism and the tenacity of its hold on the human race. Black Americans had known this for a long time. Hitler may even be understood not as an aberration of our civilization but as a logical outcome of centuries of traditional racism. DuBois could have stated the problem in stronger terms. Racism has not been confined to the 20th century but has been the main problem throughout American history, and a major factor in all Western history as well. Arnold Toynbee surveyed all known civilizations of present and past to seek lessons of value for our own. He likened the American slaves to the early Christian slaves, finding hope for our future in the black American Christian heritage, saying,

> The Negro appears to be answering our tremendous challenge with a religious response which may prove in the event, when it can be seen in retrospect, to bear comparison with the ancient Oriental's response to the challenge from his Roman masters. . . . The Negro has adapted himself to his new social environment by rediscovering in Christianity certain original meanings and values which Western Christendom has long ignored. Opening a simple and impressionable mind to the Gospels, he has discovered that Jesus was a prophet who came into the world not to confirm the mighty in their seats but to exalt the humble and meek. The Syrian slave immigrants who once brought Christianity into Roman Italy performed the miracle of establishing a new religion which was alive in place of an old religion which was already dead. It is possible that the Negro slave immigrants who have found Christianity in America may perform the greater miracle of raising the dead to life. With their childlike spiritual intuition and their genius for giving spontaneous aesthetic expression to emotional religious experience, they may perhaps be capable of kindling the cold grey ashes of Christianity which have been transmitted to them by us until, in their hearts, the divine fire flows again. It is thus perhaps, if at all, that Christianity may conceivably become the living faith of a dying civilization for the second time. If this miracle were indeed to be performed by an American Negro church, that would be the most dynamic response to the challenge of social penalization that had yet been made by man.[31]

The renewal launched by Seymour from Azusa is evidently fulfilling Toynbee's longing. If it is true that Seymour and Azusa rediscovered a certain original meaning of Christianity long ignored by our civilization, with the power to transform believers while at the same time overcoming in the church the central human problem of our age, that would be a blessing incomparable. Seymour's vision for renewal of the church included room for such a vast conception. At the height of the Azusa revival he stated, "We are on the verge of the greatest miracle the world has ever seen."[32] Seymour did not live to see the completion of his dream but he fully expected the renewal to accomplish it.

Is it not true that our nation and civilization needs as never before its historic faith to lead the way into a renewed tomorrow? In the last century, as the USA grappled with the seemingly insoluble dilemma of slavery, the main Christian denominations, which contained the overwhelming majority of church members, could not agree and finally split between North and South over the issue, ca. 1845. Once American Christianity had effectively divided over slavery, not even Abraham Lincoln, one of the greatest statesmen of all time, could heal the nation's wounds or prevent an awesome war. Lincoln went on to portray that conflict as a judgment from Almighty God, because of the offense of slavery.

In that situation, the breakdown of Christian fellowship preceded and presaged the following political collapse. May we not dare to believe that the reverse can also be true? Seymour believed that a more complete coming together in the church could serve to heal the many division of its own body and thus our modern society. Toward this goal Seymour provided the coming together at Azusa which generated previously unheard of power for Christian personal, national, and global renewal.

The explosive spread of Seymour's Azusa achievement may be understood as the power of a spirituality allowed to operate without restriction from unchristian limitations derived from race, color, gender, nation, class or status. It is instructive that the breathtaking outreach from Azusa corresponded to the original Pentecostal event it was emulating. This stood in marked contrast to the meager results from Parham's efforts of 1901 to 1905. Despite the presence of glossolalia, Parham's efforts could not explode because they were limited and hindered by the same crucial barriers which had been overcome at Azusa. Parham himself confirmed this by demonstrating his inability to compete successfully against Azusa in Los Angeles.

Seymour's genius even defied the conventional wisdom of the "homogeneous unit principle," whereby it is recognized that people prefer to join churches without crossing racial, ethnic, national, class or linguistic lines. The wonder is not that Seymour could not permanently maintain leadership of such a countercultural movement but that such a surprising historical breakthrough could happen at all and continue under him for so long.

Azusa touched some deeply hidden chord of human responsiveness to bring forth such an immediate and overwhelming response against all conventional expectations. That the movement adapted itself to prevailing cultural racial patterns does not necessarily constitute failure of the Azusa dream. This adaptation and racial separation following the Azusa years appears to bear comparison with the pattern set when the early churches gradually moved away from the interracial fellowships St. Paul labored so tirelessly to establish and keep together. Just as those early churches grew and flourished even as the dream of inclusive togetherness faded, so have the congregations and denominations resulting from Azusa. Even so, we cannot overlook the fact that the powerful memories of togetherness lingering from Azusa could not be entirely forgotten, proving sufficient to fuel the renewal with momentum for a long and worthwhile growth. Notably, even following the Azusa years the renewal remained the most effectively integrated outreach in Western church history.

The Azusa renewal began with the hope of bringing authentic elements of early scriptural Christianity to the contemporary church. Glossolalia proved sensational, but the truly revolutionary thrust from Azusa depended upon the overcoming of the color line, which opened the possibility of turning a racist world upside down. The Azusa fellowship represented an important key not only for church renewal but also for social transformation, simply by its own witness to the surrounding culture. This truth was not fully recognized at the time, or it was judged as too visionary to be practical.

We shall never know with certainty what may have happened had those early Pentecostal leaders held unflinchingly to the inclusive Christian fellowship formed at Azusa. Doubtless the host of martyrs created by such a stand would have been awesome to behold. The movement might well have fallen victim to ruthless extermination. As history actually unfolded, the movement may have survived and grown in the only way it could. What we do know is that the impetus and memory of Azusa provided the necessary ingredient for many years of spectacular expansion.

Today, the Pentecostal-Charismatic movement is viewed as a significant worldwide force, not only from the historical

Pentecostal development but also from the charismatic expansion into the more traditional churches and denominations dating from ca. 1960. So far, the movement has utterly confounded the many critics who began predicting its early demise from the very beginning. One student of the movement observed in 1913:

> That strange zeal which appears to belong to fanaticism has certainly done its work within the last seven years. . . . it is plain that the meridian of its strength and influence has been passed. In this decline it is simply following in the wake of the similar movements which went before it, and it may expect no more than they. . . . it is built upon distorted interpretation of the Bible . . . its attitude toward the present order is unwholesome and ruinous. . . its set too great value upon certain minor passages of Scripture . . . its attitude toward apocalyptic Scripture is unhistorical in the extreme; and . . . it must go the way of all followings that are not optimistic, possessed of the teachings of history, and constructive. . . . we feel safe in saying that after a few decades, possibly longer, this movement will be practically forgotten. It is bound for the unknown regions whence it came.[33]

While the movement has confounded its critics, it has not yet fulfilled the highest hopes of its Azusa roots. The movement dreamed of restoring Pentecostal spirituality to modern Christianity. Concerning evangelism, glossolalia, and related charisms, the results accomplished have been remarkable. But when one searches modern Pentecostalism to find the community wherein "There is neither Jew nor Greek, there is neither bond nor free, there is neither male nor female," one wonders if it is possible to reclaim it from the memory hole of history. Beyond doubt the movement needs to make fresh contact with those life-giving roots that gave it birth and could yet sustain it to undreamed of heights of service to the larger church.

Surely Bishop Seymour would counsel us that this renewal is fully capable of doing everything it originally set out to do, and even more. He would believe this for the same reason that he would not have approved completely of the way in which this writer has attempted to honor him and his leadership. He would have maintained that it was all the work of that divine Spirit before whom no wise man seeks to take credit. And who would dispute the truth that insofar as this renewal has been the plan and work of that same Spirit, it will continue to be?

And that being the case, what limits could some mere mortal venture to set?

Let the question be posed in another way. Can that black face of church renewal become meaningful again to this movement? If so, then truly we could be on the verge of "the greatest miracle the world has ever seen." Worldwide Christianity has already become mostly non-white.[34] In the foreseeable future, if present trends continue, it is expected to become mostly third world by location and increasingly Pentecostal-Charismatic by orientation.[35] In our nuclear age when human division and divisiveness threaten all life on the planet, the visionary dream of a spiritual community based on Pentecostal inclusiveness offers a practicality relevant as never before. Knowing that the best political solutions follow spiritual solutions, can we hope for less than the fulfillment of that dream?

The deepest truth of Azusa lay not in the simple fact that diverse people came together but in how they came together. The whites came with love and true repentance for the way they felt about blacks and had treated them. The blacks came with love and genuine forgiveness. Orientals, native Americans, and others participated similarly. Arthur Osterberg who loved Azusa from start to finish, chronicled its deepest meaning as revealed by human tears, saying,

> The Azusa Revival began, where every revival should rightly begin, in repentant tears. It began in tears, it lived in tears, and when the tears ended the Azusa Revival ended.[36]

By a strange coincidence of history the name Azusa became characteristic of this renewal because of the little two-block-long street in the first black ghetto of Los Angeles where Seymour found an old church building available for what he had in mind. No one could have known that the name Azusa meant *blessed miracle*. Considerable scholarly research has analyzed the meaning of this name. It derives from the Shoshone Indians of Southern California, who now unfortunately have all passed from the earth along with their language. But in 1813 Indian oral tradition, believed to be trustworthy, was recorded by an early researcher. The name Azusa was first noted by Father Juan Crespi in 1769 while on the Portola expedition to explore California. At that time Azusa referred to the site of an old Indian village south of present-day Los Angeles in the San Gabriel canyon, near the Portola campsite.

It seems there once flowed a spring thought to be sacred, creating a lovely pool within a remote cave, where a young Indian maiden named Coma Lee often retired to pray and fast. She was gifted with healing power as she laid hands upon the sick to pray. One day, Ohal Ya, a stranger and son of a powerful regional chief, chanced to pass through the canyon. He fell admiringly in love with the maiden without a word passing between them. Later, when the son asked permission to marry, his father refused, neither knowing nor caring to know who the maiden was. He said, "My son shall not marry the daughter of a common Indian, my son shall marry only his equal."[37] The chief happened to be lying seriously ill at this time. After his condition deteriorated further and the medicine men despaired, he was finally taken as a last resort to seek the healing touch of Coma Lee, but without anyone realizing that the maiden of reputed healing powers and the son's longed-for bride were one and the same person.

After Coma Lee prayed and ministered to the chief he slept soundly and well all night, awaking marvelously restored and healed. With great appreciation and enthusiasm the chief conferred upon Coma Lee the special name *Azusa* commemorating the blessed miracle of healing.

When the chief realized that this young maiden was the very one his son loved, he humble begged their forgiveness and ordered a huge wedding celebration.

For many years Coma Lee, known as Azusa, continued her healing ministry while her fame spread over the Californias. The account concludes,

> Wherever there was suffering and pain people said, "Go to Azusa and be healed . . . go to Azusa." Through the swift-flowing years, the promise of surcease from all ills lay in those words. . . . "Go to Azusa. . . ." In the days after the simple Indian maid had passed on to the happy haven of her faith, returning her gift to the great deities who had bestowed it, the place where she lived and ministered came to be called Azusa in memory of her healing hands of mercy.[38]

The black face of church renewal has invited us to go to Azusa to find a blessed miracle of healing for a Christianity whose body has been too long wounded and divided. When the tears of renewal return, the spirit of Azusa shall not have been in vain, and the blessed miracle of healing will come. The old Azusa Mission disappeared long ago but wherever Christians truly come together, a bit of Azusa lives on.

Notes

1. David B. Barrett, ed., *World Christian Encyclopedia: A Comparative Study of Churches and Religions in the Modern World, AD 1900–2000* (London: Oxford University, 1982). The 1985 world figure of 114 million is understated in that it contains a 30 million estimate of nonaffiliated adherents in 1980 which Barrett did not update to 1985. The 114 million should be seen in the numerical context of world Christianity for which Barrett's figures are: 1980 (1, 432, 686, 519); 1985 (1, 548, 592, 187); 2000 (projected, 2, 019, 921, 366).

2. *Time* (May 3, 1982) 67; cp. Barrett, *World*, 14.

3. Michael Ramsey, Robert E. Terwilliger and A. M. Allchin, *The Charismatic Christ* (New York: Morehouse-Barlow, 1973) 68.

4. Kenneth Kantzer, "The Charismatics Among Us," *CT* (February 22, 1980) 25–29.

5. *1984 Britannica Book of the Year*, 704.

6. Re this understanding, cf. most standard dictionary listings under "century."

7. Personal interviews with D. William Faupel, 1978, and Pauline Parham, 1979; A. C. Valdez and James F. Scheer, *Fire on Azusa Street* (Costa Mesa, California: Gift, 1980) 17–18.

8. Douglas J. Nelson, *"For Such A Time As This," The Story of Bishop William J. Seymour and the Azusa Street Revival: A Search for Pentecostal-Charismatic Roots* (Ph.D. thesis, University of Birmingham, England, 1981) 55, 66–67, n. 10.

9. *Confidence: A Pentecostal Paper for Great Britain*, Monkwearmouth, Sunderland; A. A. Boddy, editor (September 1910) 223.

10. D. William Faupel, "This Gospel of the Kingdom," first draft, unpublished Ph.D. thesis, University of Birmingham, England (1981) 1.

11. Nelson, *For Such A Time As This*, 1, 17.

12. Cf. Acts 9:4.

13. Nelson, *For Such A Time As This*, 208, 238 n. 134.

14. Charles F. Parham, *The Everlasting Gospel*, privately printed 911; reprinted 1942 (no location given for either date).

15. Vinson Synan, *The Holiness-Pentecostal Movement in the United States* (Grand Rapids: Eerdmans, 1971) 165.

16. *Confidence* (September, 1912) 209.

17. Frank Bartleman, *How Pentecost Came to Los Angeles: As It Was In The Beginning, Old Azusa Mission—From My Diary*, privately printed (no location given, but presumably Los Angeles since his Los Angeles address is given for ordering, [3]1925) 54.

18. Synan, *Holiness-Pentecostal Movement*, 114.

19. J. Roswell Flower, "Historical Review of the Pentecostal Movement," address to the World Pentecostal Conference, Stockholm, 1955.

20. Alma White, *Demons and Tongues* (Zarephath, New Jersey, 1949; reprinted privately from the 1910 version) 67-73.

21. Nelson, *For Such A Time As This*, 81-108.

22. Walter J. Hollenweger, "The Black Pentecostal Concept," *Concept* (special issue no. 30; Geneva: World Council of Churches, June, 1970) 15-17.

23. George Orwell, *1984* (rpt. 1949; with a preface by Walter Cronkite and an afterword by Erich Fromm; New York: New American Library/Harcourt Brace Jovanovich, 1983) 34-35, 40-41.

24. Nelson, *For Such A Time As This*, 6, 324-38.

25. Sydney E. Ahlstrom, *A Religious History of the American People* (New Haven: Yale University, 1972) 1059. Ahlstrom's assessment of Seymour as "the most influential black leader in American religious history" is not so astounding if he is properly credited with the decisive leadership at the Azusa Mission, the fountainhead of the current 114 million Christians in the Pentecostal-Charismatic Renewal. In the context of American religious leaders, Ahlstrom's perception of Martin Luther King, Jr., may perhaps be discerned by his description of the great gathering of 25,000 persons in Selma, Alabama in 1965 as being so momentous that "it took on almost Pentecostal significance," 1073.

26. Luther P. Gerlach and Virginia H. Hine, *People, Power, Change: Movements of Social Transformation* (Indianapolis, Indiana: Bobbs-Merrill, 1970) 34-41.

27. H. Richard Niebuhr, *The Social Sources of Denominationalism* (rpt. 1929; New York: New American Library/Times Mirror, 1957) 238.

28. Barrett, *World*, 60-62.

29. W. E. Burghardt DuBois, *The Souls of Black Folk* (rpt. 1903; New York: New American Library, 1969) 54.

30. Alain Locke, ed., *The New Negro* (rpt. 1925; New York: Arno, 1968) 385-414.

31. Arnold J. Toynbee, *A Study of History: Abridgement of volumes I-VI* (ed. D. C. Somervell; London: Oxford University, 1946) 129.

32. Nelson, *For Such A Time As This*, 216.

33. C. W. Shumway, *A Study of 'The Gift of Tongues'* (A.B. thesis, University of Southern California, Los Angeles, 1914) 191-92.

34. Barrett, *World*, 836, defines "non-white" as "A collective term referring to all races and ethno-linguistic groups distinct from the White races indigenous to Europe and North America." He gives the

global non-white population as follows: 1970 (2, 762, 999, 700); 1980 (3, 455, 726, 800); 1985 (3, 826, 509, 500). Barrett assesses the impact of numerical growth in this non-white category by observing:

> The composition of the Christian world has changed markedly since the year 1900. At the turn of the century, Christians were 88.7% Caucasian (Caucasoid) by race and 81.1% White by colour. . . . By 1980, massive church growth in the Third World had reduced these proportions to 70.0% Caucasian and to as low as 50.5% White. By 1981, Non-Whites formed a majority of all Christians for the first time for twelve hundred years. And by AD 2000, Non-White are expected to account for 60.1% of all Christians (9).

35. David B. Barrett, "AD 2000: 350 Million Christians in Africa," *International Review of Mission* 59 (January 1970) 39–54.

36. Nelson, *For Such A Time As This*, 302.

37. Ibid., 320.

38. Ibid., 321.

12

LEVI LUPTON: A FORGOTTEN PIONEER OF EARLY PENTECOSTALISM

Gary B. McGee

A MERICAN PENTECOSTALISM SUFFERED the embarrassment of two scandals in the first decade of its existence (1901–1910). Best known is the case of Charles F. Parham who directed the Bethel Bible School in Topeka, Kansas, where the first Pentecostal revival took place in which speaking in tongues was identified with a distinctive interpretation of baptism in the Holy Spirit.[1] Parham, accused of a sexual offense in 1906, refuted the charge and continued his ministry.[2]

The second and less well-known scandal involved Levi R. Lupton, a prominent early leader from Alliance, Ohio. However, unlike Parham, who denied any wrongdoing, Lupton publicly confessed to adultery and eliminated any question about his immoral behavior.[3] After his demise a virtual conspiracy of silence ensued among Pentecostal writers familiar with him. Such leaders and authors as J. Roswell Flower, a founding father of the Assemblies of God; Joseph H. King, an early leader in the Fire-Baptized Holiness and Pentecostal Holiness Churches; and Frank Bartleman, a participant at the Azusa Street Revival, and evangelist, referred to Lupton's Bible school and annual camp meeting in Ohio, but studiously avoided mentioning his name.[4] Concern to protect the offender, ironically a staunch defender of the Wesleyan-holiness view of sanctification, should not be presumed as the motivation for their omissions of his name. Rather they reflect embarrassment and moral outrage. This "conspiracy of silence" resulted in Lupton's being virtually ignored as a guiding force in early Pentecostalism, and he remains an obscure figure even to this day, despite his impact upon Pentecostalism.

Lupton's ministry falls into two distinct divisions: (1) his ministry as a Quaker evangelist, pastor, and administrator of a missionary agency; and (2) his efforts in the same capacities as a Pentecostal. This investigation examines his transition from Quaker to Pentecostal, the annual camp meetings he sponsored, and his contributions to foreign missions.

Lupton's Controversial Quaker Ministry

Levi Rakestraw Lupton (1860–1929) was born in Smith Township near Beloit, Ohio, into a devout Quaker family. Years later, Levi and his wife Laura, his brother Isaac, and other Quakers from the area migrated westward where Levi established the village of Lupton, Michigan.[5] Property was purchased and a community established.

Despite his upbringing, Lupton did not profess conversion until July of 1885. Later that year, having come into contact with the Wesleyan-holiness perspective on sanctification,[6] he reported that

> conviction again seized my heart, this time for a second work, which resulted in leading me to an altar of prayer and consecration. After three days and nights, which meant real death to carnality and a resurrection to newness of life, I received the Holy Ghost.[7]

Four days later, he felt the unmistakable call to become a preacher. Moving back to Ohio, he was ordained a minister by the East Goshen Monthly Meeting (a local church). By 1896, his health began to fail; however, at the annual gathering of the Ohio Yearly Meeting of Friends, he claimed to receive a complete healing. Lupton thereafter joined the advocates of faith healing.

Evangelistic ministry followed and he dedicated his first "tabernacle" (tent) for holding evangelistic services.[8] Sensing the need to establish a meeting house in Alliance, Ohio, and assisted by the sponsorship of the East Goshen congregation (located a few miles away), Lupton began evangelistic services in his tent there on May 1, 1900. A revival occurred and the following year the fledgling congregation dedicated a newly constructed building debt-free.[9] Lupton remained as pastor for several years and started a camp meeting in 1901 which convened annually for nine years.

Theological Perspectives Before 1907

Lupton viewed himself as a radical holiness preacher and evangelist. Even though he spent periods of time serving as a pastor, the sawdust trail had the greatest appeal for him. In his opinion, it was the responsibility of God's people "to spread holiness over every civilized land and proclaim it through the world."[10]

According to his "Cardinal Lines of Truth," the new birth ranked first. Following this experience, the second definite work of sanctification received priority because, in his words,

> the most radical preaching of the new birth will never justify you in omitting or minimizing the second definite work of grace, whereby the new-born soul is sanctified by the baptism with the Holy Ghost. Care should be taken in this connection to preach the eradication of the old man. At the same time be careful to remind all that they are yet in the world, subject to temptations, and that their safety depends, not alone upon their experience, but upon a constant reliance upon the means of Divine grace.[11]

Avoiding the fire-baptized theology of some such as Benjamin Hardin Irwin, who advocated a third experience of grace (a baptism in the Holy Spirit for power in Christian witness), Lupton taught that the "power for service" accompanied the "power for cleansing."[12]

His tenets of faith included a premillennial eschatology and belief in faith healing. In regard to the latter, he maintained that the gospel provides "a renewing for our bodies here and now, even to the extent that otherwise incurable diseases may be driven from the human system."[13]

Finally, it should be noted that Lupton's theology and approaches to ministry were deeply affected by the perspectives on faith articulated and illustrated by George Müller, the late-19th-century British philanthropist.[14]

Controversial Methods

For the conservative membership of the Ohio Yearly Meeting, Levi Lupton must have appeared as a wild-eyed visionary. His camp meetings and revivalistic evangelism created controversy, and his emphasis on faith healing further aggravated the relationship. Nevertheless, his eloquence and successful evangelism propelled him into the limelight.

In 1903 Lupton purchased a railroad car and designated it "The Gospel Car." Since the railroads at that time provided excellent passenger service, Lupton and his band of helpers utilized this means of travel to conduct revival services and camp meetings.[15]

In the summer of the same year, Lupton also purchased 12 acres of property 3 miles southwest of the public square in Alliance and built the "Missionary Home." This large, wood-framed building, three stories in height, served as a headquarters and faith home (a place where seekers could come for instruction and prayer for physical and spiritual needs). The Gospel Car and the Missionary Home became departments of the World Evangelization Company that Lupton and his associates later founded in 1904.[16] A periodical, *The New Acts*, commenced in October, 1904, to publicize the activities and teachings of the organization.[17]

On October 4, 1905, Lupton opened the Missionary Training School at the Missionary Home "to Scripturally teach and train laborers on radical, Apostolic lines . . . seeking under God to lead them into the deepest spiritual life and to the use of the best possible methods of work for the Master."[18] The curriculum included the following courses: Old Testament, Bible on Missions, The Gifts, New Testament, History of Missions, and Doctrines.[19]

The highlight of this period came when the World Evangelization Company attempted to establish a mission station in Africa in 1905. Following the pattern of faith advocated by George Müller, a party of seven (Levi R. Lupton, William M. Smith, Jefferson W. and Helen M. Ford and their daughter Clara, Charles and Kitty Kurtzhalz) set out for England and eventually Nigeria with only their railroad and steamship

tickets and eight dollars in cash.[20] Their needs were supplied
by gifts along the way. After locating a site for mission
work, Lupton and his associate, William M. Smith, returned to
America, leaving the others to continue the work.

The lack of preparation for the field, the faith approach to
financial resources, which did not work as well in practice as it
did in theory, and illnesses that the missionaries contracted in
the field, forced their departure shortly after Lupton's return
to America. This experience on the mission field, although
devoid of lasting results, moved him into the position of a
missionary statesman both among his Quaker and holiness
followers and the Pentecostals with whom he later identified.

Difficulties Increase

Because of the African venture and for other reasons, the
Ohio Yearly Meeting of Friends and its district in the Alliance
area, the Damascus Quarterly Meeting, kept a sharp eye on
the independent enterprises which Lupton had developed.
Otherwise, he usually followed their ecclesiastical policies. The
beginning of a breach dated back at least to 1904 when Lupton
sought permission to journey to Africa.[21] The Alliance congregation granted him permission, but this decision found opposition within the Quarterly Meeting. The representatives to
this body did not criticize his burden for evangelizing the lost,
but stated:

> we do not as a meeting see our way clear to endorse . . . an individual and
> independent work of the character and magnitude proposed. We trust that
> in humble, patient, prayerful waiting before God the brother will see his
> way clear to affiliate with some missionary organization in the opening
> and development of the work to which he feels himself called.[22]

Ignoring this advice, Lupton took a leave of absence from his
congregation and traveled to Africa. When he returned, pressure from the membership forced him to resign and pursue
itinerant evangelism.[23]

Difficulties multiplied in 1906. Financially, the World Evangelization Company was overextended and mismanaged. The
organization sold the Gospel Car to pay off its mortgage and
the plight of the entire operation required a new financial
policy.[24] Furthermore, the Quarterly Meeting appointed an

oversight committee in May to ensure "that the work may harmonize with the various lines of work under the care of the Yearly Meeting."[25] Finally, in September, Lupton suspended publication of *The New Acts*. Presumably his evangelistic work continued, but the hopes and aspirations for his enterprises must have dimmed. Perhaps he hoped for a brighter day.

Lupton's Pentecostal Experience

News of the Azusa Street Revival[26] set in course a chain of events that changed Lupton's ministry and breathed fresh hope into his vision for world missions and into his ministry in Alliance. Pentecostal meetings began on December 5, 1906, at the Union Gospel Mission in Akron pastored by C. A. McKinney,[27] a former Christian and Missionary Alliance missionary to Africa. They were conducted by Ivey Campbell of East Liverpool, Ohio, who had just returned from Los Angeles. She was the first person to bring the Pentecostal message of a baptism in the Spirit evidenced by speaking in tongues to Ohio. Lupton and some of his co-workers went to Akron and were convinced that her teaching was genuine. Upon returning to Alliance, he began to conduct services hoping for such a revival.

On December 30th Lupton professed to receive this new baptism of power. At 10 a.m., the service began with from thirty to forty people in attendance. He recounted later that after he began to pray

> I soon found myself on the floor under His gracious power, where I remained for nine hours. . . . My prayer upon this morning was one of consecrating my body as I had never understood it before. He took me at my word and really took possession. I then became perfectly helpless and for a season my entire body became cold, and I was unable to move even to the extent that I could not wink an eye for a short time.[28]

Full consciousness returned and after four hours of prayer,

> I began to speak in other tongues. The dear Lord had taken my jaws and vocal organs and moved them in His own peculiar manner, as was witnessed by many of those who stood by. . . . I was given a number of messages to people in a personal way, and was permitted to interpret many things which I spoke. At this time I wish to have it well understood that I was not seeking the gift of tongues, but the gift of the Holy Ghost,

> holding myself open to receive any of the promised gifts, (I Cor. 12:7-11) which He saw fit to bestow upon me, and it pleased Him to give me the gift of tongues.[29]

Lupton's wife, Laura, reported that "a halo lit upon his brow."[30] Ivey Campbell as well as some of his followers recalled that he spoke in five different languages.[31]

To these early Pentecostals, speaking in tongues represented the evidence for the Pentecostal baptism. Their holiness theology, with its emphasis on a subsequent experience of sanctification following salvation, laid the groundwork for a third experience, a baptism of power. The apostolic power of the early church had reappeared "in the last days" before the premillennial coming of Christ. Only those who had received this experience would be ready when Christ returned.[32]

Like other early Pentecostals, in particular Charles F. Parham, William J. Seymour, Florence Crawford, and A. G. Garr, world missions and speaking in tongues were closely linked. This new gift was thought to be xenolalia, the ability to speak in a human language otherwise unknown to the speaker, but understood by the hearer. By this means, they reasoned, the pace of world evangelism would increase, since the missionaries could immediately receive the necessary language preparation and the dynamic power of the Holy Spirit. It is unclear whether Lupton changed his perspective on the meaning of tongues (as most Pentecostals did) before his demise in 1910.

Local controversy over the recent happenings at the Missionary Home erupted almost immediately. Reporters flocked to interview Lupton and others who professed receiving the Pentecostal baptism. One reporter commented that

> he [Lupton] was not known to the world until during the past week when he sprang into sudden prominence by his claim of the gift of tongues. His name is now known from ocean to ocean and the public are anxiously awaiting the sequel to the strange gifts received at the Home.[33]

Much of the publicity took a skeptical turn.[34] The recent events at the Home proved particularly painful to the local Quakers and the Damascus Quarterly Meeting. Local members had mixed reactions to the news. Even though Lupton had resigned from the church in 1905, some remained loyal to him.

A parting of the ways followed quickly. William M. Smith, his associate in the World Evangelization Company, left the

Missionary Home and Lupton. More seriously, Edward Mott, the clerk of the Ohio Yearly Meeting, traveled to Alliance and from the pulpit of the Friends Church denounced Lupton for teaching the "third blessing" heresy.[35] He maintained that "the gift of tongues or languages was taught in our schools today and in this way the Lord expected man to learn the languages." When he personally queried Lupton as to the evidence for the new gift, the latter replied that it was the ability to converse with another person in a foreign language given by the Holy Spirit. Mott denied that such evidence could be found.[36]

Dismissal by the Quarterly Meeting followed swiftly on February 9, 1907, when the oversight committee submitted its report. Interestingly enough, it mentioned two reasons: (1) disloyalty for holding services within the area of the Alliance Monthly Meeting after Lupton had been expressly requested not to do so, and (2) refusal to abandon all independent work and support only the ministries of the Ohio Yearly Meeting.[37] Nothing is said about the gift of tongues. Apparently the Quarterly Meeting preferred to bypass the theological issue which had probably precipitated the submission of the report at that time.

Pentecostal Ministry

Lupton's evangelistic background, fiery preaching, former Quaker status, and recent "persecution" for his Spirit-baptism must have impressed the early Pentecostals. In view of such established institutions as the Missionary Home, the Missionary Training School, and the annual camp meeting, Lupton, C. A. McKinney, Ivey Campbell, and others agreed that Alliance, Ohio, should serve as "the headquarters for this gracious Pentecostal movement in this part of the country."[38] His plans for the future began to take shape with the republication of *The New Acts* in February of 1907.

In league with McKinney and Campbell, Lupton continued the annual camp meeting in Alliance. This event, particularly the one held in June of 1907, proved to be a significant milestone in the advance of the Pentecostalism in the Northeast. Fanny Van Dyke, who traveled from Youngstown, Ohio, to attend, called this the first Pentecostal camp meeting in the East.[39] More accurately, Frank Bartleman referred to it as the first in the Northeast.[40] Historians of Pentecostalism have taken little note of this event; what little mention has been made is partially marred by inaccuracy.[41] Perhaps if Lupton had remained as a leader in the movement, the memory and significance of this gathering would have endured.

Several factors point to the importance of the gathering. First of all, prominent early Pentecostals participated in the services. Frank Bartleman may have been second only to Lupton in directing the services.[42] Speakers also included A. S. Copley, W. A. Cramer, A. F. Mitchell, C. A. McKinney, Ivey Campbell, Joseph H. King, and E. B. Walker from as far away as Winnipeg, Canada. Others such as J. Roswell Flower, T. K. Leonard, Alice C. Wood, and George Fisher from Toronto also attended.[43] In addition, two later women missionaries from Zion City, Illinois, Bernice Lee and Edith Baugh, journeyed to the meeting.

People came from California, Tennessee, Georgia, Delaware, Pennsylvania, Ohio, Massachusetts and other states, as well as Canada. Many came seeking the Pentecostal baptism. The attendance indicates the importance attached to the occasion. One estimate placed the number at 700 persons from 21 states. The figure may have been larger.[44]

A second factor reminiscent of the Azusa Street Revival was the report that although Lupton was the nominal leader, the Holy Spirit provided the real direction for the services, which sometimes lasted all night. Men as well as women participated. Bartleman, reflecting a radical restorationist's perspective on worship, reported,

> no organ or hymn books were used. The Spirit conducted the services and there seemed no place for them. Numbers were saved, baptized in the Spirit, and healed. Many received a call to foreign fields, to prove God along real faith, Bible lines. The rapid evangelism of the world, on real apostolic lines, was the goal set.[45]

However, the reporters for the Alliance newspaper viewed the events differently: "The best of order prevails outside the tent, but within, it is bedlam, when once in full swing."[46]

The attendance of blacks and whites constitutes a third factor which also parallels the Azusa Revival. It is noteworthy that Lupton welcomed both, and their tents were intermingled. This open attitude toward blacks characterized other Pentecostals at the time; however, Lupton's Quaker heritage was a key factor here.[47]

The ecumenical tone of the gathering represents a fourth point of importance. Creedal backgrounds were minimized. One writer recounted that "churches, creeds, beliefs and doctrines are not touched upon. They all belong to one family."[48] This minimizing of doctrinal distinctives to focus on Spirit-baptism and evangelism also characterized early Pentecostalism.

Finally, the camp meeting attempted to establish a permanent institution to expedite world evangelization. Unlike the Azusa Street Revival, which produced no agency for this purpose, those in attendance witnessed on June 25, 1907, the formation of the Apostolic Evangelization Association with Lupton as the director. This happened, however, after many had already left for their homes. The new organization designated him the "Apostle Levi." The signatures of George E. David, I. O. Courtney, Frank Bartholomew, and Lewis C. Grant joined that of Lupton on the document of incorporation.[49] The objective was to establish

> an interdenominational association, and did not require one to sever his connection with the church to which he belonged. This association would have its headquarters in Ohio. The school was to be run under its auspices, and a printing plant was to be established at that place. . . . Many leaders from various parts of the state were included in this association. The prospect for a great work to be accomplished throughout the world seemed to be held out before this representative body.[50]

While many, including Lupton, had left or been dismissed from their churches because of their new-found theology, and consequently often held strong anti-organizational sentiments, those who gathered on this occasion were willing to foster an agency to aid the cause of evangelism before the imminent return of Christ. This could possibly be attributed to the presence of Pentecostals who had left the Christian and Missionary Alliance and had a more positive view toward organization. The initial willingness of Joseph H. King, general overseer of the Fire-Baptized Holiness Church and thus a recognized denominational leader, to edit *The New Acts* might have been another influence.[51] Indeed, the perceived stature of Lupton, particularly his previous world travel and missionary endeavor in Africa, probably helped to convince those in attendance that a mutual effort was the order of the day.

Later Activities

In the months and years that followed, Lupton continued his climb into prominence. This was partially assisted by preaching engagements around the country, including the missions conventions at the Stone Church in Chicago, his popular annual camp meeting in Alliance, and the growing recognition of the Missionary Training School, one of the earliest in the movement.[52] One student, Harry Horton, traveled from as far as Winnipeg, Canada, in 1908, to attend classes. His son, Stanley M. Horton, later became one of the foremost theologians of modern Pentecostalism.

The sources which describe Lupton's activities after 1907 to the end of his ministry in December of 1910 are limited and only a few issues of *The New Acts* are currently available. Although the camp meetings continued, the crowds declined in size. Nevertheless, notable Pentecostal speakers, such as Minnie T. Draper,[53] Elizabeth R. "Mother" Wheaton, [54] and Alexander Boddy[55] from England, addressed those who came.

The interest in missions continued. Even though the Apostolic Evangelization Association failed (for reasons currently unknown), the 1908 camp meeting adopted a "missionary manifesto" stating: "We believe that the formation of any ruling body would not meet the approval of God's baptized people, but that such an affiliation of Pentecostal Missions is desirable as will preserve and increase the tender sweet bond of love and fellowship now existing and guard against abuse of legitimate liberty."[56] This may have been the first call among independent Pentecostals for a missionary agency.

An important development occurred with the establishment of the Pentecostal Missionary Union (U.S.A.) following the annual camp meeting on July 6, 1909.[57] Lupton, of course, was chosen to direct it. The new organization supported approximately seventy-five missionaries, some of whom had been trained at the school in Alliance. It should be noted however, that many of these individuals simply advertised their ministries through *The New Acts* and received assistance from the readerships of other periodicals as well.

Conclusion

The Azusa Street Revival sparked similar spiritual awakenings around the country. Such was the influence behind the 1907 camp meeting at Alliance, Ohio, sponsored by Lupton. While it attracted believers from many parts of the country, it also resulted in the early establishment of a beachhead for Pentecostalism in the Northeast.

In some ways, it was reminiscent of the happenings at Azusa Street. The similarities appear in the recognition of the Spirit's leadership in the services, the emphasis on Spirit-baptism with speaking in tongues, the priority of signs and wonders in world evangelism before the imminent return of Christ, the underlying belief of sanctification as a second definite experience in the life of the believer, the elimination of racial lines in worship and participation, and the role allowed for women. The Quaker heritage of Lupton, however, contributed a distinctive influence (particularly on racial attitudes) which may have been unique.

While Alliance never became the center for Pentecostalism that Lupton envisioned, his Missionary Home and Training School, annual camp meetings, and *The New Acts* influenced many early believers. In a period of strong anti-organizational inclinations, Lupton and his associates convinced a large number of Pentecostals to support two nondenominational agencies for overseas evangelism: the Apostolic Evangelization Association and, later, the Pentecostal Missionary Union. These probably represent the earliest efforts among independent Pentecostals to establish an organization to accomplish their objectives in foreign missions.

Finally, Lupton had become one of Pentecostalism's better-known preachers and advocates of foreign missions. His institutions at Alliance, forceful pulpit ministry, and recent "persecution" by the Quakers propelled him into an instant leadership role. It should be noted that the Pentecostals were probably unaware of the controversy that surrounded his Quaker ministry. With his moral failure in 1910 and the considerable publicity which it received, his followers and associates felt betrayed. This embarrassment led Flower, King, and Bartleman to bar his name from their memoirs, but not the significance of what was achieved at Alliance.

While this turn of events caused considerable damage to the new movement in Alliance it did not retard the expansion of Pentecostalism in Ohio and the adjoining states. For the most part, the belief in the sanctified life and the reality of the baptism in the Holy Spirit—held by so many—could not be shaken by one man's failure. With the great outpouring of the Holy Spirit taking place at the end of time, Satan's hostility could be expected. A leader had fallen, but God would nevertheless triumph now that human history was drawing to a close.

Notes

1. "Evangelist is Arrested," *The San Antonio Light*, July 19 1907, p. 1; "Voliva Split Hits Preacher," *The San Antonio Light*, July 24, 1907, p. 2. For some historical perspective on this distinctive interpretation, cf. William W. Menzies, "The Holy Spirit in Christian Theology," *Perspectives on Evangelical Theology* (ed. K. Kantzer and S. Gundry; Grand Rapids: Baker, 1979) 67–80.
2. For more information on the charges against Parham, cf. Robert Mapes Anderson, *Vision of the Disinherited: The Making of American Pentecostalism* (New York: Oxford University, 1979) 272–73, n. 8.
3. "Founder of Missionary Home Confesses to Sin," *The Alliance Daily Review*, December 13, 1910, pp. 1, 3.
4. J. Roswell Flower, "Historical Review of the Pentecostal Movement," *The Pentecostal Testimony*, September 1955, p. 13; Joseph H. King and Blanche L. King (Franklin Springs, Georgia: Pentecostal Holiness Church, 1949) 131–32, 136–37; Frank Bartleman, *How Pentecost Came to Los Angeles* (2nd ed.; Los Angeles: By the author, 1925) 104–5, 115–16, 122; the earlier historians of the Ohio Yearly Meeting of Friends (now known as the Evangelical Friends Church) have generally given only passing reference to his ministry and have completely ignored the widely known controversy within their ranks in the first decade of this century. For a significant history which omits all reference to the issue, see Edward Mott, *The Friends Church: In the Light of Its Recent History* (Portland: Loomis, n.d.). Mott had strongly condemned Lupton's Pentecostal theology and urged his ouster from the Damascus Quarterly Meeting and hence from the Ohio Yearly Meeting in 1907.
5. C. E. McPherson, *Life of Levi R. Lupton: Twentieth Century Apostle of the Gift of Tongues, Divine Healer, Etc.* (Alliance, Ohio: By the author, 1911). This may be the first biography to have been written about a Pentecostal leader. The author, perhaps a local reporter, focuses much

of his attention on Lupton's adultery and the events surrounding the public disclosure of it. The book, nevertheless, contains important information on the earlier part of his life. As there are some inaccuracies in the book, an examination of pertinent information in *The New Acts* and *The Alliance Daily Review* helps to establish a more precise perspective on Lupton's life and ministry.

6. For information on the Wesleyan-holiness view of sanctification, cf. Vinson Synan, *The Holiness-Pentecostal Movement in the United States* (Grand Rapids: Eerdmans, 1971) 13–34.

7. Levi R. Lupton, "My Conversion and Call," *The New Acts*, October 1904, p. 3.

8. Ibid.

9. Minutes of the Eighty-Eighth Ohio Yearly Meeting of the Friends Church held at Damascus, Ohio, 1900, p. 17; *Pictorial Directory of the First Friends Church* (Alliance, Ohio, 1976).

10. "'Ye Shall Be Witnesses:' An Exhortation to the Holiness Preachers and Evangelists of America," *The New Acts*, May 10, 1906, p. 1.

11. Ibid.

12. Ibid., p. 2.

13. Ibid.

14. For example, see "George Müller's Acts, IV," *The New Acts*, May 1905, p. 7.

15. L. R. Lupton, "Origin, Review and Prospects," *The New Acts*, February 15, 1906, p. 2.

16. For information on the objectives and departments of the World Evangelization Company, see the Appendix in William M. Smith's *Chapters from the New Acts: An Account of the First Missionary Journey of the World Evangelization Company to Africa—1904-1905* (Alliance, Ohio: World Evangelization Company, ca. 1906).

17. The inspiration for the name of the new publication came from Arthur T. Pierson's addresses at the Duff Missionary Lectureship given in Scotland in 1893 which were later published as *The New Acts of the Apostles or the Marvels of Modern Missions* (London: Nesbit, 1894).

18. "Opening of School," *The New Acts*, October 12, 1905, pp. 1–2.

19. Ibid., p. 2.

20. "Brought to Completion," *The New Acts*, February 1, 1906, pp. 1–4; McPherson, *Life*, 89–96.

21. Minutes of the Alliance Monthly Meeting, August 4, 1904.

22. Minutes of the Alliance Monthly meeting, September 1, 1904. It is interesting to note that the Ohio Yearly Meeting had no African missionaries at the time. Their attention seems to have focused on the Orient. For information, cf. Walter Rollin Williams, *These Fifty Years With Ohio Friends in China* (Damascus, Ohio: Friends Foreign Missionary Society of Ohio Yearly Meeting, ca. 1940) 11–17. This interest on the part of the Friends may have been partially

responsible for Lupton's willingness to attempt an independent African venture.

23. "No Evidence of Gift of Tongues," *The Alliance Daily Review*, January 14, 1907, p. 1.

24. "Rigid Future Faith Policy," *The New Acts*, May 31, 1906, pp. 4–6.

25. "Damascus Quarterly Meeting Minute," *The New Acts*, May 31, 1906, p. 6.

26. For more information on the Azusa Street Revival and its significance, cf. Synan, *Holiness-Pentecostal Movement*, 95–116; for a more recent perspective, cf. Douglas Nelson's contribution to this volume, "The Black Face of Church Renewal: The Meaning of a Charismatic Explosion, 1901–1985."

27. For information on Claude Adams McKinney, cf. "Our Heritage," (Akron, Ohio: First Assembly of God, n.d.) pp. 1–6. (Mimeographed.)

28. Levi R. Lupton, "Testimony," *The New Acts*, February 1907, p. 3.

29. Ibid.

30. "Claim Gift of Tongues," *The Canton Repository*, January 4, 1907, p. 6.

31. Ivey Campbell, "Report from Ohio and Pennsylvania," *The Apostolic Faith*, February–March 1907, p. 5.

32. "This is That," *The New Acts*, February 1907, p. 1.

33. "The Gift of Tongues; Is It From God?" *The Alliance Daily Review*, January 7, 1907, p. 1.

34. For further information, see "The Day of Miracles; The 'Gift of Tongues,'" *The Alliance Daily Review*, January 2, 1907, p. 1.; "Mystic Creed Mere Frenzy," *The Alliance Daily Review*, January 8, 1907, pp. 1,3; "Claim Gift of Tongues," *The Canton Repository*, January 4, 1907, p. 6; one writer contributed a poem to the Alliance newspaper which mocked speaking in tongues and was printed on the front page; for the poem, see James W. Harter, "That Gift of Tongues," *The Alliance Daily Review*, January 9, 1907, p. 1.

35. "No Evidence of Gift of Tongues," *The Alliance Daily Review*, January 14, 1907, p. 1. For a brief account of the penetration of holiness theology into the Ohio Yearly Meeting, cf. Charles Edwin Jones, *Perfectionist Persuasion: The Holiness Movement and American Methodism, 1867–1936* (ATLAMS 5; Metuchen, New Jersey: Scarecrow, 1974) 60–61.

36. Lupton did attempt to provide the necessary proof in "Pentecost Proved," *The New Acts*, April 1907, p. 4.

37. Minutes of the Damascus Quarterly Meeting, February 9, 1907. For a description of Lupton's perspective on the dismissal, see Lydia Markley Piper, "A Journey and Its Lessons," *The Latter Rain Evangel*, April 1909, p. 10.

38. "Publication Resumed," *The New Acts*, February 1907, p. 1.

39. Fanny Van Dyke, *History of the Full Gospel Work in Youngstown*, n.d., p. 10. (Typewritten.)

40. Bartleman, *How Pentecost*, 104.

41. A. W. Tozer in his biographical account of A. B. Simpson, president of the Christian and Missionary Alliance (CMA), relates that since an outburst of Pentecostal activity had developed in the organization, Simpson sent his trusted associate, Dr. Henry Wilson, to Alliance, "a hot-bed of the new phenomenon, to study the meetings and report back. After a careful study Dr. Wilson made the following report, and it stands today as the crystallized utterance of the Society: 'I am not able to approve the movement, though I am willing to concede that there is probably something of God in it somewhere.'" *Wingspread* (Harrisburg, Pennsylvania: Christian, 1943) 133. However, early reports indicate that Wilson visited the annual convention of the CMA in Cleveland, March 25-29, 1907. Furthermore, it was reported that Wilson had concluded "that this work is of God, and no man should put his hand upon it." See "An Influential Endorsement," *The New Acts*, April 1907, p. 3. W. A. Cramer, a CMA pastor in Cleveland, corroborated this report in "Pentecost at Cleveland," *The New Acts*, June 1907, p. 4.

42. Bartleman, *How Pentecost*, 104-5.

43. For lists of those in attendance, see Flower, "Historical Review of the Pentecostal Movement," *The Pentecostal Testimony*, September 1955, p. 13; "Many Ministers from Many States," *The Alliance Daily Review*, June 11, 1907, p. 1; "The Outlook Bright," *The New Acts*, June 1907, p. 7.

44. For a description of the camp meeting and the attendance, see "'Gift of Tongues' Creed is Now on Exhibition," *The Alliance Review*, June 17, 1907, pp. 1,8; "Continuous Performance," *The Alliance Daily Review*, June 18, 1907, p. 1; "At the Camp, At the Home," *The Alliance Daily Review*, June 15, 1907, p. 1.

45. Bartleman, *How Pentecost*, 104-5.

46. "Continuous Performance," *The Alliance Daily Review*, June 18, 1907, p. 1.

47. *The New Acts* occasionally reflected the social concerns of Lupton and his associates. For example, the paper condemned the lynching of three blacks on the public square in Springfield, Missouri, in "Liberty Not Complete," *The New Acts*, April 19, 1906, p. 8; Lupton and his associates also supported legislation in Ohio which would have eliminated the death penalty; see "Limiting Capital Punishment," *The New Acts*, March 1, 1906, p. 7; for Lupton's pacifism, see Levi R. Lupton, "'Wilt Thou Go With This Man?'" *The Latter Rain Evangel*, June 1910, p. 22; for the mixing of blacks and whites at the camp meeting, see "At the Camp, At the Home," *The Alliance Daily Review*, June 15, 1907, p. 1; "'Gift of Tongues' is Now on Exhibition," *The Alliance Daily Review*, June 17, 1907, pp. 1,8; "Day's Doings at Camp Lupton," *The Alliance Daily Review*, June 21, 1907, p. 1.

48. "Continuous Performance," *The Alliance Daily Review*, June 18, 1907, p. 1.

49. "Apostle Levi, Says Vision," *The Alliance Daily Review*, June 26, 1907, p. 1; "Lupton Again," *The Alliance Daily Review*, June 25, 1907, p. 1.

50. King, *Yet Speaketh*, 132.

51. Ibid.

52. "Apostolic Faith Directory," *The Pentecost*, September 15, 1909, p. 8.

53. For information on Minnie T. Draper, cf. Gary B. McGee, "Three Notable Women in Pentecostal Ministry," *Assemblies of God Heritage* (Spring 1986) 3–5, 12, 16.

54. For information on the activities of Elizabeth R. "Mother" Wheaton before the Azusa Street Revival, see Elizabeth R. Wheaton, *Prisons and Prayer or a Labor of Love* (Tabor, Iowa: C. M. Kelley, ca. 1906).

55. The visit by Alexander Boddy to Alliance, Ohio, is found in McPherson, *Life*, 133. For more information on Boddy, cf. Edith Blumhofer, "Alexander Boddy and the Rise of Pentecostalism in Great Britain," *JSPS* 8/1 (1986) 31–40.

56. "Important Pentecostal Manifesto," *Confidence*, August 15, 1908, pp. 9–10.

57. Alice C. Wood, personal diary, July 1909; *Confidence*, September 1909, p. 200. For information on the missionaries who had been trained in Alliance or received support through Lupton, see McPherson, *Life*, 106–7; also, "Many Missionaries," *The Alliance Daily Review*, June 27, 1909, p. 7.

13

BAPTISM IN THE HOLY SPIRIT AND THE EVANGELICAL TRADITION

Richard Lovelace

I. Ancestral Roots of Charismatic Renewal in the Great Awakenings

AS W. S. GILBERT OBSERVES, "Things are seldom what they seem." My Charismatic students, searching for the historical roots of their movement, often seize upon every group that legitimized tongues-speaking as an honorable precursor. This puts modern Pentecostals in some rather strange company. Heretical "spirit-movements" like the Cathari, the Brethren of the Free Spirit, the Ranters, and the Shakers support J. S. Whale's dictum that the inner light is often the shortest pathway to the outer darkness.

One is inclined to ask, "Why does the Holy Spirit have such odd theological preferences?" The deepest theologian in the Pentecostal succession as it is sometimes portrayed is John Wesley. After him, the list runs downhill, through thinkers like Edward Irving, the Pelagian evangelist Charles Finney, and the later 19th century perfectionists. Bishop Ronald Knox would have found this group even more vulnerable than the Evangelical heroes he assassinates in his instructive work on *Enthusiasm*.[1]

Clearly the main criterion for Pentecostal ancestry should be *the manifest presence of the Holy Spirit in renewing power*, and not the single gift of tongues. Speaking in tongues has occurred outside movements of spiritual awakening. And powerful levels of spiritual awakening have occurred apart from tongues.

In this paper, I want to suggest that the real ancestry of modern Pentecostalism has far stronger roots in the tradition of the Evangelical awakenings—despite the fact that the major awakeners usually kept their distance from the acceptance of tongues. I would argue that if Pentecostals can affirm their basic continuity with this stream of church renewal, they will be much better understood by church leaders today. Not only will they be closer to unity with "standard brand Evangelicals," but they will also find themselves historically closer to the other two main streams in the church, the Protestant and Catholic traditions.

Elsewhere I have suggested that the actual rootage of the Protestant Evangelical tradition also differs from popular misconceptions. In *The Fundamentalist Phenomenon*, for example, historian Edward Hindson links the Evangelical succession to a long string of heretical and sectarian movements.[2] But a stronger case can be made for the thesis that the Protestant Reformers are rooted in the orthodox reform movement led by the ascetic church fathers from Athanasius through Augustine. These leaders wanted neither to divide the church nor to leave it. They simply wanted to perfect its witness to the deity of Christ, the grandeur and sufficiency of his saving work, and the renewal of the church according to biblical norms of faith and experience.[3]

We could try to limit Pentecostal roots to the Montanists and others outside this stream. But it may be both truer and safer to insist that Pentecostalism is rooted also in the tradition of renewing activism which runs from patristic spirituality up through the Reformers.

One could make a case that weaker elements in today's Charismatic Renewal are closely related to spirit-movements in the Radical Reformation, and in the next century to the Puritan Left Wing as Geoffrey Nuttall has described this.[4] But the Pentecostal movement as a whole seems to be seeking balance and avoiding enthusiasm, with a caution born of painful firsthand experience.

Beyond the Reformation, I would suggest that Pentecostals and Charismatics find their strongest ancestry not only in John Wesley, but in the other great leaders of the Evangelical awakenings, whether or not these leaders promoted glossolalia.

It is true that most of these men carried over the resistance to "extraordinary gifts of the Spirit" which the Reformers inherited from Augustine. Still, if we want to see the deepest work of the Spirit in the time between the Reformation and our own century, we must go to the Puritans, the Pietists, and the great awakening movements of the 18th and 19th centuries. Further, I would suggest that Pentecostal Christianity cannot be either fully Charismatic, or adequately filled with the Spirit, unless it strives after some of the less dramatic gifts and graces, and the culture-transforming goals, sought by the Evangelical awakeners.

If this thesis is true, it means that "the baptism in the Holy Spirit"—in a sense which may be deeper than any of our experience today, whether among Pentecostals or Evangelicals—can occur in a context where the nine gifts mentioned in 1 Corinthians are not apparent. Nevertheless, I believe that both Scripture and recent history argue incontestably that all the gifts mentioned in Scripture should be present in every congregation which is fully awakened and renewed. And I affirm that the nine gifts celebrated by Charismatics will be shared and celebrated in the future church if it is truly filled with the Spirit.

II. The Evangelical Stream Before the Awakenings

In Scripture we can distinguish two kinds of spirituality. The first, which I call *the ascetic model*, is rooted in the spiritual disciplines, described ably for our generation in Richard Foster's *Celebration of Discipline*.[5] *Askesis* means *exercise*. The Christian ascetic is like an athlete in training. He or she is busy eradicating bad habits (the process of sanctification), taking in healthful foods (using the means of grace), and following vigorous programs of exercise that build self-control (the spiritual disciplines). The main text for this model of spirituality is 1 Cor 9:24-27: "Everyone who competes in the games goes into strict training. . . . Therefore . . . I do not fight like a man beating the air. No, I beat my body and make it my slave . . ." (1 Cor 9:25-27, NIV).

This text has a lot to say to Protestants today who do not work very hard at cultivating the Christian life. It speaks especially to some Charismatics who lack the last fruit of the Spirit, self-control. Still, the ascetic model of spirituality can easily fall into a religion of achievement, a reliance on works and law that eclipses Christ and substitutes willpower for faith in his saving work.

Thus the second kind of spirituality, which I call *the Pentecostal model*, is essential as a balance to the first kind. This model can be explained by referring to a strong text in Galatians:

> I would like to learn just one thing from you: Did you receive the Spirit by observing the law, or by believing what you heard? Are you so foolish? After beginning with the Spirit, are you now trying to attain your goal by human effort? . . . Does God give you his Spirit and work miracles among you because you observe the law, or because you believe what you heard? (Gal 3:2–3,5)

Thus both kinds of spirituality are present in the NT. By the 2nd century, however, the ascetic model had come to predominate, due to the eclipse of the doctrine of justification. Judging from the writings of the apostolic fathers, the early church by the 2nd century seems to have mislaid the full Pauline understanding of our acceptance in Christ. It also apparently lost sight of the priority of faith in spiritual growth, and the Pentecostal pattern of the Holy Spirit's initiative in equipping the Christian community with both gifts and graces.[6]

These losses led the Western church to adopt the belief that we are justified by being sanctified. The Hellenistic disjunction between spirit and matter, involving distrust of the body and its drives and a special fear of sexuality, further distorted the understanding of sanctification. Godliness became associated with an extreme form of ascetic spirituality. Keep in mind that one of the worst offenders in this distortion was Tertullian, whose Montanist "Charismatic connection" did not prevent him from originating many of today's Fundamentalist taboos, which reject the drama, the dance, cosmetics and other elements of culture and creativity because of their pagan origins.

By the 4th century it was commonly understood that spiritual perfection could best be gained by the amputation of whole areas of life, and by an almost masochistic attack on the body. Thus the ascetic reformers invited those who would be perfect to join a monastic community, and in effect to strap themselves into a sanctification machine. The machine would keep them from sexual impurity by amputating sex; it would deliver them from greed by eliminating property; and it would free them from pride by demanding absolute obedience to another human being.[7]

According to this analysis, Christian spirituality from the 2nd century through late Medieval mysticism remained captive to an extreme and distorted form of the ascetic model of spirituality. In the mystical tradition from Augustine through Bernard and the Rhineland mystics, we regularly encounter experiences of communion with God. And we also find "extra-ordinary works of the Spirit" such as visions and healings. But this is only among those who have climbed the difficult ladder of ascetic discipline, only among the rare and selected few. Only these spiritual athletes could achieve something resembling an assurance of acceptance with God. Only they could expect with some confidence that they might be given conscious experience of the Holy Spirit. Among the majority in the church, there was no encouragement toward faith in these supernatural operations—and without faith, the main artery of spiritual growth is cut.

This confusion in the realms both of justification and sanctification is a main cause of the clergy/laity split in the early church. Even the average priest could hardly hope to achieve the level of spiritual heroism needed for mystical experience. This was sought according to the threefold pattern derived from Neo-Platonism: purification of life through repentance and ascetic discipline; then illumination of the mind and heart through the Holy Spirit; and finally conscious union with God. Climbing such ladders requires the leisure available to philosophers. To the average layperson, the goal and even the process seem remote from daily experience.

Luther suggests that the whole structure of Medieval Catholicism grew out of the soteriological confusion at the root of its views on Christian experience. The entire system was a product of the missing sense of assurance among the people of God. They tried to fill up a yawning gulf of insecurity with everything they could throw into the breach: the works of martyrs and ascetics, the intercession of saints, a pastoral ministry reinterpreted as priesthood, the sacramental system, and strange inventions like the treasury of merit which could be tapped through indulgences.[8]

Luther's discovery of justification by faith alone, on the basis of the imputed righteousness of Christ, freed parts of the Western church from captivity to a distorted and exaggerated asceticism. The great wind of freedom which blows through his works is indeed the Pentecostal wind of the Spirit. His writings are electrified by the same spiritual power that we find in the Fathers of the early church and the greatest mystics. He has a basic spiritual realism, and an understanding of biblical spiritual dynamics, which often shows up the shallowness in modern spiritual movements.

Of course Luther, like the other conservative Reformers, squared off against the Schwärmer, the spiritualists of the Radical Reformation. "I wouldn't believe Luther if he swallowed the Bible," said Thomas Muntzer. "And I wouldn't believe Muntzer," replied Luther, "if he swallowed the Holy Ghost, feathers and all."

The Reformers were fighting a battle on the right with an established church claiming validation by miracles, and on the left with fanatics who discounted Scripture and theological tradition because they were directly inspired by the Spirit. Facing warfare on two fronts, Luther and Calvin found it convenient to assume Augustine's position against the Montanists, and broaden it to exclude all "extraordinary works of the Spirit" since the days of the apostles. This is not the only case where Protestants have cut off their nose to spite Rome's face.

Still, we cannot forget how fanatical and divisive much of the Radical Reformation was. And we must remember the volcanic spiritual power in Luther, which could erupt in sparkling wit and brilliant biblical insights. Calvin, also, has a balance and a solid focus on spiritual reality which has given his work a staying power unmatched by any writings from the Protestant Left Wing.

But there is no doubt that the magisterial Reformation neglected or even reacted against the role of the Holy Spirit in producing sanctification and providing spiritual gifts for the body of Christ. Though the Reformers sought to destroy the clergy/laity separation which the Medieval church had fostered, and to encourage lay vocations and the priesthood of all believers, they failed to equip the laity in two ways.

As H. Richard Niebuhr has commented, they did not provide an overarching theology of the kingdom of Christ which would organize each believer's life around mission, rather than around individualistic goals like piety and prosperity.[9] Beyond this, they did not envision the church as a body in which each part is spiritually gifted with enzymes which are vital to the health of all. Instead, they simply sought to purify the older pattern of church attendance. Laypeople who were used to passive attendance at a sacred drama became students passively involved in a sacred classroom.

Since the sacred seminar met only once a week, it is not surprising that many among the laity failed to experience the deep conviction which had prepared the Reformation leaders for conversion. Most laypeople remained solidly mired in the individualistic struggle for survival or success. The pastors who preached to them soon found it convenient to adjust to this unawakened mass by preaching what Bonhoeffer has called "cheap grace."[10] "Everything is admirably arranged," as Heinrich Heine said; "I like committing sin, and God likes forgiving it."

Reacting against this incompleted Reformation, and responding to the serious challenge of Catholic spirituality in the Counter-Reformation, Calvinists and Lutherans in the late 16th century began to build a distinctively Protestant spirituality. They did this, in part, by returning to patristic spirituality and adopting many aspects of the ascetic model. But they connected these to the new understanding of justification by faith. They balanced this Reformation emphasis—and sometimes almost obscured it—by an increased stress on sanctification, especially the first stage of this process: regeneration, or being born again.

Puritans were concerned to make sure each congregation was composed of "visible saints." They did not want churches full of persons who professed Christian faith, but had only a "notional" orthodoxy devoid of trust in Christ and commitment to obey him. They therefore "loaded" initial conversion with all the content which the Catholic model would expect as the product of a lifetime of sanctification. As Gordon Wakefield has commented, Roman Catholics saw conversion as the first step in a long journey of growth in holiness. Accepting Christ as Savior, for Catholics, was like the prelude to a three-act opera.[11]

For Puritans, on the other hand, the whole opera often seemed condensed into the prelude. Seekers after conversion were marinated in the Law for weeks of conviction, before they broke through to an understanding of the gospel and its personal relevance to their needs.

The Puritans had also adapted a pattern of progressive growth in holiness from Calvin's careful development of sanctification in the *Institutes*. This pattern was based on mortification of sin in every part of the personality, leading to revitalization of every department of life. John Owen even went so far as to say that "The vigor and power of spiritual life are dependent on mortification of sin."[12] Owen's statement implies that we are only filled with the Spirit in proportion to our actual growth in holiness. This is a biblically refined version of the ascetic model of spirituality.

In practice, however, Calvinist Puritans and their Lutheran siblings, the Pietists, put most of their emphasis on the powerful surge of spiritual growth accompanying initial conversion, rather than on the process of progressive sanctification. They practically regarded regenerate Christians as presanctified— like a modern watch which has been so carefully tuned at the factory that it will never break down or need adjustment. And it is clear that Puritan converts were spiritually much deeper than the products of modern mass evangelism. At the end of the process of conversion, they expected, and may have experienced, much of what we call "the baptism in the Holy Spirit."

Is it possible that Puritans, so carefully searched out by the rigorous "law-work" required before the acquisition of saving faith, may have experienced more of the Spirit than we do— minus the working of the nine gifts in 1 Corinthians? Perhaps not. But we may at least say that by homing in on this great leap of spiritual growth at the outset of the Christian life, the Puritans were groping toward the Pentecostal model of spirituality.

Still Puritan spirituality retains an individualism that reminds us of its ascetic forerunners in the monasteries and nunneries. Ernst Troeltsch calls Puritanism *"Innerweltliche Askese,"* inner-worldly asceticism, a monastic movement with the walls knocked off, and with married monks and nuns. The component of ascetic legalism taken over from patristic spirituality is strong enough so that second- and third-generation Puritans found difficulty relating to the high spiritual rigors of their leaders. In the Puritan theocracy of New England, the clergy/laity gap reappears in the spiritual decline of the second and third generations after the founders.

Of course there is more than one possible explanation for "New England's Spiritual Decline" between 1652 and the late 1720s. Immigration produced worldly neighbors. Anticlerical reaction against theocratic legalism appeared. The hypercalvinist conversion pattern, which simultaneously called men to Christ and told them that they were naturally unable to come and might not be elected if they did, discouraged lay initiative. As the popular rhyme put it: "You can but you can't, you will but you won't; You're damned if you do, and damned if you don't." And there were other causes of the pathology of decline. The continuing lack of any theology of the kingdom made it easy for the laity to neglect the arduous ascetic disciplines needed to cultivate "the power of godliness."

As Edmund Morgan points out, the Puritan leaders had talked about world mission as a goal of the New England settlement: outreach to the Indians, and witness to the unreformed church through the erection of a "city on a hill," a showcase of godliness in America. But lay expectations were drawn from an OT paradigm rather than the NT model: the pattern of Abraham, whose piety was rewarded by prosperity. New Englanders were more interested in forming personal dynasties than they were in conquering the world for Christ. And when their piety did beget prosperity, as Cotton Mather points out, all too often the daughter devoured the mother.[13]

Mather, who Sydney Mead has called the first American Evangelical, turned away from OT models. He was deeply concerned to reverse the spiritual decline in New England and in the rest of Western Protestantism, where the wind had also been out of the sails since the middle of the 17th century. Like

John XXIII, Mather felt that nothing would reverse the decline
except a new Pentecost.

> We can do very Little. Our Encumbrances are insuperable; our Difficulties
> are infinite. If He would please, to fulfill the ancient Prophecy, of *pouring*
> *out the Spirit on all Flesh*, and revive the extraordinary and supernatural
> Operations with which He planted His Religion in the primitive Times of
> Christianity, and order a Descent of His holy *Angels* to enter and possess
> His Ministers, and cause them to speak with the Tongues of Men under
> the Energy of Angels, and fly thro' the World with the *everlasting Gospel* to
> preach unto the Nations, wonderful Things would be done immediately;
> His Kingdome would make those Advances in a Day, which under our
> present and fruitless Labours, are scarce made in an Age. I pleaded, that
> His Word had given us Reason to hope for a return of these Powers, and
> for the making bare the Arm of the Lord before the Nations; and He has
> promised His holy Spirit unto them that ask Him. . . . And having made
> this Representation, that Orders may be given by the glorious Lord, for a
> Descent of His mighty Angels, to give wonderful Shakes unto the World,
> and so seize upon the Ministers of His Kingdome, as to do Things which
> will give an irresistible Efficacy unto their Ministry; I concluded with a
> strong Impression on my Mind; *They are coming! They are coming! They will*
> *quickly be upon us; and the World shall be shaken wonderfully!*[14]

It is hard to imagine a better prayer for the arrival of the
Charismatic renewal. But what God gave the 18th century, in
response to Pentecostal prayers, was the Great Awakening.
This began in Germany in the same year that Mather died
(1727), at a time when he had almost despaired that his prayer
would be answered.

Keep in mind that the Evangelical awakenings are not local
or national in character. They take place within spiritual eco-
systems that are international in scope. We need to look hard
at the Awakening as it developed in Germany, in England and
in America, to see how God was moving us gradually toward a
fully charismatic experience of renewal.

III. Evangelicalism in the Great Awakenings

The Lutheran Pietists in the late 17th century had formed a
"born-again" movement with many of the same characteristics
of Puritan Calvinism, though it was blessedly free of some of
the quirks and kinks the Puritans had developed by trying to
be more Calvinistic than Calvin. Philipp Spener had produced a
"secret ecumenical theology" which attacked cheap grace and

made room for Catholic and Calvinist elements rejected by Lutheran orthodoxy. Spener cherished the "hope of better times" for the church. He expected that continued reformation and renewal would purify the Gentile churches and lead to a massive ingathering of the Jews, as Martin Bucer had first taught in the 16th century. Spener also said privately that the Protestant churches would be reunited after they had been renewed. He did not challenge the common Protestant identification of Rome with Antichrist, although he intimated that at times the Lutheran church was just as problematic.[15]

August Herrmann Francke, Spener's pupil, had started a university at Halle to promote the Lutheran renewal—a 17th century equivalent of Fuller or Gordon-Conwell. The most illustrious graduate of Halle was not a pastor but a layman, Count Nicolaus von Zinzendorf. Zinzendorf saw that the needed renovation in the body of Christ must be even broader and deeper than Halle's goal of Lutheran renewal. Alone among his generation, he had the good sense and the courage to believe that even the Roman Catholic Church was not a permanent villain in history, but could be reformed and renewed.

Zinzendorf was the architect who designed all the ecumenical networks around us today, from the World Council of Churches to the World Evangelical Fellowship. We might be tempted to feel that Zinzendorf—like the Anabaptists, the Quakers and so many modern Charismatics—did not know enough theology to confuse him. But we should remember that Karl Barth has called him the most original theologian since Luther.

In 1724, Zinzendorf began to assemble on his estate a sort of microcosm of the divided world church, a community made up of refugees from the religious wars—Catholics, Calvinists, the Moravian Hussites, and Lutherans thrown in for the sake of respectability. These representatives of the shattered body of Christ proceeded to fight like cats and dogs for three years. Meanwhile the Count resorted more and more to systematic prayer in order to achieve his goal: an ecumenical task force which would be separated like the Anabaptist communities, but facing outward in concern for worldwide spiritual awakening and missionary expansion.

Zinzendorf's community was named Herrnhut, "the Lord's watch," after the image of the renewing remnant presented in Isaiah 62: "I have posted watchmen on your walls, O Jerusalem; they will never be silent day or night. You who call on the Lord, give yourselves no rest, and give him no rest till he establishes Jerusalem and makes her the praise of the earth" (Isa 62:6-7 RSV). This passage is the basis for one of the Count's most famous innovations, the round-the-clock prayer-watch, which continued during the next hundred years of Protestant missionary expansion. Here is something a stage closer to the monastic model in Catholic circles—except that the inner-worldly asceticism here is anchored closely to the end of Acts 2.

The reference to Acts is appropriate, since the Count could not unite his ecumenical task-force for renewal without a baptism in the Holy Spirit. As in Acts 1, Zinzendorf fought back against division in Herrnhut by escalating prayer. He cultivated especially the "bands," or small groups of mutual confession and prayer—another innovation which paved the way for the Class Meetings of John Wesley.

The result of all this prayer sounds remarkably like the New Pentecost for which Mather had been praying. The morning of August 13, 1727, began at Herrnhut with a sunrise communion. A. J. Lewis describes the scene:

> Several brethren prayed with great power and fervour. . . . An inner anointing flowed through every person and with inexpressible joy and love they all partook of one bread and one cup and were "baptised into one spirit." All were convinced that, partaking of the benefits of the Passion of the Lamb in real fellowship with one another, the Holy Spirit had come upon them in all his plenitude of grace. [16]

There were no "extraordinary gifts" in conjunction with this baptism in the Spirit, only an extraordinary catholicity of love and mutual forgiveness. We should recognize that these qualities are sometimes missing from Charismatic communities today, especially as they relate to other parts of Christ's body. Zinzendorf certainly had the faith to believe in "extraordinary gifts," though he probably did not expect that they would come. He would have had even more trouble explaining them to orthodox Lutherans than he had defending his incredibly daring ecumenical experiment. Still, eyewitnesses present us with a remarkably Pentecostal scene:

"On the 13th day of August 1727," wrote Arvid Gradin, "all the members of this flock in general were touched in a singular manner by the efficacy of the Word of reconciliation through the Blood of Christ, and were so convinced and affected that their hearts were set on fire with new faith and love towards the Saviour, and likewise with burning love towards one another" . . . Christian David wrote: "It is truly a miracle of God that out of so many kinds and sects as Catholics, Lutheran, Reformed, Separatist, Gichtelian and the like, we could have been melted together into one." "From that time on," said David Nitschmann, "Herrnhut became a living Congregation of Christ." "Then were we baptized by the Holy Spirit Himself to one love," said Spangenberg. 13 August, Zinzendorf concluded, "was a day of the outpouring of the Holy Spirit upon the Congregation"; it was "its Pentecost."[17]

The similarity to Pentecost here lay not with the outward phenomena of tongues and the sound of rushing wind. It consisted in the explosion of mission activity that followed the event, the first great expansion of Protestant world missions. Herrnhut began to revolve like a spiral nebula, throwing off arms of witness in two forms. Mission teams took the gospel to places as yet untouched by Protestant Christianity. Renewal teams took the message of born-again Christianity to every major communion including the Roman Catholic Church. The Pope's favorable reception of Moravian leaders was the first of a series of positive contacts between Catholics and Protestants during Awakening periods.

The Herrnhut experience is the nearest analogue in the Great Awakening to the Pentecostal outpourings in Acts 2 and Acts 4. It has everything in these texts except tongues. We can see reasons in the historical context why this gift was not given. Herrnhut would have been disabled for its task of unifying mission if God had added glossolalia to the Pentecostal empowering the community undoubtedly received. Pietists had been under attack as enthusiasts by the orthodox for decades— and Herrnhuters were attacked even by the Pietists, because of their radical witness to Christian unity. Ironically, the very gift that had unified Jewish and Gentile Christians in the 1st century would have divided believers in the 18th.

This does not mean that the other sectors of the Awakening were devoid of the spiritual power visible in Herrnhut. All of Northampton received the outpouring of the Spirit in 1734, under the ministry of Jonathan Edwards. The remarkable phenomenon in this case was the exact reversal of "New England's

Spiritual Decline," which had left the laity totally absorbed in the daily concerns of business. They went to church, and they could recite orthodox doctrines from memory. But their ultimate concern was certainly prosperity, and they were losing their children to unbelief.

In 1734, Northampton went through a kind of collective dark night of the soul. The townspeople were transfixed by an awareness of the holiness of God and the death of their sin. Their convictions followed the regular Puritan pattern, leading from this deep sense of personal estrangement from God and to an understanding of the gospel, assurance of salvation, and peace and joy in the vision of the glory of God.

Their experience exactly paralleled Edwards' prayers for them. These followed the lines of Paul's prayer in Eph 1:17-19:

> That the God of our Lord Jesus Christ, the Father of glory, may give you a spirit of wisdom and of revelation in the knowledge of him, having the eyes of your hearts enlightened, that you may know what is the hope to which he has called you, what are the riches of his glorious inheritance in the saints, and what is the immeasurable greatness of his power in us who believe.

In typical Puritan fashion, Edwards had told his people that what they needed was not a notional belief in doctrine, but "a true sense of the divine excellency of the things revealed in the word of God, and a conviction of the truth and reality of them." In the great sermon on "A Divine and Supernatural Light," preached in 1734, Edwards dealt with the whole age surrounding him as well as with his people's lack of awakening. "It is not a thing that belongs to reason, to see the beauty and loveliness of spiritual things; it is not a speculative thing, but depends on the sense of the heart."[18]

This may sound like rather abstruse material, preached as it was by a theologian reading from a manuscript and staring at the bell rope. The effect upon the townspeople, however, was thoroughly Pentecostal. "Our public praises," says Edwards, "were then greatly enlivened. . . . There has been scarce any part of divine worship, wherein good men amongst us have had . . . their hearts lifted up in the ways of God, as in singing his praises."[19]

The Awakening created a revolution among the laity. Families which had been used to letting the pastor handle the complicated brain-surgery of Puritan conversion suddenly began to practice it on one another, as they were burdened by the Spirit for the salvation of the lost. Laypeople began to preach, and women began to pray and exhort in "promiscuous assemblies." Perry Miller and Alan Heimert comment that the groundwork for the American Revolution was laid during the Great Awakening. It turned New England society upside down and inside out, exalting the poor and ignorant and bypassing the learned and proud.[20]

From another perspective, of course, the Awakening created a lot of wreckage, in the form of shattered congregations and alienated onlookers. It would be remembered by many as a time when "Multitudes were seriously and soberly out of their wits," as Ezra Stiles put it.[21] It is to Edwards' credit that after pointing out that the Awakening had distinguishing marks of a work of the Spirit of God, he went on to criticize its defects with increasing severity. I have summarized his critique in a chapter of *Dynamics of Spiritual Life* called "How Revivals Go Wrong."[22] It is to be hoped that Evangelical and Charismatic leaders will note the similarities in this summary with current renewal, although my criticism there of the misuse of prophetic gifts could now be supplemented by Sullivan's discussion.[23]

Edwards has given us the second best analysis of religious flesh, or carnal religiosity, in theological literature. John of the Cross before him had pointed out that the seven deadly sins take on new forms among those who are growing in the Spirit: spiritual pride, spiritual gluttony, spiritual envy, and so on.[24] Edwards homes in on spiritual pride as a major problem in young converts, which leads them toward censorious judgment of others and sectarian division. Waking up in the midst of congregations of sleepwalkers, they too often assume that they are among zombies, and that their first duty is to split the church and go somewhere else with those who are as zealous or holy as they are. This is complicated by the adoption of wrong theological principles, such as the Donatist heresy, or a presumption of direct guidance which is not sufficiently guarded.[25]

Having issued these warnings in the *Thoughts on the Revival in New England* in 1742, Edwards went on in the *Treatise on Gracious Affections* in 1744 to point out that many forms of religiosity were "insufficient signs" of a work of the Spirit. Some kinds of experience may stem either from the flesh, or from the Spirit, or from a mixture of the two. Edwards included much in this category that we rather too easily assume must always come from the Spirit: high experiences of joy, involuntary bodily effects, talkativeness on spiritual matters, and even love for others and praise of God when these issue from a selfish motive.

In order to be genuine, these signs must be accompanied by an experience of the Holy Spirit which produces, not mere "animal spirits" (Edwards' term for a nonsupernatural emotional high), but affections of the heart which are centered on God. Such an experience leaves the recipient humble, meek toward others, concerned for the public good, hungering and thirsting after righteousness with a sharpened sense of sin, and bearing the fruits of the Spirit.[26] (St. Ignatius, St. Teresa, and John of the Cross give substantially the same counsel as Edwards on the distinction between true spirituality and that which is false or defective.)

On the subject of the *charismata* in 1 Corinthians, Edwards did not rise above the common assumptions of Puritan Calvinism. In the great sermon series on *Charity and Its Fruits*, he limits the "extraordinary gifts of the Spirit" to the apostolic era, and states that the greatest miracles of grace are produced when hearts are transformed and filled with Christian love.[27] There is a hint of the Hellenistic spirit/matter distinction here, and a lack of faith as well as a lack of solid exegetical backing.

Still, are the multitudes we process through "the baptism in the Holy Spirit" as Spirit-filled as the converts of the Great Awakening? Have they produced a similar impact on American society? Some frivolous teaching on health and wealth[28] seems to baptize the very flaw that led to New England's spiritual decline: a self-centered concern for personal affluence and success. America's characteristic sin in the pursuit of prosperity and dynastic success apart from the interests of Christ's kingdom. But we are proposing to renew America spiritually by reinforcing these concerns!

I sometimes think that if Edwards were among us today he might say that much of what we experience is the effect of ordinary causes. He might tell us that we need to combine in "explicit agreement and visible union in extraordinary prayer" for a new outpouring of the Spirit, which will effect something deeper than either Evangelicals or Charismatics have so far produced in their processing of individuals.

The English phase of the Great Awakening, like the American, shows us a variety of workings of the Spirit which have great power but little resemblance to our standardized understanding of "the baptism in the Holy Spirit" today. Pentecostals are happy about Wesley because he defended the legitimacy of extraordinary works of the Spirit, and because he made a place for a second experience of grace in his problematic doctrine of Christian perfection.

Still, his own experience of the Spirit is described as a heart strangely warmed through the understanding of Luther's teaching on justification. We cannot deny that a profound "baptism in the Spirit" accompanied this growth in faith. It seems to have been the one key which needed turning to release the power of the Spirit in Wesley's ministry.

The Wesleyan impulse, like modern Pentecostalism, was especially powerful in its outreach to the poor. When it penetrated the Anglican system through John Newton and the Clapham Sect, it ultimately transformed English society by the middle of the 19th century.[29] As we analyze the culture-changing power of this revival, we must conclude that its deep impact was due to a "United Evangelical Front" across denominational lines, an activated laity, and continued prayer for the outpouring of the Spirit.

John Calvin had told the Puritans they could not properly disciple England with a divided church. He had urged them to give up the quest for presbyterian church order, accept bishops, and use the Prayer Book with its "tolerable stupidities."[30] The Puritans had ignored this counsel during the revolutionary period, had generated many of the denominational divisions we suffer today, and had discredited their cause and lost the culture. The Wesleyan renewal thrust had been locked out of the centers of power through the Methodist separation. But the Second Awakening drove the Wesleyan impulse home by penetrating the established church.

Part of the genius of the English phase of this Awakening was the ability of the leaders to combine Wesleyan evangelistic outreach and Edwardsian spiritual death with Zinzendorf's ecumenical agenda. The opening of the empire to missions, the abolition of the slave trade, the release of the slaves compensated by 20 million pounds from the British treasury, and all the other social reforms of the Awakening could not have been achieved without an "Evangelical United Front," as Charles Foster has shown.[31]

It would also have been difficult to do these things without laypeople who were praying three hours daily. They were pouring their money and their energy into an expansion of the kingdom of Christ, which goes far beyond the agenda of our laity today, including those who are Pentecostals and Charismatics. The Holy Spirit was working in this Awakening at a depth which turned individuals and churches inside out. Laypeople baptized in the Spirit found their attention fixed on issues of moral reform and social justice which our own Spirit-filled believers either ignore or deliberately resist addressing. All of this, as far as we know, took place without tongues and prophecies.

The same patterns were at work in the American phase of the Second Awakening. C. C. Cole notes that the revival typically began with an extremely broad evangelistic outreach, and then moved into five levels of additional activity. These included a wave of home and foreign missions; a wave of producing edifying literature for the converts; a wave of establishing educational institutions (or reviving colleges which had drifted from their Christian foundations); a wave of moral reform or "reformation of manners"; and the great social justice crusades, particularly the attack on slavery.[32]

Most of this activity emerged from Jonathan Edwards' disciples, the "New School Presbyterians," such as Timothy Dwight and Lyman Beecher. But of course the epitome of the expanded kingdom vision of the "Benevolent Empire" was Charles G. Finney, whose experience duplicates our modern approach to "the baptism in the Spirit" better than any other phenomenon in the Evangelical awakenings. Finney experienced a typically Puritan conversion, complete with a sense of total inability to change—an Augustinian conversion for a Pelagian evangelist, B. B. Warfield wryly comments—and then almost immediately went on to a second level of experience:

... As I turned and was about to take a seat by the fire, I received a mighty baptism of the Holy Ghost. Without any expectation of it, without ever having the thought in my mind that there was any such thing for me, without any recollection that I had ever heard the thing mentioned by any person in the world, the Holy Spirit descended upon me in a manner that seemed to go through me, body and soul. No words can express the wonderful love that was shed abroad in my heart. I wept aloud with joy. . . . [33]

Here "the baptism" is individualized in a way which we have not yet seen. Finney universalized his own experience and made it nomative for all Christian workers in his *Memoirs* and *Lectures on Revival*. From these sources it passed into the teaching of D. L. Moody, R. A. Torrey, and a host of Evangelicals both in America and Europe. As Donald Dayton and others have shown, by the end of the 19th century it was very widely assumed that all mature Christians should duplicate Finney's experience. It remained only for Charles Parham to add the teaching that tongues was the initial evidence of baptism in the Spirit, and the modern Pentecostal movement was launched.

Perhaps it is a little unfair to add that the rest of Finney's theology, adapted from the liberal N. W. Taylor, went on to blow up the Presbyterian Church in 1837 and 1838. This effectively destroyed the "Evangelical United Front" in America, so that slavery had to be abolished through a Civil War rather than a bloodless moral revolution led by Christians in the North and South. Finney had his own response, with which I have often agreed: "Every time there is a Presbyterian General Assembly, there is a jubilee in hell." Still, whatever kind of perfection Finney's baptism produced in his life, it did not guarantee sound theology. As my colleague Roger Nicole comments: "My students ask me, What did Finney have that Pelagius didn't? I answer, A revival!"

Nevertheless, Finney had an aggressive kingdom theology, which, as Timothy Smith has shown, blended spiritual awakening with the attempt to bring every phase of individual and corporate life into harmony with God's will. Thus Finney helped guide the last great expression of Evangelical awakening which did not merely multiply the number of Christians, but also transformed American society.[34]

The subsequent Prayer Revival of 1857–58 establishes an admirable pattern of daily prayer for awakening among the laity. The revival of 1904–05, as J. Edwin Orr has shown, was international in scope and not limited to Wales or to the Pentecostal Movement.[35] But Evangelical theology began to decline in the late 19th century. The result was division among Evangelicals, with the ensuing loss of the controlling influence they had maintained both within most historic churches and within American society since the early 19th century. Only with the Neo-Evangelical and Neo-Pentecostal recoveries in recent decades have we begun to dream again about regaining the level of spiritual awakening which prevailed between 1727 and 1837.

IV. Conclusions

God writes straight with crooked lines. He used the ascetic movement to establish Trinitarian orthodoxy and preserve the church from being dissolved by the influx of half-converted pagans. He used Luther's solafideism to offset Catholic legalism, and Puritan spirituality to rebuild an understanding of holiness. He used Edwards to fight the Enlightenment's confidence in reason and human ability, and Finney to counter the hypercalvinist passivity Edwards had failed to correct.

God also used Charles Parham and William Seymour to break through the church's resistance to the supernatural gifts listed in 1 Corinthians 12. Parham may have been extreme in insisting that every Christian must experience the baptism of the Holy Spirit as a second work of grace, and that the inevitable sign of this baptism is speaking in tongues. But God has made an essential point through this extreme. By segregating out one strain of Christianity which operates with these particular gifts, and giving it an unparalleled rate of growth and numerical expansion, God has proved once and for all that "first-century Christianity" is not obsolete. It is not mere history; it is an option for today.

Still Charismatics must ask whether the Pentecostal model is the only container in which renewal can appear. Do we really assume that every member of Christ's body must manifest *our* gifts and assume *our* habits of worship before he or she is renewed in the Spirit? Doesn't this verge on the Galatian heresy—the claim that first-class Christianity depends on the adoption of the particular cultural style?

Further, is a particular way of processing individual Christians what spiritual renewal is really *about*? Every cell in the body of Christ must experience conversion and the infilling of the Holy Spirit, manifested both by gifts and graces. But is not Zinzendorf correct when he says that the diversity of worship forms, and even of orthodox creeds, is a manifestation of the variety in God's nature, and of the variety he has created in human beings? Were not Mather and Edwards right when they said the Holy Spirit initiates and perfects Christian experience in various and subtle ways? Part of the reason the larger church draws back from the different forms of revivalism is that it senses that there is about them some of the predictability, and the monotony, of the assembly line.

The material we have covered suggests that "the baptism in the Holy Spirit" can mean many things in the church's experience. It can mean the release of the Holy Spirit's gifts and graces through individual recognition of his indwelling and dependence on his enabling. It can mean individual empowering for service. It can also mean an extraordinary outpouring of the Holy Spirit upon a community, in answer to united prayer, usually to equip that community for spiritual warfare, as in Acts 4. The Holy Spirit seems to honor urgency in seeking for further dimensions of his indwelling, more than he does the assumption that we are already blessed possessors of his fulness.

In our stress on the single gift of tongues, we may have failed to recognize what God is getting at in his own concern for his people's gifts. As we look at the Evangelical Awakenings and the present manifestations of renewal to discern what God is building in history, we see an increasing trend toward *enabling the laity for ministry.*

Luther freed the laity from the weight of earning salvation by heroic asceticism and taught the priesthood of believers. The Great Awakening galvanized laypeople into action through the development of small groups of Herrnhut and in Methodism. In the English phase of the Second Awakening the main actors were laypersons—we all know Wilberforce, but few remember the names of John and Henry Venn. D. L. Moody was a layperson, and the best thing we can say about the dispensational theology he imported is that it was connected with the Plymouth Brethren, who emphasized lay activity to a fault. And Pentecostal and Charismatic Christianity have introduced a pew-centered Christianity that demands lay activism even by its worship pattern, which returns to the diversified experience described in 1 Cor 14:26ff.

At a crucial moment in the Second Vatican Council, one of the leaders articulated the old assumption that extraordinary gifts of the Spirit are limited to the apostolic era. At that juncture, Cardinal Suenens rose, long before his contact with Pentecostal teaching, to insist on the continuation of the gifts in the present age. He sensed that the thing at issue was the gifting of the laity for ministry. He saw that without the *charismata* in action, the church would continue to be a hierarchical monolith. The body of Christ would be paralyzed, as the clergy dominated the laity, smothered their gifts, and were in turn smothered themselves, as they tried to care for an unawakened church.[36]

This may be the most important link connecting the *gifts* of the Spirit with the *baptism* in the Spirit. Those in whom the Spirit is released and working manifest a plenitude of gifts which are essential for the health of a fully awakened church. As Kilian McDonnell has pointed out, the signs of the Spirit's working include both the gifts A through P (those we commonly find among non-Pentecostals), and the gifts Q through Z (the nine gifts of 1 Corinthians 12). Unless all these gifts are fully distributed and in use in individual congregations and in the church at large, it will be operating at less than optimum spiritual health.[37]

This illuminates the importance of another statement by Suenens. He says that there are two great streams of renewal running through the 20th century. One is the broad Evangelical current of which the Charismatic renewal is a particularly strong component. The other is the Ecumenical Movement! This would shock the socks off your local congregation and mine . . . but it is implicit in the data we have reviewed.

It may be no accident that the most Pentecostal event in this history was the unification of Herrnhut. Zinzendorf was the architect of Protestant ecumenism. Deficient as that has been, it is responsible for triggering the Second Vatican Council, which has threatened the devil with the worst nightmare he has ever had to face: the possibility of the largest body of Christians on earth waking up in the power of the Holy Spirit. This implies that we may not fully understand what "the baptism in the Holy Spirit" is all about until we are living in a body which is substantially whole once more. In order for the body of Christ to be fully baptized in the Spirit, we need a church in which Protestant zeal for biblical reforms is balanced by Catholic concerns for tradition and unity, and Charismatic faith and openness to the Spirit are balanced by the current Evangelical concerns for reason and organization. As John Mackay used to say, we need both *ardor* and *order*.

The great eras of Awakening take us back to a time when we experienced these qualities in balance. Actually, no single part of the body of Christ today preserves all of the genes which were at work in the Awakening eras. The genetic pool has been shattered, and we desperately need one another to recover our full inheritance in Christ. The life-giving river of the church has been split into three streams which must be reunited. May we avoid every theological definition of "the baptism in the Holy Spirit" which hinders the recovery of unity and wholeness, and thus of the Spirit's fulness.

Notes

1. Ronald Knox, *Enthusiasm* (Oxford: Clarendon, 1950).
2. Jerry Falwell, Edward Hindson, and Ed Dobson, *The Fundamentalist Phenomenon* (Garden City, New York: Doubleday, 1981).
3. Richard Lovelace, "A Call to Historic Roots and Continuity," *The Orthodox Evangelicals* (eds. Robert Webber and Donald Bloesch; New York: Nelson, 1978) 43–67.
4. Geoffrey F. Nuttall, *The Holy Spirit in Puritan Faith and Experience* (Oxford: Blackwell, [2]1947).
5. Richard Foster, *A Celebration of Discipline* (San Francisco: Harper and Row, 1978).
6. Thomas F. Torrance, *The Doctrine of Grace in the Apostolic Fathers* (Grand Rapids: Eerdmans, 1959).
7. Cf. H. B. Workman, *The Evolution of the Monastic Ideal* (rpt. 1913; Boston: Beacon, 1962).

8. Martin Luther, *Table Talk* (ed. and tr., Theodore Tappert; Philadelphia: Fortress, 1967) 340.

9. H. Richard Niebuhr, *The Kingdom of God in America* (New York/ Chicago: Willett and Clark, 1937).

10. Dietrich Bonhoeffer, *The Cost of Discipleship* (tr. R. H. Fuller; New York: Macmillian, 1959) 34–37.

11. Gordon Wakefield, *Puritan Devotion* (London: Epworth, 1957).

12. John Owen, *Of the Mortification of Sin in Believers, Works VII* (ed. Thomas Russell; London: Baynes, 1823) 350.

13. Cotton Mather, *Magnalia Chrisiti Americana.* (2 vols.; London: Parkhurst, 1702) 1:63.

14. Cotton Mather, *Diary* (2 vols.; New York: Unger, 1957) 2:265–66.

15. A. W. Nagler, *Pietism and Methodism* (Nashville, Methodist Episcopal Church, n.d.) 41.

16. A. J. Lewis, *Zinzendorf the Ecumenical Pioneer,* (Philadelphia: Westminster, 1962) 58.

17. Lewis, *Zinzendorf,* 59.

18. Jonathan Edwards, "A Divine and Supernatural Light," *Works,* (2 vols.; ed. Sereno Dwight; rpt. 1834; Edinburgh: Banner of Truth, 1974) 2:12–17.

19. Jonathan Edwards, "Narrative of the Surprising Work of God," *Works,* 2:348.

20. Cf. Perry Miller and Alan Heimert, eds., *The Great Awakening* (Indianapolis: Bobbs-Merrill, 1967), "Introduction" and Alan Heimert, *Religion and the American Mind* (Cambridge, Massachusetts: Harvard University, 1966).

21. Quoted in Edwin Scott Gausted, *The Great Awakening in New England* (New York: Harper, 1957) 103.

22. *Dynamics of Spiritual Life: An Evangelical Theology of Renewal* (Downers Grove: Inter-Varsity, 1979) 239–70; or in the German edition, *Theologie der Erweckung* (Marburg/Lahn: Franke, 1984) 251–58.

23. Francis Sullivan, *Charisms and Charismatic Renewal: A Biblical and Theological Study* (Ann Arbor, Michigan: Servant, 1982) 91–119.

24. John of the Cross, "The Dark Night of the Soul," *The Complete Works of John of the Cross* (ed. and tr., E. Allison Peers; Westminister, Maryland: Newman, 1964) 332–49.

25. Jonathan Edwards, "Thoughts on the Revival in New England," *The Great Awakening* (ed. C. C. Goen; New Haven: Yale University, 1972) 414–23.

26. Jonathan Edwards, "Treatise on the Religious Affection, Part III," *Works I.* This point summarizes the whole thrust of this treatise; actually it ought not even be limited to Part III.

27. Jonathan Edwards, *Charity and Its Fruits* (ed. Tryon Edwards; London: Banner of Truth, 1978) 26–49.

28. *Contra,* Sullivan, *Charisms,* 160–65; Gordon Fee, "Some Reflections on the Current Disease: Part I, The Cult of Prosperity" and

"Some Reflections on a Current Disease: Part III, The Gospel of Perfect Health," *Agora* 2/4 (Spring 1979) 12–16 and 3/1 and 2 (Summer/Fall 1979) 12–18.

29. Cf. E. M. House, *Saints in Politics* (Toronto: University of Toronto, 1952) and Ford K. Brown, *Fathers of the Victorians* (Cambridge: Cambridge University, 1961).

30. Cf. John T. McNeill, "The Ecumenical Idea and Efforts to Realize It, 1517–1618," *A History of the Ecumenical Movement* (2 vols. ed. Ruth Rouse and Stephen C. Neill; Philadelphia: Westminster, ²1967) 1:27–69.

31. Charles Foster, *An Errand of Mercy* (Chapel Hill, North Carolina: University of North Carolina, 1960).

32. C. C. Cole, *The Social Ideas of the Northern Evangelists* (New York: Octagon, 1966) 102–103.

33. Charles G. Finney, *Memoirs* (New York: Barnes, 1876) 17.

34. Timothy L. Smith, *Revivalism and Social Reform in Mid-Nineteenth Century America* (New York: Abingdon, 1957).

35. J. Edwin Orr, *The Flaming Tongue* (Chicago: Moody, 1975).

36. Elizabeth Hamilton, *Suenens: A Portrait* (Garden City, New York: Doubleday, 1975) 107–11.

37. Kilian McDonnell, "Theological and Pastoral Orientations on the Catholic Charismatic Renewal: Malines Document I," *Presence, Power, Praise: Documents on the Charismatic Renewal* (Collegeville, Minnesota: Liturgucal, 1980) 13–70.

PART III:
CONTEMPORARY STUDIES

14

THE CHARISMATIC MOVEMENT
AND LOVING COMMUNITIES:
AN ANALYSIS OF GROWTH

Margaret M. Poloma

Introduction

A SIGNIFICANT BY-PRODUCT of the second wave of the charismatic movement that gained momentum in the 1960s is the rise of Christian intentional communities. In an increasingly individualistic society where often even family ties are transient, neighborhood seemingly anachronistic, and long-term friendship an increasing rarity, many began a quest for community. This search for community was evident in the short-lived era of communes in the 1960s and early 1970s—a search that gave rise to communal living among members of new religious movements (including the Hare Krishnas and the Moonies) as well as among some followers of the charismatic movement.

The desire for a new depth of fellowship among believers baptized in the Holy Spirit should surprise no one; nor should the problems in living out new levels of commitment. The first fires of Pentecost gave rise to a community that is described in Acts 2:44–47 (NAS) where

> All those who had believed were together, and had all things in common; and they *began* selling their property and possessions, and were sharing them with all, as anyone might have need. And day by day continuing with one mind in the temple, and breaking bread from house to house, they were taking their meals together with gladness and sincerity of heart, praising God, and having favor with all the people. And the Lord was adding to their number day by day those who were being saved.

Yet this community was not without its problems, as the account of Ananias and Sapphira demonstrates, and the Scriptures are silent about the existence of other similar intentional communitites. A study of the history of Christendom, however, is not complete without acknowledging the role played by post-biblical religious communities. Charismatic communities are simply the most recent development of a long history of communities within Christianity, particularly Catholic Christianity.

Religious Communities Within Historical Perspective

Within the Catholic religious tradition one can observe an unbroken history of intentional communities, ranging from the third-century desert monks to the rise of teaching congregations of religious brothers and sisters in the 19th century.[1] Protestants, particularly Reformation churches, tended to reject religious intentional communities, although they have had a place in Anglicanism and Lutheranism. Well-known to students of intentional communities are the histories of now defunct Protestant communities, including the Zoar community and the Shakers, as well as the successful ventures of the four centuries of Hutterite community life and the 20th-century development of the Bruderhof.[2] Although Protestant churches have demonstrated a relatively sparse history of intentional communities, some increased interest has been noted during more recent times.[3]

A major difference, however, may be observed between historic Reformation and Catholic communities. With the noteworthy exception of the Shakers, Reformation communitites (excluding most Anglican and Episcopalian communities which have utilized a Catholic model) have included the nuclear family, whereas Catholic communities have required celibate living. Although the Catholic church has kept alive the ideal of living Christian community through its numerous religious orders of sisters, brothers, and priests, it is largely the Protestant model of family communities that has developed among both Protestant and Catholic charismatics.

For the purpose of discussing charismatic communities, they may be typed as denominational, interdenominational, or nondenominational. Many differences, particularly with regard to living arrangements and sharing a common purse, may be found within each category. What these communities do share with each other, as well as with historical communities, is a belief that more intense commitment among believers, than what typically might be found in most church congregations, is both necessary and desirable.

Types of Charismatic Communities

Denominational Communities

Given the important role that religious communities have played in the history of Catholicism, it is not surprising that Catholic charismatics are at the forefront of the rise in charismatic intentional communities. Not only has the charismatic movement influenced many traditional celibate communities, but it has given rise to new communities within the Catholic Church.[4] One identifiable type is that of charismatic monasticism as found within the Pecos Community, an all-male community that follows the Benedictine monastic rule. Another type entails the development of a covenant community as part of a larger Catholic parish structure. This would include married couples and single people who choose to make more extensive commitments to each other than normally found in parishes. The third type is a community replacement for the traditional Catholic parish.[5] Covenant communities, both parochial and transparochial, represent one stream within the Catholic charismatic renewal (the other consists of more loosely knit prayer groups). They frequently developed out of prayer groups as members desired to share more of their lives with one another.[6]

Although Catholic communities dominate the denominational community scene, they are found in other denominations, particularly among Episcopalians. A variant of intentional communities may also be found within evangelical and pentecostal denominations, including the Assemblies of God. Influenced by the ministry of Dr. Paul Yonggi Cho, pastor of a 600,000 member congregation in Seoul, Korea, some Assemblies of God, particularly in very large congregations, have established cell churches. These cell or home churches (house groups) are intended to supplement gatherings of the larger congregation to promote more intensive fellowship among believers.

Transdenominational Communities

Some communities stemming from prayer groups are ecumenical or transdenominational. While many of these communities were founded under the leadership of lay Catholics, those joining from other denominations are encouraged to maintain their denominational ties. Unlike nondenominational communities, transdenominational ones do not represent an attempt to establish a new church. Their emphasis is on creating a type of religious suprafamily that helps members enrich their lives as Christians, while maintaining membership and involvement with established churches.

Lifestyles within transdenominational communities vary. Some members remain single while others marry; some live in extended households while others reside in nuclear families. Some live off an allowance from a larger salary given to the community; others pledge only a percentage of their income to the group. Regardless of the particular living arrangement, all members strive to develop interpersonal relations with one another which they believe are necessary to living out a deep Christian commitment in a modern secular society.

Nondenominational Communities

Both denominational and interdenominational communities remain linked to established churches. Each community seeks to spread the charismatic movement within the denominations of members. Those in nondenominational communities, on the other hand, tend to view the community as their church. It appears that many such communities have developed, particularly as small home churches. Many have thrived for a time only to disappear as quietly as they appeared. The most likely to succeed are those which have a specified ministry that provides members with a common goal. Often such communities are small, with fifteen or fewer adults, but their efforts, resources, and very lives are joined together to further what they perceive to be an important Christian ministry.

It is perhaps the nondenominational community that has generated some of the most controversy among charismatics. Having no official relationship with a larger church body, it is more prone to controversial teachings and practices than those retaining denominational ties. Of particular concern to outsiders and ex-members is the potential abuse of authority and the extreme attitudes or overemphases which may develop from a continual stress on one doctrine.[7]

Charismatic Communities and the Family

A community may be viewed as a kind of suprafamily, and as such, it may experience tension with the nuclear family. Intentional communities have traditionally treated the family in one of two ways: (1) as a source of strife and disharmony which must be eliminated if the intentional community is to succeed in achieving its vision of a more perfect social order or (2) as building blocks from which the larger intentional community is formed. Catholic religious orders are prime examples of the first model, but other examples, both religious and nonreligious, are also available. Those range from the Shakers to the aberrant Christian Oneida Community of the 19th century, to the writings of Plato and Karl Marx.[8]

Although there is some support for the thesis that nuclear family ties weaken communal solidarity, successful intentional communities have generally modified rather than eliminated the nuclear family. Kantar,[9] for example, notes that most communes are a larger social order that contain smaller family units. The contemporary Israeli kibbutz serves as a prime example of a successful intentional community which sought to eliminate family ties, only to find them strengthened in the modified family system of the adults who were born and raised in kibbutzim.[10]

Most charismatic communitites are examples of the second model where the family serves as the base for the larger intentional community. They are not alternatives to family life, but rather are intended to strengthen the nuclear family. It is the conviction that the isolated family needs support in living out a total Christian commitment that has given rise to charismatic communities.

Given the urban nature of these communities, most differ markedly from the Hutterian rural communities or from those of earlier centuries. The prevalent mode of living appears to be in neighborhood clusters where families purchase or rent homes in a particular area. Single people may live with non-related nuclear families, but more likely single members will form same-sex households of their own. Both in living style and in monetary sharing, such communities resemble more the historical extended family system than communes. The nuclear family unit is clearly identifiable and viable, but·it is blanketed with the protection of the extended "family" of the intentional community.

Cell or home churches found in some Assemblies of God and Episcopalian churches generally require less commitment to the cell group than do other intentional communities. They resemble intentional communities in providing emotional support, some financial assistance when needed, and more intense fellowship that go beyond the Sunday-morning church ties, but they are generally more loosely structured than the groups who have formed intentionally for establishing community ties.

Functions of Charismatic Communities

Charismatic intentional communities have played a key role in the larger charismatic movement. Having a greater commitment from members and increased resources stemming from this commitment, their influence exceeds the actual number of members. It appears that they function to meet both personal and social needs, in providing a response to deep psychic needs as well as in performing certain functions for the larger social structure.

Personal Needs: Community and Dependence

Charismatic intentional communities appear to be a response to three human desires frustrated by American culture that are vividly described in Philip Slater's account, *The Pursuit of Loneliness*.[11] These human desires are:

(1) The desire for *community*—the wish to live in trust and fraternal cooperation with one's fellows in a total and visible collective entity.

(2) The desire for *dependence*—the wish to share responsibility for the control of one's impulses and the direction of one's life.

(3) The desire for *engagement*—the wish to come directly to grips with social and interpersonal problems and to confront on equal terms an environment which is not composed of ego-extensions.[12]

Most institutions in our advanced industrial society frustrate such desires. Our cultural values, including those of individualism utilitarianism, and pragmatism (all commonly accepted guiding ideologies), war against such desires. The family seems to stand alone as an institution where the desire for community and dependence may be partially satisfied; but even in this already overburdened institution, such values have come under attack. While modern humankind may be questing community, our guiding cultural values are largely anti-community.[13]

In providing a type of suprafamily, intentional communities do meet a need for fraternal and sororal relations. They also provide for meeting the need for healthy dependence where the religious family members do share responsibility "for the control of one's impulses and the direction of one's life."[14]

Most communities, however, go beyond narcissism and also strive to meet the need for engagement through a communal sense of purpose. Roberts[15] has cited a community's sense of purpose as one of the most important ingredients for any successful intentional community and one that religious communities are more likely to meet than their nonreligious counterparts. This sense of purpose goes beyond personal and even the community's immediate needs. In the case of charismatic communities, the sense of purpose usually stems from one or both interrelated Christian concerns: evangelism and social action. Both concerns extend beyond the intentional community to the larger charismatic movement and/or to meeting needs in other institutional structures. Responding to needs outside the community may be viewed as a means of evangelism or primarily as a ministry to the poor.

Institutional Functions: Engagement

The purposes of intentional charismatic communities usually go beyond meeting personal needs of members. Communities view themselves as corporate persons that have identities extending beyond the individuals who comprise them. As such communities have goals or purposes as communities to minister to a larger world. This engagement with their noncommunity environments may take the broad forms of evangelism or social action.

Evangelism implies using the community to spread the good news of the gospel, in general, and the works of the Holy Spirit, in particular. Fellowship meetings, often held in members' homes, provide a place to bring noncommunity members to introduce them to their beliefs. These small meetings often provide a forum for training members in the use of the gifts of the Holy Spirit and a place where both members and nonmembers may be ministered to by them. Such meetings allow an intimacy to develop that is usually not possible in larger urban churches, providing an atmosphere of love and warmth that is attractive to many.

Evangelistic efforts, however, often go beyond the highly personal recruitment found in small fellowship groups. Community members may pool resources to further the spread of the charismatic movement through such efforts as sponsoring conferences, publications, or sending personnel to assist new prayer groups and communities. The People of Praise Community (South Bend, Indiana) and the Word of God Community (Ann Arbor, Michigan) are good examples of such evangelism, working to spread the charismatic renewal among Catholics in the United States as well as in Europe.

Other communities see their primary purpose as ministering to the physical needs of the larger society. This may be done through diverse ventures, including establishing day care centers, food cooperatives, clothing centers, and through taking political action. Pooling resources permits the community to support workers for these activities as well as it provides needed resources for these various ministries. Such communities usually establish themselves within deteriorating neighborhoods and often their very presence adds a stability to such urban areas.

Dilemmas Facing Intentional Communities

Spittler[16] has observed a serious problem in much of pentecostal-charismatic experience for which he believes community is a cure. Religious experience is usually a highly individual affair, making individualism "something of an occupational hazard." He continues, "Add in some dominant personality traits, take away an acquaintance with the church's collective past, delete theological sophistication, and the mix can be volatile, catastrophic." It is precisely this individualism that has led some observers to label the charismatic religious experience as narcissism.[17] Although the cure reportedly may be community, the tension between individualism and collectivism manifests itself in a number of dilemmas facing intentional communities. Two that warrant special attention are personal freedom versus community structure and religious experience versus its insitutionalization.

Personal Freedom Versus Community Structure

Lack of structure and leadership is fatal to an intentional community. Yet at the same time, Christ's followers have a freedom in him. As Paul exclaims: "It was for freedom that Christ set us free; therefore keep standing firm and do not be subject again to a yoke of slavery" (Gal 5:1). In spite of this biblical admonition and others like it, historically, Christians have become enslaved by new Pharisaic laws that replace the ones Jesus had freed them from. Similarly in intentional communities there is the ever-present danger of members being enslaved by the leadership and rules of the community.

This is a dilemma that will always be present as long as the community is a viable one. Its resolution once and for all would result in either the end of the community or the loss of this freedom. The history of communal failures testifies to the dangers of condoning the extremes that are inherent in rampant individualism; yet Christ's free power should not be sacrificed, even in the name of community. Overstructuring and overregulation confuse community with conformity, and their danger may be empirically demonstrated from the rigidity of many Catholic religious orders (priests, nuns, and brothers) before the liberating Second Vatican Council of the Catholic Church in the 1960s.

Complaints of misplaced authoritarianism in some communities reflect the controversy over the larger issue of discipleship in the charismatic movements.[18] Yet given the importance of religious experience in charismatic communities, order and disciplines can be problematic. Normative controls are necessary, but the nagging question is the degree to which authority should be invoked. This is a dilemma of all institutions, but one that is particularly salient within intentional communities.

Religious Experience Versus the Institutionalization of Religion

Another dilemma that intentional charismatic communities share with the larger Christian church is the problem of attempted institutionalization of religious experience. The late humanist psychologist Abraham Maslow has proposed that the attempt to institutionalize experiences of God to the subsequent loss of the experience for followers has been an age-old problem of established churches. For Maslow, the great religions of the world and their religious writings have been founded by those who have experienced a sense of the Ultimate. As these experiences are put into writing, they become concretized, and a form of idolatry comes into being where sacred things and sacred practices are worshipped rather than a living God. Maslow concludes that this idolatry "has been the curse of every large religion."[19]

The charismatic renewal within the churches and offshoot intentional communities have represented a fresh outpouring of the Holy Spirit on the church. Establishing a personal relationship with Jesus through the power of the Holy Spirit is central to this renewal. It allows Christians to see the Scriptures not as dry historical documents but as a personal word of God's love which all of Jesus's followers may experience. The dilemma is that as social beings we cannot live by feelings alone. Coming together in groups, men and women attempt to develop theology and social structures based on the experience. In the case of covenant communities, instructional programs (Life in the Spirit workshops, teaching weekends, and other foundational courses) have been instituted to socialize interested persons into the structure and presumably into the experience. The danger, as Maslow points out, is a routinization of the practices.[20] In this case it can mean losing sight of the power of the Holy Spirit who began the entire process. When the programs rather than the Voice of the Lord become the invitation to graduate to a new spiritual level, when the community rather than Jesus becomes the center of life, when religious practices become ends in themselves other than means to achieve a closer walk with the Lord, charismatic communities will have experienced Maslow's curse of idolatry.

These and other dilemmas exist, the balancing of which will permit the growth and development of loving communities. A problem with rigidly organized groups is in their effort to be rid of as many dilemmas as possible. Rigid organization spells an end to life and growth in a community. The direction that different communities take depends on the wisdom of their leadership. If they are able to live with dilemma situations, rather than making concerted efforts to eliminate them, they will come closer to their own goals of being living organisms rather than petrified structures.

Notes

1. Lawrence Cada et al., *Shaping the Coming Age of Religious Life* (New York: Seabury, 1979).

2. Williams M. Kephart, *Extraordinary Groups: The Sociology of Unconventional Life-Styles* (New York: St. Martin, 1982).

3. Donald G. Bloesch, *Wellsprings of Renewal: Promise in Christian Communal Life* (Grand Rapids: Eerdmans, 1974).

4. Margaret M. Poloma, *The Charismatic Movement: Is There a New Pentecost?* (Boston: Twayne, 1982) 137-42. Cf. Leon Joseph Cardinal Suenens, "The Holy Spirit and New Communities," *A New Pentecost?* (New York: Seabury, 1975) 131-50; René Laurentin, *Catholic Pentecostalism* (ET; London: Darton, Longman and Todd, 1977) 180-84.

5. Margaret M. Poloma, "Christian Covenant Communities," *Reader in Sociology: Christian Perspectives* (ed. C. P. Santo et al.; Scottdale, Pennsylvania: Herald, 1980) 609–30.

6. Kilian McDonnell, "Prayer Groups and Communities," *New Covenant* 8 (July, 1978) 23–27. Cf. Donal Dorr, "Letting Go to the Group," *Remove the Heart of Stone: Charismatic Renewal and the Experience of Grace* (Dublin: Gill and Macmillan, 1978) 119–38; David Parry, "The Charismatic Prayer Meeting," *Not Mad Most Noble Festus: Essays on the Renewal Movement* (London: Darton, Longman and Todd, 1979) 79–103.

7. For a discussion of alleged abuses of authority/submission/government teachings in one such community, cf. Leon Howell, "The Controversial Community of Jesus," *Christian Century* (April 1983) 307–12. A competent proposal to handle new doctrines (such as potential authoritarianism) which may threaten charismatic unity has been tabled by Charles Farah, "Towards a Theology of Ecumenicity or Doctrinal Disagreements and Christian Fellowship," *ThRen* 19 (October, 1981) 21–30.

8. Cf. Poloma, "Christian Communities."

9. Rosabeth Moss Kantar, *Communes: Creating and Managing the Collective Life* (New York: Harper & Row, 1973).

10. George A. Hillery, Jr., *Communal Organizations* (Chicago: University of Chicago, 1968).

11. Philip Slater, *The Pursuit of Loneliness* (Boston: Beacon, 1970).

12. Slater, *Pursuit*, 5.

13. Benjamin D. Zablocki, *The Joyful Community* (Baltimore: Penguin, 1971) 295.

14. Slater, *Pursuit*, 5.

15. Ron E. Roberts, *The New Communes* (Englewood Cliffs, New Jersey: 1971) 81.

16. Russell P. Spittler, "Bar Mitzvah for Azusa Street," *Theology, News and Notes* (a publication of Fuller Theological Seminary) (March, 1983) 13–17.

17. Mary Jo Neitz, *Slain in the Spirit: Creating and Maintaining a Religious Social Reality* (unpublished Ph.D. dissertation; University of Chicago, 1981).

18. Poloma, *Charismatic Movement*, 235–36.

19. Abraham H. Maslow, *Religions, Values and Peak Experience* (New York: Viking, 1964) 24.

20. Ibid., 26–29. Maslow refers in his discussion to the "paraphernalia of organized religion" (28).

15

THE CHURCH AS COMMUNITY:
SMALL GROUPS IN THE LOCAL CHURCH

Galen Hertweck

I. Biblical Background

A. *Biblical Emphasis on Relationships*

T HE HEART OF THE GOSPEL is relationship. Jesus Christ came calling men and women into a new relationship with God. This relationship involves knowing God, i.e., having an intimate knowledge of him (e.g., John 17:3; 14:7). The new covenant between God and humanity which Jesus inaugurated was the covenant that Jeremiah foresaw in which the Lord declared, "no longer will a man teach his neighbor, or a man his brother saying, 'know the Lord,' because they will all know me, from the least of them to the greatest." This relationship further involved loving God. Thus, the greatest commandment is "Love the Lord your God with all your heart and with all your soul and with all your mind" (Matt 22:37).

This relationship with God involves trust. Although *pistis* carries with it the sense of intellectual belief in God's existence (Heb 11:6), the essence of saving faith is trust. Thus, faith is not simply acceptance of a dogma, but "an existential personal happening,"[1] a commitment of oneself to God in a personal relationship. Jesus calls men and women to precisely such a relationship of love for and trust in God.

Jesus uses the analogy of the relationship between a father and his son to explain that between God and humanity. The Prodigal Son, for example, comes back to his waiting father and is received with open arms of love (Luke 15:11-32). Jesus further told his disciples that unless they become like little children, i.e., live their lives in trusting dependence upon God, they would never enter the kingdom of heaven (Matt 18:3). Jesus' own life showed the importance of his relationship with the Father.

The Apostle Paul also sees salvation as a proper relationship with God. Salvation involves not only propitiation, justification, and redemption, but also reconciliation and adoption, both of which clearly refer to a personal relationship. Romans 5:6–11 shows that the whole of the atonement, even those aspects in which a personal relationship with God are not central, are a result of God's love for humanity.

The new life in Christ is entered by faith, i.e., by putting one's trust in Jesus Christ alone. To do that is to receive God's love and to enter into a relationship of love with him. The Christian life and Christian ethics are an outworking of that relationship of love. In sum, salvation is a proper relationship with God.

But people were also created for relationships with other human beings. God's statement that "it is not good for the man to be alone" (Gen 2:18) shows us that there are human needs which even God himself cannot meet and that can be met only by other human beings. Individuals by nature have an inherent need for relationships with others.

Jesus' life was no exception. He cherished and nurtured deep relationships with others. He called the Twelve *"that they might be with him* and that he might send them out to preach." This seems to imply that the purpose of companionship was the first reason for their call. This companionship was also for their training. Jesus' teaching method was to give himself to them completely and constantly, not only that they might learn about the kingdom of God conceptually, but that they might see the lifestyle of the kingdom lived before their eyes. He called them personally to himself. And from that relationship came their training.

Within the circle of the Twelve there were three with whom Jesus was especially close. Time and again the Gospels recount special times when Jesus was accompanied by Peter, James, and John (Matt 17:1; 26:37; Mark 5:37; 13:3, with Andrew). Further, the Gospel of John mentions one disciple who seemed to be closer to Jesus than any other, for he was called "the one whom Jesus loved" (13:23; 19:26; 20:2; 21:7, 20).

Jesus also understood the importance of companionship in the ministry of his followers. In sending out the Twelve (Mark 6:7) and the Seventy (Luke 10:1), he sent them out two by two, not alone. Some of the last words Jesus said on the cross were instructions to the disciple whom he loved to care for his mother. Jesus realized the deep human need for relationships.

B. New Testament Teaching on Relationships in the Church

The New Testament teaching on the nature of the church is rich and varied. Paul Minear sees ninety-six images of the church in the New Testament.[2] Here we will look at Paul's images of the church as the body of Christ and as a family.

1. *The body of Christ.* One of Paul's favorite metaphors for the church is the body of Christ. He uses it in Romans, 1 Corinthians, Ephesians, and Colossians to show the unity and interrelatedness of believers. Paul's most extensive treatment of the church as the body of Christ is found in 1 Corinthians 12. There he shows that the same Spirit apportions the gifts to the individual members of the body as he wills. Therefore, as in a physical body, each member is necessary to the functioning of the body as a whole. There is therefore no place for feelings of superiority or inferiority among the members because all are important. There should be no divisions (*schisma*) in the body; rather, each member should have concern for the others (12:25), whether it means suffering or rejoicing (12:26).

In Romans 12 Paul deals with the distribution of the spiritual gifts among the members of the body of Christ. Again he stresses the unity of the body ("we who are many form one body"), the diversity of function of the various members ("these members do not all have the same function"), and the interdependence among the members ("each member belongs to all the others"). In Romans 12, Paul goes beyond the gifts exercised in the context of worship and includes gifts such as serving and showing mercy.

In the later epistles of Ephesians and Colossians, Paul uses the analogy of the body in a slightly different way. There the references to the body of Christ refer to the universal church, whereas in Romans and 1 Corinthians they referred to the local church. In Ephesians and Colossians Paul further equates

Christ with the head of the church, whereas in 1 Corinthians all the body, including the head, is identified with the church.

In Ephesians 4, after stressing the unity of the church and the fact that Christ gave gifts to her, Paul lists the gifts in v 11. There were apostles (referring primarily to those specifically commissioned by Christ to be instruments of revelation, although there are apostles, i.e., "sent ones" today, but only in a secondary sense), prophets (those with the gift of inspired utterance), evangelists (those who preach the good news primarily to the non-Christian), and pastor-teachers (those who tend the local congregation, as a shepherd does his sheep, and minister to them through teaching). When all of these are fulfilling their calling, the result will be that the Christians will be equipped to do the work of the ministry, so that the body of Christ is built up,[3] in one accord, mature, and united to Christ, the head of the body.

From this passage are derived the following principles concerning the church:

(1) *The function of the offices of the church is to equip the laity for the work of the ministry.* In a real sense there is no laity or priesthood in the church of Jesus Christ. The "ministers" are really "enablers" to help the laity be ministers. They are generals engaged in battle with the rest of the soldiers. They are player-coaches spurring the team to victory. So in the truly biblical church there can be no dichotomy between ministers and laypersons. The "laypersons," i.e., those not holding an office in the church, are truly ministers, and the "ministers" are truly laypersons.

(2) *The work of the ministry of the members results in the building up of the body of Christ.* Each activity of the ministry is to be judged by this criterion—does it build the body? It is truly a proper function of the ministry only when it does.

(3) *The goals of the ministry are unity in and the maturing of Christ's body.* According to Eph 1:10, God's plan is to unite all things in Christ. The church as the prototype of God's will for the universe must also be united in Christ. Thus, as God's masterpiece (Eph 2:10) the church is a tangible demonstration of the fact that God is interested in breaking down barriers between people.

The church is to be mature (literally, "perfect"), i.e., it is to get beyond the immaturity shown in factions and to reflect the image of Jesus Christ. It is to have in operation all the gifts which Christ has given (Eph 4:11).

(4) *This maturity takes place in a lifestyle characterized by truth and love.* Paul deliberately contrasts "speaking the truth in love" (v 15) with "cunning," "craftiness," and "deceitful wiles" (v 14) which would destroy God's work. Rather, truth (the objective aspect) and love (the subjective aspect) are to characterize the members of Christ's body. The verb *speak the truth* (*alētheuō*) means more than just the utterance of correct words. It means to deal truthfully, to *be* truthful.[4] Thus it encompasses one's entire lifestyle.

Love (*agapē*) is the specific context in which the edification of the body takes place (v 16). It is the *sine qua non* of a Christian lifestyle.[5]

(5) *Jesus Christ is central to the growth of the body.* He is the head of the body (v 15), without whom the body is dead and meaningless. It is to Christ's full stature that the body is growing (v 13), and it is through him that bodily growth takes place. Christ is the measure of the church's maturity and lifestyle, corporately and individually. It is he who gave the gifts to the church, without which its existence would be impossible in the first place (vv 8–11).

2. *The church as family.* The idea of the church as a family finds its basis in the Christian's relationship to God. Through the process of spiritual adoption (Rom 8:15) the Christian has become a child of God and a sibling and co-heir of Christ (Rom 8:17; Heb 2:11–12). By the Holy Spirit, the Christian calls God "Abba, Father" (Rom 8:15; Gal 4:6).

Since Christians have a common Father, it follows that they form a spiritual family. In Ephesians 2 Paul relates how through the death of Jesus Christ God has united Jew and Gentile in him. He goes on to say, "Consequently, you are no longer foreigners and aliens, but fellow citizens with God's people and members of God's household" (Eph 2:19). In Gal 6:10, Paul urges the Galatians to "do good to all people, especially to those who belong to the family of believers."

So the Christian's relationship with God the Father has brought him into a family relationship with other Christians, who are now his brothers. In fact, the word "brother" is one of Paul's favorite words for addressing his fellow Christians. It speaks of a close relationship—the intimate relationship of a family. Paul also uses the word "sister" to describe women who were fellow Christians such as Phoebe (Rom 16:1) and Apphia (Phlm 2). Paul, further, can claim to be a spiritual father to the Corinthians (1 Cor 4:14–15), whom he repeatedly addresses as "brothers" (4:6; 7:24). He says that the mother of Rufus had been a mother to him (Rom 16:13). All of this indicates that Paul lived by the instruction laid down in 1 Tim 5:1–2: "Do not rebuke an older man harshly, but exhort him as if he were your father. Treat younger men as brothers, older women as mothers, and younger women as sisters, with absolute purity."

The church is to be a family—a network of close relationships in which love is the rule. Thus, Paul can exhort the Romans to "be devoted to one another in brotherly love (*philadelphia*)." Paul describes his relationship with the Thessalonians as that of a father with his children, which he characterizes as "encouraging, comforting, and urging you to live lives worthy of God" (1 Thess 2:11–12).

3. *The nature of relationships within the church.* We have seen that the church is the body of Christ—an organism of interdependent members who partake of the same life and work in close relation with each other. The church is a family whose relationships are ruled by brotherly love.

But what specific actions should characterize the relationships of one Christian for another? Gene Getz has helped clarify these actions by isolating the instances of the use of the pronoun *allēlōn*, usually translated "one another" or "each other," in the NT epistles. His list gives us an idea of what relationships in the church should look like:

Romans
12:10	Be devoted to one another.
	Give preference to one another.
12:16	Be of the same mind toward one another.
13:8	Love one another.
14:13	Let us not judge one another.
14:19	Pursue the things which make for peace for the building up of one another.
15:5	Be of the same mind with one another.
15:7	Accept one another.
15:14	Admonish one another.

1 Corinthians
12:25	Care for one another.

Galatians
  5:13   Serve one another.
  6:2   Bear one another's burdens.

Ephesians
  4:1-2   Show forebearance to one another.
  4:32   Be kind to one another.
  5:18-21   Speak to one another in psalms and hymns and spiritual
              songs.
              Be subject to one another.

Colossians
  3:9   Do not lie to one another.
  3:12-13   Bear with one another.
              Forgive each other.
  3:16   Teach and admonish one another.

1 Thessalonians
  3:12   Increase and abound in love for one another.
  4:18   Comfort one another.

Hebrews
  3:13   Encourage one another.
  10:23-25   Stimulate one another to love and good deeds.

James
  4:11   Do not speak against one another.
  5:9   Do not complain . . . against one another.
  5:16   Confess your sins to one another.
              Pray for one another.

1 Peter
  1:22   Love one another.
  4:9   Be hospitable to one another.
  5:5   Clothe yourselves with humility toward one another.

1 John
  3:11   Love one another.
  3:23   Love one another.
  4:7   Love one another.
  4:11   Love one another.
  4:12   Love one another.

2 John 5   Love one another.[6]

Each of these exhortations presupposes a depth of relationship. They cannot be carried out among strangers. Caring, humble service, admonition, the bearing of burdens, mutual subjection, honesty, forgiveness, the confession of sins, love—none of these can take place where the relationships are superficial. They require personal commitment, trust, and in-depth acquaintance with one another. This is the flesh-and-blood outworking of those who have been incorporated into Christ's body and adopted into his family.

What would a church look like if it were based on these exhortations to mutual ministry? Such a church would be made up of people who knew each other well—who spent time with each other, talked together about the important issues and experiences in their lives, and upheld one another in prayer. It would be a learning community devoted to the study of God's Word in which there was mutual accountability for its application to members' lives. It would be a community of honest sharing, including the confession of sins. And above all, it would be a community of love in which the members shared burdens, comforted and encouraged, and humbly served one another.

II. Small Groups in the Contemporary Church

To much of the church today, many of the epistolary exhortations listed above are seemingly irrelevant. They presuppose an audience of people living in close relation with one another. But to many church members the experience of deep spiritual relationship is completely unknown. Why is that?

A. Sociological Background—Trends that Make Small Groups So Necessary

American society and Western culture in general have undergone changes over the past fifty years which have contributed to the anonymity and isolation of church members. There has been a devastating breakdown in the natural networks of relationships and caring. Before the past few decades' upsurge in mobility, neighborhoods and rural areas tended to stay fairly stable. But the increase in mobility has made that a thing of the past. This means that the possibility of neighbors maintaining close, long-lasting friendships has been greatly reduced. This mobility has also had its effect on the family, separating children from parents, grandparents, and siblings.

Another factor is the breakdown of the American home. With divorce rates remaining high, many families are being broken apart. Thus, the most important unit of caring is for many people fractured, and its function of healing and nurturing has been greatly impaired. These factors have been accompanied by a subtle change of values from the personal to the material and by the necessary increase in anonymity and depersonalization in an ever-growing, urbanized population, resulting in a greatly increased sense of personal isolation.

B. *The Need in the Contemporary Church*

This widely felt sense of anonymity would be perfectly met by a church which fulfilled the New Testament exhortations listed above. But the contemporary church, being a part of society, bears the marks of that society's sociological changes. The feeling of personal isolation persists as strongly within many churches as outside it. And to the extent that the size of local congregations has increased, so their ability to be personal networks of caring has decreased, with the exception of those which have intentionally created small groups designed specifically to meet that need. The point is that a group of 100 or 1000 people, while it can fulfill many vital functions in the life of the church, cannot function in such a way as to fulfill the New Testament exhortations to be a personal, sharing, confessing, touching, comforting community. That kind of deep relationship can develop only as a small number of people over a period of time get to know one another intimately, develop mutual trust, and commit themselves to one another.

But other factors also prevent the church from being a personal community. The architecture of the typical church—straight pews facing the "stage"—would effectively stifle any great amount of personal interaction. It is also true that many clergy and church members do not believe that such relationships are needed. American rugged-individualism, which envisions the lonely hero standing for right when no on else does, makes it seem that only the weak need other people. This is subtly taught by the members' closed lifestyles, by church programs that do not encourage or allow for in-depth sharing, and even by the words of some of the popular gospel songs. Yes, the Lone Ranger Complex is alive and well.

But another factor that is perhaps more influential than any of those mentioned so far is the tendency, especially in many Fundamentalist and Holiness churches, toward perfectionism.

While perfection of attitude, thought, and deed is our goal, perfectionism holds that it must be attained now and that any person living below that standard is unacceptable. But, in fact, no Christian has reached that goal, for "if we claim to be without sin, we deceive ourselves and the truth is not in us" (1 John 1:8). Having to maintain a standard of perfection while knowing in his heart that he is not "without sin," can cause a person to retreat from deep fellowship with the church body lest the discrepancy become known. It can take the form of hypocrisy, putting on airs of perfection when the person knows that that is not the case, or the form of hyperindividualism, when the person is desperately trying to live the Christian life in relational (though not physical) isolation.

C. *The Place of Small Groups in the Church*

Small groups[7] are not new to the church. Since the birth of the church as recorded in Acts, small groups have been an important form of Christian gathering. A classic example of the role of small groups is the Methodist Class Meeting which was formed originally to facilitate discipline. John Wesley describes their benefits this way:

> It can scarce be conceived what advantages have been reaped from this little prudential regulation. Many now happily experienced that Christian fellowship of which they had not so much as an idea before. They began to "bear one another's burdens," and naturally to "care for each other." As they had daily a more intimate acquaintance with, so they had a more endeared affection for, each other. And "speaking the truth in love, they grew up into Him in all things, who is the Head, even Christ."[8]

Over the past thirty years small groups have become a major factor in church renewal. They have taken a myriad of forms. They exist in Catholicism, Protestantism, liberal and conservative churches, and they have been both hailed and resisted at various times by the clergy in every sector of Christianity. But one thing that can be said is that in our day God has used small groups as a means of renewal all around the globe. In fact, Larson and Osborne say, " . . . we do not know of a single church now producing live laymen that does not have at its heart some form of small group fellowship."[9] It has been my experience that virtually any church that has enjoyed significant renewal and growth has probably done so with the help of small groups.

D. What Is a Small Group?

A small group is a gathering of three to twelve people who meet together regularly for the purpose of spiritual and personal growth. The group's main objective is to do the work of God in an atmosphere of love and care. The emphasis is on relationships—not merely doing a task or drawing closer to God independently, but drawing closer to him while at the same time "drawing closer" to one another. That is the distinct contribution of the small group.

There are basically three kinds of small groups. The first exists primarily for edification of its members and emphasizes the elements of sharing, Bible (or book) study, and prayer. Most small groups are of this nature.

Another kind of small group exists for the purpose of evangelism, forming a beachhead for the penetration of the gospel into the world. Many people will not come to a church building because they are uncomfortable with or feel antagonism toward the institutional church. But some will participate with a group of friends who meet together to talk about where "they're at" and to explore the possibilities of the Christian life. In that way they can come into contact with the word of God and with growing Christians on their own territory. And thus they can come face to face with Christ.

The third kind of small groups is the mission group which meets to accomplish a task such as planning a church building program, helping the needy with housing, or developing a drug prevention program. Every church committee has the possibility of becoming a mission group by incorporating the relational elements of the small group.

E. What Does a Small Group Do?

The three basic elements which make up a small group agenda are sharing, Bible (or book) study, and prayer.

Sharing. Although many groups, either large or small, meet for Bible study or prayer, the distinctive element in the small groups with which we are dealing is the personal nature of the group. Bible study is not dealt with merely in an abstract fashion, but each person in the group relates to it personally and applies it directly to his or her own life. In prayer immediate, personal, felt needs are prayed for.

This personal element comes to the fore in the element of sharing. For a group to function in accordance with the exhortations of the biblical writers (see the list above), the members of the group must come to know and trust one another. That process of increasing intimacy takes time and requires that all members allow the others to know them. That process should not be forced—indeed it cannot be. It must come as the person is comfortable with revealing his or her feelings, experiences, fears, and dreams.

At first, sharing will be primarily in the form of history-giving, as people begin to share the experiences which have made them who they are. But as people develop a trust level, more intimate sharing can develop in which burdens can be borne (Gal 6:2) and eventually sins can be confessed that healing may occur (Jas 5:16; cf. *Did.* 4:14; 14:1,2).

Bible Study. It is important that a group get outside input, the best of which is God's Word. At times the study of other Christian books can be valuable,[10] but generally the Bible will be the text. There are two tendencies in small group Bible study which must be avoided. The first is to deal with the text in abstraction without allowing each person to apply it to his or her life personally. If the Bible study of a small group is to be successful, each person must relate individually immediately to the text. Someone may ask questions like: "With whom do I relate in this parable or episode?" "Where in my life do I need to apply this?" "If I did what the text says, what would it look like in my life?" The answers should be shared with the group, and in that way the group members can help one another come to a fuller understanding of the meaning and application of the text.

The opposite tendency is for a group to study the Bible in a completely relational way, so that the text is used as simply a springboard for the group members' own thoughts. That kind of "Bible study" does not let the text speak for itself—the group might as well use Shakespeare. Although the text should be related to personally, the text itself should be taken seriously and its message should be clearly understood prior to its application.

The best form of Bible study for a small group is the inductive method in which the group leader, by asking key questions, allows the members to discover for themselves the meaning of the text. He or she then helps them draw out its implications for their lives.

Prayer. Prayer is the third vital element in a small group. When we pray, we communicate with God, bringing to him the things that are truly important in our lives and thanking him for what he has done for us. Without prayer, the sharing and Bible study will not be as beneficial as they should be.

Jesus said, "Again I say to you, if two of you agree on earth about anything they ask, it will be done for them by my Father in heaven" (Matt 18:19).[11] This promise has often been relegated to the category of unattainable promises which we can never see fulfilled. After all, many typical "prayer meetings" involve the same people each week praying the same prayers about the same things using the same King James English vocabulary and getting the same results! This situation has disillusioned many new converts who have taken Christ's promise at face value and expect to see answers to their prayers. But today more and more people are seeing new power in their prayers in and through small groups.

Why is it that small groups are effective in having prayers answered? First of all, small groups tend to place a high priority on honesty, i.e., they encourage people to share in prayer what their real needs and concerns are. This is not to say that the typical midweek prayer meeting is dishonest; it is just that the *real* needs—the needs that are ultimately important such as spiritual struggles or problems in relationships—seldom get shared there. The only deep needs that are often shared are *someone else's* spiritual struggles! Personal needs that are shared usually consist of physical afflictions or unsaved loved ones. The really important needs, which according to Jesus should be agreed upon, are shared as "unspoken requests"!

Secondly, in the small group prayer is usually corporate, i.e., done as a body. In many traditional prayer meetings, needs are shared, but then each person individually takes them to God in prayer (if they can be remembered) or one person leads everyone else in prayer for all the needs. The small group, however, generally employs conversational prayer. Conversational prayer is praying as a group in a way that we would talk to one another. It first of all presupposes the presence of Christ in the group, and the group's conversation is directed to him. The prayer is done in short sentences by subject, so that everyone can participate in the prayer for a need in the particular way that the Holy Spirit impresses him or her. Thus the melding of minds and hearts takes place when the group as one takes the needs to God in prayer. It is conversational in that the group is directing its conversation to God.

But it is conversation in another way. When a pause takes place in the prayer, there is a great opportunity to let God talk back to the members of the group as they are sensitive to his presence. Thus, the members are agreeing together at a very deep level about the things that really matter in their lives, and they also allow God to speak to them as they are sensitive to the Holy Spirit's working in their hearts.

F. *What Is the Style of a Small Group?*   Evans, in his book *Creative Love*,[12] lists eight "covenants" which I would term "key ingredients in koinonia." These eight ingredients summarize the dynamics necessary for a small group to accomplish the biblical standards of Christian community:

> (1) *Affirmation.* This is an attitude of acceptance of the others in the group, regardless of their shortcomings. As Spicq (n. 5) has observed, this attitude of acceptance and respect is perhaps one of our best contemporary equivalents for the NT Greek concept of *agapē*. (2) *Availability.* Here a person makes himself available to the others in the group. A minimum commitment of availability is to be consistent in attendance at group meetings. (3) *Prayer.* Prayer is important in that it opens up channels of God's power to do his work in the group. Some groups covenant to pray for each other outside group meetings. (4) *Openness.* This implies a desire to become a more transparent person, open to letting others know who one really is as a person. (5) *Honesty.* This refers to giving other members accurate feedback about oneself, always done in love at the right time for the purpose of edification. (6) *Sensitivity.* Sensitivity indicates a desire to be able to identify with the other members of the group and to understand what they feel. (7) *Confidentiality.* This means simply that what is shared in the group stays in the group and is not repeated elsewhere. (8) *Accountability.* This is committing oneself to be accountable to the other members of the group in the pursuit of spiritual growth in those areas of one's life where he feels God would most have him grow.

III. Conclusion and Summary

Salvation is a right relationship with God which makes possible a right relationship with others. The importance of human relationships is shown in the life and teaching of Jesus. The analogies of the body and the family show the great importance of relationships in the church. The specific nature of Christian fellowship is shown in the exhortations in the epistles which employ the pronoun *allēlōn* ("one another"). These give the picture of a church of mutual edification based on love, burden-bearing, comfort, encouragement, and humble service.

Recent sociological trends and factors in the church itself have hindered the formation of deep relationships, and have made them all the more necessary. Small groups where these relationships can grow are not new, but have been in existence in the church since they were first mentioned in the book of Acts. But over the past thirty years they have been an especially important means of renewal in the church.

There are three different kinds of small groups designed to fulfill one of three different primary purposes: edification, evangelism, or mission. Most small group agendas consist of three elements: in-depth sharing, inductive Bible study, and conversational prayer. The style of the group involves the ingredients of affirmation, availability, prayer, openness, honesty, sensitivity, confidentiality, and accountability.

Small groups have been a great source of spiritual renewal in our day as men and women have begun to live a lifestyle of in-depth, open relationships which is part and parcel of being a member of the body of Christ and of God's family. They continue to hold the promise of renewal to those who are willing to take the step of commitment to open, in-depth relationships. It is only as the members of Christ's body take that step that they can truly minister and be ministered to as the apostolic writers envisioned.

Notes

1. Emil Brunner, *The Christian Doctrine of the Church: Faith and the Consummation* (Philadelphia: Westminster, 1962) 371.

2. Paul S. Minear, *Images of the Church in the New Testament* (Philadelphia: Westminster, 1960).

3. Cf. KJV, "For the perfecting of the saints, for the work of ministry" and RSV, "For the equipment of the saints, for the work of ministry" or RSV (2nd ed.), "To equip the saints for the work of

ministry." A thorough discussion may be found in Markus Barth, *Ephesians*, (AB 34A; Garden City, New York: Double day, 1974) 477-84.

4. BAGD, 36; cf. Rudolf Bultmann, *TDNT*, 1:251.

5. For the distinctiveness of the Christian *agapē* concept, cf. Ceslas Spicq, *Notes de lexicographie néo-testamentaire* (OBO 22/1; Göttingen: Vandenhoeck & Ruprecht, 1978), 19, 20; E. Stauffer, "*Agapē*," *TDNT*, 1:44–47.

6. Gene A. Getz, *Sharpening the Focus of the Church* (Wheaton, Ill.: Victor Books, 1974), 115, 116.

7. They are also called covenant groups, koinonia groups, growth groups, fellowship groups, agape groups, support groups, and mission groups.

8. John Wesley, *The Works of John Wesley* (ed. Thomas Jackson London: John Mason, 1829–31) 8:254, quoted in Howard A. Snyder, *The Radical Wesley and Patterns of Church Renewal* (Downers Grove, Illinois: Inter-Varsity, 1980) 37.

9. Bruce Larson and Ralph Osborne, *The Emerging Church* (Waco, Texas: Word, 1970) 94.

10. In this category the pastoral value of Clement's "Exhortation to Endurance or To the Newly Baptized," *Clement of Alexandria*, transl. G. W. Butterworth, (Loeb 92; Cambridge: Harvard University, 1929) 370–77, is often overlooked.

11. Not following here the legal interpretation of J. Duncan M. Derrett, "Where two or three are convened in my name . . . a sad misunderstanding," *ExpTim* 91/3 (1979) 83–85; nor the Matthean creation hypothesis of Robert H. Gundry, *Matthew: A Commentary on His Literary and Theological Art* (Grand Rapids: Eerdmans, 1982) 369.

12. Louis H. Evans, Jr., *Creative Love* (Old Tappan, New Jersey: Revell, 1977).

16

THE AMERICAN ASSEMBLIES OF GOD: SPIRITUAL EMPHASIS AND SOCIAL ACTIVISM

Sharon Linzey Georgianna

Introduction

OVER A HALF-CENTURY AGO Ernst Troeltsch developed his church-sect typology.[1] According to his theory, new religious bodies begin as sects in a high state of tension with society. But as they accommodate to society they tend to take on more traits of "church" bodies. The church is viewed as an inclusive group that encourages all members of society to join and that requires less specific commitment and conformity than the sect. While the church accepts the secular order, the sect rejects the social order and maintains a prophetic ministry. The church may be characterized by its compromise of Christian values and accommodation to secular society whereas the sect is counterposed to it. Though America has no pure church in the Troeltschian sense, virtually all religious bodies in American began as sects.[2] As they grow and acquire wealth, religious groups move toward the end of the church-sect continuum. But because "church" status as defined by Troeltsch can never be attained in America, due to religious plurality, denominational status is to what American sects tend to evolve.

As American religious bodies move from sect to denomination, important changes take place doctrinally. There seem to be grounds for assuming that the typical Episcopalian or Congregationalist in the mid-19th century believed in orthodox tenets now held by the more conservative denominations of today. Only a minority of members within contemporary traditional religious denominations adhere to the beliefs originally held by members when that denomination was a sect.

While only 19% of Congregationalists today believe that Jesus walked on water, 99% of Southern Baptists believe it.[3]

Sectarian religious bodies tend to be more orthodox in their beliefs, more in agreement as to which beliefs are crucial, and more committed to those beliefs as well. Mainline denominations, however, tend to be more heterodox, less in agreement as to which beliefs are crucial and less committed to the church in general. Liberal congregations are often likened to theatre audiences where members are strangers to one another, whereas conservative congregations often tend to be more close knit, united by widespread bonds of personal friendship and common beliefs. This is one reason why conservative religious bodies grow at faster rates than the more liberal bodies. Sociologists of religion have demonstrated that strong beliefs, interpersonal cohesion, commitment, and sense of purpose and meaning are often found in religious groups that are set apart from the dominating culture, whereas weak beliefs, anonymity, and loss of commitment, purpose, and meaning are often found in mainline traditional religious bodies.[4]

Why do religious groups that originate with a vision and strong goals lose their distinctiveness? Why do they gradually adopt society's value system instead of maintaining their witness to society? The "why" for this transition may be due, in part, to the pluralization of world views which exists and is encouraged especially in America. This diversity of beliefs allows particular religious orientations to be valid and meaningful only to a given group of adherents. No religious orientation or organization is considered by society to have a monopoly on the definition of truth and reality. "Whatever works for you" is reason enough for believing a particular creed or belonging to a particular religious organization. In a world where there is no monopoly on the definition of reality, it is difficult to maintain any superempirical certitudes or beliefs in reality that are not directly accessible through the senses. This may be one reason why the pluralistic situation may be a secularizing one and tends to plunge religion itself into a crisis of credibility.[5]

Religion that is accommodated to society tends to be more receptive to values of that society instead of contributing values to that society. Thus the conclusion is often drawn that, at present, religion found in liberal denominations appears to be neither a prominent witness to its own value system, nor a major focal point around which ultimate commitment to norms, values, and beliefs are found.

Religious groups remaining in a state of tension with society (closer to Troeltsch's "sect" on the church-sect continuum) have been better able to maintain orthodox positions and traditional value systems. By embracing an all-encompassing world view based on a strict interpretation of Scripture, members of some sectarian religious bodies have been protected from the pluralism of world views which exists outside of the group's confines. A firm and viable belief system and definition of reality may thus be maintained. Certain values and norms within a given subculture may operate to keep members uncontaminated by outside views and values.

If it is the tendency of religious groups to grow more liberal doctrinally and consequently more liberal in social values through time, it may then be wondered if religious groups presently closer to the sectarian end of the church-sect continuum (e.g., the Assemblies of God, although reasonably well-related to the larger evangelical world) will follow the liberalizing tendency of their predecessors.

The Assemblies of God

The Assemblies of God began as a Pentecostal sect in 1914, but since its inception it has grown at a faster rate than most, if not all, of the mainline churches, and since World War II it has achieved denominational status. It is the fastest growing Protestant denomination in America at present.[6] The issue this paper addresses is whether the Assemblies of God denomination will liberalize in the manner that traditional religious bodies did a century or so ago. One of the marks of the liberalizing tendency in religious bodies is a deemphasis on evangelism and spiritual growth and an emphasis on social action directed toward changing society to the exclusion of evangelism and spiritual growth. There appears to be a connection between the social action orientation and liberal religious beliefs on the one hand, and evangelism and orthodox religious beliefs on the other.[7] While it is not impossible for denominations to emphasize both social activism and evange-lism, the tendency seems to be that they don't.

From its origin, the Assemblies of God has stressed the importance of a simple upright life and the acceptance of Jesus as one's personal Savior. Standards of separation from norms of society were an important heritage from the Holiness roots of the Assemblies of God.[8] Assemblies of God religious expres-sion has the character of a "witness" experience. This oral wit-ness is suited for preaching, testifying, and relating to people on a one-to-one basis.[9] Among Assemblies of God doctrines is a premillennial view of the future. This view holds that born-again Christians will be "raptured," Jesus will defeat the Anti-christ in battle and will reign for a thousand peaceful years on Earth before the last judgment. Because the Assemblies of God, along with other Fundamentalist groups, holds that the state of society will continually worsen until Christ returns, there has been little motivation by Fundamentalists, histori-cally speaking, for getting involved in social activism to alle-viate social ills.[10] But a great deal of motivation exists to work for the salvation of individual souls. When a person genuinely accepts Jesus as Savior, salvation occurs. However, one can work a lifetime attempting to alleviate social ills and see very little reward for one's efforts.

Having rejected the religious expression of the mainline de-nominations, the Assemblies of God worked hard at building a spiritual body in which an honest quest could be made to God and spiritual needs fulfilled. Because this world was con-sidered to be only temporary, material wealth was originally discounted and spiritual gains were stressed. Among the major emphases of the Assemblies of God were evangelism and spiri-tual growth through the baptism in the Holy Spirit spoken of in Acts 2. The practice of "speaking in tongues" has been branded as the "Pentecostal experience" and has since spread into most of the traditional church bodies, described there as "neo-Pentecostalism," "Charismatic renewal," or by other re-lated terms.

In its origins the Assemblies of God was not interested so much in having a great social impact in the world other than what might be accomplished through evangelism and the bap-tism in the Holy Spirit. Social gospel methods practiced in the mainline denominations were frowned on by the Assemblies of God, which was concerned foremost with making a spiritual impact in the world through saving souls. Consistent with Troeltsch's concept of sects, the Assemblies of God, in its attempt to restore and/or emulate NT Christianity, stressed the simple but radical opposition of the kingdom of God to secular interests and institutions.

By focusing on the spiritual needs of people, the Assemblies of God was successful in maintaining the purity of its beliefs over the years and the dedication of its pastors and laypeople. Focusing on spiritual needs also is undoubtedly the key to the phenomenal growth of the Assemblies of God and its international missionary enterprises.

After World War II the American Assemblies of God as a denomination experienced upward social mobility and found the evangelical world now accepting and making room for them. Thomas F. Zimmerman, former general superintendent of the Assemblies of God for over two decades, served as president of the National Association of Evangelicals for a term. However, the Assemblies of God also began to take on more of the outward characteristics of mainline Protestant churches. Agreement on behavioral standards diminished. Social programs with a spiritual emphasis, sprang up such as David Wilkerson's "Teen Challenge" program, the national prison ministry, and other socio-religious works such as programs for the aged and youth. The social conscience within the Assemblies of God has continued to develop since the forties.

Today written liturgies, printed programs, choir robes, and beautifully architectured buildings all point to a formalization process taking place within the Assemblies of God, making it resemble traditional denominational bodies. Along with phenomenal growth a steady evolution from social isolationism to social involvement has become evident. While the Assemblies of God has emerged as a stable and influential body, some ministers who witnessed its rapid growth saw that increasing social involvement could potentially present a problem. The sound sociological principle was observed that on the road from sect to denomination, there was a danger of the message changing also. The question began to be asked by many within the Assemblies of God—pastors and laymembers alike—whether the Assemblies of God would also lose its distinctiveness and liberalize as mainline denominations had years earlier. Menzies ties the degree of accommodation to prevailing social norms to the size of the local congregation.[11] The larger the congregation the more the accommodation to social values and norms. The question has been asked by many: Will the Assemblies of God lose its Bible-centered emphasis and standards? Would the staunch emphasis on the Holy Spirit be lost? Would the spiritual distinctiveness and zeal for evangelism be lost?

Hypothesis

I wanted to know, how active were Assemblies of God people in social issues? With what kinds of social issues were they concerned? And what mechanisms of social action would be engaged in to achieve goals? Because I believe the primary emphasis of members of the Assemblies of God is still evangelism and life in the Spirit, I have hypothesized that though Assemblies of God members now engage in a degree of social action, it would necessarily be related to the moral and spiritual norms that the Assemblies of God denomination holds as a whole. Specifically, social action would almost always be directly linked to the motive of evangelism.

Methodology

A questionnaire was mailed to fifty-one district superintendents of the Assemblies of God in the United States in the fall of 1979. The motive for polling the district superintendents rather than pastors or members of the congregations themselves is that I wanted to see the organized and developed rationale for involvement or noninvolvement in social action issues. I assumed that the district superintendents would be in touch with the major social issues their members and pastors would be involved in, as well as what social action tactics would be used.

Questions asked were open-ended and dealt with matters such as the Equal Rights Amendment, liquor control, Bible in the schools, controversial textbook adoptions, abortion, homosexuality and busing children to schools. I asked which tactics were used as social pressures, e.g., letter writing, telephone calls, picketing, or joining rallies. I asked the superintendents how the people in their districts would explain their involvement or lack of involvement in issues. Seventy percent of the district superintendents returned their questionnaires (n = 36).[12] The results are set out below.

QUESTION ONE	Yes	No
Would individual members of the Assemblies of God churches in your district be inclined to participate in various types of social pressures to influence liquor control? (Letter writing, telephone calls, etc.)	87% (n = 31)	13% (n = 5)

—by what means? (% of those answering "yes")

Letter writing, telephone calls or visits	61% (n = 19)
Distribution literature, participation in campaigns circulating petitions	26% (n = 8)
Legal action[13]	6% (n = 2)
No Answer	6% (n = 2)

QUESTION TWO	Yes	No	Maybe
What about controversial textbook adoptions, Bible in the schools, or homosexual teachers? Would individual members be inclined to get involved in any of these issues via picketing, letter writing, phone calls, or visits?	77% (n = 28)	6% (n = 2)	19% (n = 6)

—breakdown (% of those responding "yes")

Homosexual teachers	36% (n = 10)
Textbook adoptions	21% (n = 6)
Bible in the public schools	7% (n = 2)
Other (pornography, evolution and miscellaneous)	36% (n = 10)

QUESTION THREE

Would members of your churches be inclined to picket or join in rallies or other form of social pressure for any reason?

Rallying only	50% (n = 18)

No picketing or rallying   25%
                                                          (n = 9)
    Yes rallying and yes picketing   20%
                                                          (n = 7)
    Maybe rallying and picketing   5%
                                                          (n = 2)

QUESTION FOUR   Yes   No   Maybe

Have members of your churches become   65%   10%   24%
involved in letter writing to legislators or   (n = 23)   (n = 4)   (n = 9)
officials for any reason?
    For what reason?
    Prayer in schools   28%
                                                (n = 10)
        Government control of Christian schools 20%
                                                (n = 7)
        To fight Madelyn Murray O'Hare   20%
                                                (n = 7)
        Religious broadcasting   13%
                                                (n = 5)
        Church taxation   8%
                                                (n = 3)
        Gambling   5%
                                                (n = 2)
        Busing   5%
                                                (n = 2)

QUESTION FIVE   Yes   No

Do you know of any women in your   16%   84%
congregations who were or are involved in   (n = 6)   (n = 30)
the Right to Life movement regarding
abortion issues?

QUESTION SIX

Do you know of any women in your   16%   84%
congregations who were or are involved with   (n = 6)   (n = 30)
the Equal Rights Amendment?

QUESTION SEVEN

Basically, how do the people within your
district explain their involvement or lack of
involvement in these issues?
    It depends on how strongly they feel the   29%
        issues relate to personal concerns   (n = 10)
    Social actions are determined by pastor   17%
                                                (n = 6)
    There is no social interest; they don't get 17%
        involved   (n = 6)

Emphasis is only on the Gospel	17%
	(n = 6)
Issues are of moral significance	13%
	(n = 5)
Make the world a better place to live	8%
	(n = 3)

QUESTION EIGHT

How would you explain their involvement or
lack of involvement in social action issues?

They get involved to the degree that it affects the family	25%
	(n = 9)
It depends on local leadership	25%
	(n = 9)
Public demonstrations do little good	21%
	(n = 8)
To protect the moral fiber of homes and churches	8%
	(n = 3)
There is no relation between the social and the religious	8%
	(n = 3)
People lack initiative to become involved	8%
	(n = 3)
Jesus will correct social injustices when he returns	4%
	(n = 1)

Discussion

Though the Assemblies of God as a denomination has engaged somewhat in social activism, district superintendents
tend to perceive members as disassociating from the socio-
political arena except when issues affect the membership directly or the congregation/denomination as a whole. When
socio-political involvement is engaged in, it seems to be limited
to areas relative to the group's moral stance, i.e., alcohol control, prayer in the schools, homosexuality, textbook adoptions,
government control of Christian schools and fighting Madelyn
Murray O'Hare. Areas such as the Right to Life movement
and the Equal Rights Amendment were largely ignored by
female members. In the six cases where women had been
involved in these issues, they were working for the rights of
unborn babies and against the Equal Rights Amendment. Assemblies of God women spend a good deal of time involved in
church and family activities and have traditionally not been directly involved in feminist political issues. The fact that several

women were involved in these issues may indicate that issues once considered to be outside the domain of one's personal faith and testimony are increasingly thought of in these terms. In two cases where liquor licenses had been illegally granted in areas not zoned for selling alcohol, the district superintendents reported that legal action they had initiated had been successful and as a result liquor licenses were revoked.

Political involvement also appears to be resorted to when the autonomy of the church organization is threatened, e.g., government control of Christian schools, religious broadcasting, and church taxation.

District superintendents believe their members tend to avoid public demonstrations such as strikes and picketing, This may be due to the conservatism of the group as a whole and their tendency toward noninvolvement in the purely secular social arena. In relation to socio-political involvement three district superintendents reported the following:

A Our people feel that public demonstrations accomplish very little, are a waste of time, and that issues are not settled that way. As a leader, I encourage our people to vote and run for public office. The way to influence the issues is to elect people whose position you know and that can be trusted. [However,] if there were to come a threat to our religious rights, you can be sure we would demonstrate, politic, and vote!

B We have not traditionally been involved in socio-political activism. Historically this is thought to be the province of "liberal" Christianity and unacceptable in the orientation of the Fundamentalist/conservative/right-wing.

C Lack of involvement in side issues is explained in involvement in our primary task—taking the gospel to the lost.

Comment "C" reveals that socio-political activism is still considered to be a "side issue" and not the central focus of Assemblies of God members' lives. However, there are subtle indications that the membership of the Assemblies of God may becoming less restrained in exercising political rights. Though individuals appear to involve themselves in social issues to the degree that an issue threatens themselves directly, there is also evidence that church members may become involved in social issues to the degree that the local leadership, i.e., the pastor, influences them.

In comment "A" we are assured that "if there were to come a threat to our religious rights, you can be sure we would demonstrate, politic, and vote!" This district superintendent appears to be confident that he could persuade members to rally to the cause if religious rights were threatened.[14]

Social action seems to be appropriate by the Assemblies of God when it relates to individual moral and religious freedoms or the organizational integrity of the local church. From a Bible-centered point of view, members see their actions to be what Christ would have them do. The Bible for the most part provides a clear guide to human behavior and there seems to be a right and wrong decision to make in most circumstances.

Being a patriotic group, Assemblies of God members believe in influencing society quietly through conventional channels. Members tend not to get involved in purely secular issues; but they do believe that getting involved in the lives of needy individuals is the model of social action appropriate to their aim of spreading the gospel. Individuals are dealt with on a one-to-one basis through witnessing efforts which one hopes will lead to conversion and a new walk with the Spirit.

More research is necessary for a clearer understanding as to what segments within the Assemblies of God are more active in social issues than others and why. It may be that those involved in social action are members who are more involved in society. Perhaps they are more affluent, more successful, and less threatened by the secularism of society.

For those who remain uninvolved, it might be explained as part of the cultural complex acquired and passed from one generation to the next. Evangelism has been and still is the most important social activity of Assemblies of God members. This is one of the reasons for their phenomenal growth and vital ministry. Another issue that deserves time and research is the process of norm-enforcement within the Assemblies of God denomination. For instance, are core values or values that the denomination holds to be most important used to inhibit social involvement? If so, how is this enforced?

Social activism by members of the Assemblies of God may be generally limited to issues concerned with the moral and organizational integrity of the individual and group. A strict sense of morality has been carefully cultivated within the denomination, which tends to keep members' focused on spiritual and moral concerns. It also guards members from straying from the central goals before them which are evangelism and growth in the Spirit.

Though with time members of the Assemblies of God have become somewhat accommodated to the surrounding culture, they have not lost their stress on spiritual values and orthodox beliefs. These emphases are not likely to be diminished as long as members remain faithful to Scripture. In a world where traditional religious teachings have increasingly become questioned, the Assemblies of God has constructed and maintained a viable spiritual orientation where orthodox beliefs, spiritual values, and stress on the Holy Spirit can be affirmed. While many denominations have become more recalcitrant when faced with a society that has itself become increasingly secularized, the Assemblies of God has chosen to carry on a ceaseless theoretical warfare, a kind of permanent apologetic to maintain its unique emphasis on the gospel and the life in the Spirit.

While the Assemblies of God operates a bureaucratic organizational form and has adapted rationalistic modes of communication to send its evangelistic message around the world, it has maintained an inspired leadership in this matter and a staunch belief that it is God who "giveth the increase."

Notes

1. Ernst Troeltsch, *The Social Teaching of the Christian Churches* (New York: Macmillan, 1931).

2. Rodney Stark and William Sims Bainbridge, "American Born Sects: Initial Findings," *JSSR* 20/2 (1981) 130–49; cf. also H. Richard Niebuhr, *The Social Sources of Denominationalism* (New York: Holt, 1929).

3. Rodney Stark and Charles Y. Glock, "Are We Entering a Post-Christian Era?" *Religion in Sociological Perspective* (ed. Charles Y. Glock; Belmont, California: Wadsworth, 1973).

4. Cf. Dean Kelly, *Why Conservative Churches are Growing* (San Francisco: Harper & Row, 1972); David Moberg, *The Great Reversal* (Philadelphia: Lippincott, 1972); and Niebuhr, *Social Sources*.

5. Peter L. Berger, "A Sociological View of the Secularization of Theology," *JSSR* 6 (1967) 3–16.

6. Cf., e.g., the reports: "The Fastest growing American Denomination," *CT* (January 7, 1983) 28–34; "Assemblies of God Sunday schools are the fastest growing in 20 of the 50 states," *CT* (January 1, 1982) 41; and Kenneth Kantzer, "The Charismatics Among Us," *CT* (February 22, 1980) 25–29.

7. Cf. Kelly, *Conservative Churches*; Stark and Glock, "Are We Entering?"; Moberg, *Great Reversal*; and Dean R. Hoge and David A. Roozen, *Understanding Church Growth and Decline, 1950–1978* (New York: Pilgrim, 1979).

8. William Menzies, *Anointed to Serve: The Story of the Assemblies of God* (Springfield, Missouri: Gospel Publishing House, 1971); "Giving Thanks for Our Heritage," *PE* (November 24, 1974) 4–6.

9. William G. MacDonald, "Pentecostal Theology: A Classical Viewpoint," *Perspectives on the New Pentecostalism* (ed. Russell P. Spittler; Grand Rapids: Baker, 1976) 62–68.

10. Barbara Hargrove, *The Sociology of Religion* (Arlington Heights, Illinois: AHM, 1979).

11. Menzies, *Anointed*, 377.

12. Seventy percent is a respectable response rate for sociological studies.

13. Six percent (n = 2) of the respondents stated that legal action resorted to had been successful.

14. This, in large part, is how the Moral Majority became involved in social activism; cf. my *Fundamentalism and the Moral Majority: Plausibility and Dissonance* (Lewiston, N.Y.: Edwin Mellen, forthcoming).

INDEX OF NAMES

INDEX OF REFERENCES